ROCK

FAITH
How to Sustain It

Bert Thompson, Ph.D.

APOLOGETICS PRESS

Apologetics Press, Inc.
230 Landmark Drive
Montgomery, Alabama 36117-2752

Library of Congress Cataloging-in-Publication
Thompson, Bert, 1949 -
  Rock-Solid Faith: How to Sustain It / Bert Thompson
  Includes bibliographic references and subject, name, and Scripture indices.
  ISBN 0-932859-40-2
  1. Apologetics and polemics. 2. Christian theology. I. Title.

239—dc21   2002100213

Dedication

This volume is affectionately dedicated to two good friends and respected biblical scholars, Dr. Earl Edwards, Chairman of Graduate Studies at Freed-Hardeman University, and Dr. Dave Miller, Director of the Brown Trail School of Preaching, whose kindness in disposition, courageousness in spirit, balanced defense of the Christian Faith, and contributions to the Cause of Christ, have meant so much to so many for so long.

TABLE OF CONTENTS

PREFACE

When the apostle Paul penned his epistle to the Galatians, he made the following observation: "But when the fulness of the time came, God sent forth his Son..." (4:4). For generations, scholars have offered insightful opinions on all that they believe to be entailed in this short-but-powerful verse. Some have suggested that Christ arrived when He did because Greek had become practically a universal language that afforded ease in communicating the Gospel. Others have suggested that the intricate system of Roman roads, plus the fact that the *pax Romana* (the peace of Rome) was in place, made it a perfect time for Christ to arrive. Still others have suggested that the spiritual state of the Jewish nation was such that "the fulness of time" had come for its redemption. And so on.

While we may not presume to know with certainty all that the apostle Paul had in mind when he spoke of "the fulness of time," one thing is certain: the birth, life, death, and resurrection of Christ left this planet and its inhabitants reeling. Christianity did not come into the world with a whimper, but a bang. For millennia, Old Testament prophets sent forth their predictions about a coming Messiah. Suddenly, those predictions were being fulfilled—before the eyes, and within earshot, of the common man. Christ and His Gospel message turned the world of the first century "upside down" (Acts 17:6). Even His worst enemies recognized the impact He was having. When the Pharisees and chief priests sent their officers to seize Christ on one occasion, the officers returned empty-handed. When asked why they had failed in their quest, the only answer they could offer was, "Never man so spake" (John 7:46).

While there were those who were willing to accept the Gospel, there likewise were many who were not. Some of Christ's most hateful enemies were the Jewish chief priests and scribes. The Pharisees and Sadducees also belonged to that infamous crowd; they wanted no part of this "good news" that shed the floodlight of Truth on their manifold errors. And it was not just groups that opposed the Lord. Even individuals became disenchanted with the Lord's message. Acts 19 records the efforts of Demetrius the silversmith to incite a riot in an attempt to discredit Paul because of the impact he was having on the trade of making idols dedicated to the Greek goddess Diana.

As Christianity spread, its enemies became more determined. They no longer were content merely to object to its central tenets or those who espoused them. Eventually, vocal disagreement gave way to physical violence. The efforts of the Roman emperor Nero to obliterate Christ's message by charging His followers with all manner of falsehoods and killing them by the thousands are well documented. Later, the Roman emperor Domitian was even more hostile in his attempts to destroy Christianity. The attacks made upon Christianity, and the deaths of those who had become its faithful adherents, became innumerable (see Revelation 6:9-11).

Try as they might, however, Christ's enemies could not accomplish their ill-fated goal. While its foes consigned it to die a thousand deaths, the "corpse" of Christianity never remained in the grave. With each persecution, it grew stronger and spread farther. Rather than eradicating Christianity, its enemies somehow had infused it with new growth. Christianity flourished, even amidst persecution, because it was based on matters of the head and the heart —not of the bow and sword.

Advance forward twenty-one centuries. Even today, a Christian's faith can find itself under attack. When Paul wrote to the young evangelist Timothy in order to warn him that "all that would live godly in Christ Jesus shall suffer persecution" (2 Timothy 3: 12), he did not intend for that warning to apply **just** to Timothy.

Sadly, the apostle's warning is just as applicable today as it was in the first century. Yet, truth be told, such persecution is not always physical in nature (although on occasion it may well be). At times, the persecution may be mental—which is no less devastating, nor any less destructive, to a person's faith. In fact, persecution may take any number of forms. It may indeed be the result of physical pain and suffering in the life of a Christian or someone near and dear to him or her. It may present itself as public or private ridicule from a friend or family member—either behind a person's back or directly to his or her face. Or it may occur because of a seemingly inexplicable bout of injustice or unspeakable evil. Perhaps Paul had some of these things in mind when he encouraged the Christians in Ephesus to

> be strong in the Lord, and in the strength of his might. Put on the whole armor of God, that ye may be able to stand against the wiles of the devil. For our wrestling is not against flesh and blood, but against the principalities, against the powers, against the world-rulers of this darkness, against the spiritual hosts of wickedness in the heavenly places. Wherefore take up the whole armor of God, that ye may be able to withstand in the evil day, and, having done all, to stand. Stand therefore, having girded your loins with truth, and having put on the breastplate of righteousness, and having shod your feet with the preparation of the gospel of peace; withal taking up the shield of faith, wherewith ye shall be able to quench all the fiery darts of the evil one. And take the helmet of salvation, and the sword of the Spirit, which is the word of God: with all prayer and supplication praying at all seasons in the Spirit, and watching thereunto in all perseverance and supplication for all the saints (Ephesians 6:10-18).

The Bible not only warns us to "be strong in the Lord and in the strength of his might," but also gives us examples (sad, yet instructive, examples) of those who were not. Today, when we read the names of people like Demas (who Paul said "forsook me, having loved this present world"—2 Timothy 4:10) or Hymenaeus and Alexander (who Paul said "made shipwreck concerning the faith" and therefore were "delivered unto Satan"—1 Timothy 1:19-20), do we esteem them highly and remember them fondly? When we recall the vicious lies of Ananias and Sapphira in Acts 5, are we encouraged by their fate to follow in their footsteps, or inspired by their actions to imitate them? No, instead we remember such people with sadness (and in some cases, disgust) because although they once possessed a living, vital, active faith, they abandoned it for a mess of earthly pottage. Peter discussed this very thing when he wrote of those who,

> after they have escaped the defilements of the world through the knowledge of the Lord and Saviour Jesus Christ, they are again entangled therein and overcome, the last state is become worse with them than the first. For it were better for them not to have known the way of righteousness, than, after knowing it, to turn back from the holy commandment delivered unto them. It has happened unto them according to the true proverb, The dog turning to his own vomit again, and the sow that had washed to wallowing in the mire (2 Peter 2:20-22).

It does not make for a very pretty picture when a Christian who once "walked in the light" (1 John 1:7), and who once possessed what Peter called a "a like precious faith" (2 Peter 1:1), willingly leaves behind his or her faith, only to be compared to a dog that returns to lap up its own vomit or to a washed sow that returns to wallow in the muck and mire of her former pig pen. No doubt that was exactly Peter's point! He desperately wanted to remind Christians of the importance of sustaining their faith, and he just as desperately wanted to dissuade them from abandoning that faith and the salvation that accompanied it ("the free gift of God"—as Paul called it in Romans 6:23), lest they return to the sin-sick world whence they came and be lost forever.

While it admittedly is important to know how to **build** a personal faith, it is just as important to know how to **sustain** that faith. Jesus, speaking through the apostle John, could not have been any more serious about this matter when he said: "Be thou faithful **unto death**, and I will give thee the crown of life" (Revelation 2:10, emp. added). It is that "unto death" part that so many Christians seem not to grasp. When persecution comes, when ridicule arrives, when pain attends their every waking hour, or when suffering seems their lot in life, their faith wanes, weakens, crumbles, and finally disappears altogether. They, personally, are poorer for the loss ("it were better for them not to have known the way of righteousness, than, after knowing it, to turn back from the holy commandment delivered unto them," as Peter put it). But so is the family of God. The church has lost one of its own, and a precious soul made in the image and likeness of God now finds itself in the clutches of "the evil one." The words of poet John Greenleaf Whittier describe the situation better than I ever could: "For all sad words of tongue or pen, the saddest are these: 'It might have been.'"

The first in this planned three-volume series, *Rock-Solid Faith: How to Build It*, explained how a person can **build** a biblical faith exactly like that of the people in the Bible (Abraham, Moses, Esther, Elijah, Hannah, Paul, Peter, Lydia, Timothy, and so many others) whose names are synonymous with an unshakable, unbending faith in their Creator, His Son, and His Word. The volume you now hold in your hand, *Rock-Solid Faith: How to Sustain It*, is the second in the series and concentrates on how, once a person has built such a faith, he or she can **sustain** it amidst the vicissitudes of life. Volume three, *Rock-Solid Faith: How to Defend It*, will provide ammunition that can be used to **defend** that faith against the attacks made upon it by a society that all too often is becoming increasingly unbelieving and frequently hostile. It is my hope that reading and applying the concepts found in each book in the *Rock-Solid Faith* trilogy will help you build a foundation upon which you can construct a genuine, abiding, personal faith in God, His Word, and His Son. If, along the way, I may be of any assistance to you in attaining that goal, please call on me. I gladly will do whatever I can to help.

Bert Thompson
March 1, 2002

CHAPTER 1

BIBLICAL FAITH—
DEFINING AND
SUSTAINING IT [PART I]

"As indicated earlier, there is not enough evidence anywhere to absolutely **prove** God, but there is adequate evidence to justify the assumption or the faith that God exists" (Thomas, 1965, p. 263, emp. in orig.).

Faith implies something less than knowledge.... Faith, by standing between knowledge and ignorance, certainty and credulity, in a sense partakes of the essence of both. It has some evidence, which relates it to knowledge, yet it has some uncertainty, because the evidence is indirect (Hoover, 1976, p. 27).

"Now we **believe**, not because of thy speaking: for we have heard for ourselves, and **know** that this is indeed the Savior of the world" (John 4:42).

If a person wants to build, and sustain, a rock-solid biblical faith, then he or she first must know exactly what faith is—and what it is not. And that is why the first two chapters of this book stress the definition and workings of **biblical** faith.

For example, even a cursory reading of the three quotations shown above reveals that the first two stand in stark contradistinction to the third. The first two advocate the view that faith is based on unprovable assumptions that produce a personal belief system fraught with uncertainty. The third statement, from the pen of the inspired apostle John, describes some of the people from Samaria whose faith in the Lord's deity was based on the fact they **knew**—as a result of the evidence—that He was the Savior.

Obviously, both sentiments cannot be correct, for they represent mutually exclusive ideas of biblical faith. On the one hand, we are asked to believe that faith is an "assumption" made by a person who simply desires to believe something in a rather credulous manner. On the other hand, the biblical record teaches us that knowledge is an integral part of faith, and that faith is not based on merely an educated guess or unfounded assumption. Why does this confusion over the topic of biblical faith exist? What is the relationship between faith, belief, sincerity, testimony, reason, and knowledge? And exactly how does one sustain a rock-solid faith?

Why the Confusion?

On an unnumbered page titled "Introductory Comments" at the front of his book, *Dynamics of Faith*, theologian Paul Tillich observed: "There is hardly a word in the religious language, both theological and popular, which is subjected to more misunderstandings, distortions and questionable definitions than the word 'faith' " (1957). Dr. Tillich's assessment was correct in 1957 when he first made it, and remains just as true today. But why is this the case? Perhaps there is so much confusion regarding the concept of faith because there are so **many** definitions from such a wide variety of sources —and yet so **little** understanding of what the Bible actually teaches on the subject. Consider, first, the following definitions of the word "faith" from both the religious and the nonreligious sides of the spectrum.

False Views of Faith Offered by Unbelievers

Through the years, faith has been defined by its opponents in numerous uncomplimentary ways, such as "the power of believing what you know isn't true," or "an illogical belief in the occurrence of the improbable." In his book, *Atheism: The Case Against God*, George H. Smith lamented:

> Faith depends for its survival on the unknowable, the incomprehensible, that which reason cannot grasp. Faith cannot live in a natural, knowable universe.... A man committed to reason, a man committed to the unswerving use of rational guidelines in all spheres of existence, has no use for the concept of faith. He can adopt faith only at the expense of reason.... The Christian wishes to claim knowledge beliefs that have not (and often cannot be) rationally demonstrated, so he posits faith as an alternative method of acquiring knowledge. Faith permits the Christian to claim the status of truth for a belief even though it cannot meet the rational test of truth (1979, pp. 108,105, parenthetical comment in orig.).

In the chapter on "Religion and Reason" that he wrote for the book, *Critiques of God* edited by Peter Angeles, atheistic professor Richard Robinson accused religious people who harbor a personal faith of abandoning both human rationality and available evidence in exchange for intellectual dishonesty and blissful ignorance. He wrote:

> It seems to me that religion buys its benefits at too high a price, namely at the price of abandoning the ideal of truth and shackling and perverting man's reason.... The main irrationality of religion is preferring comfort to truth; and it is this that makes religion a very harmful thing on balance, a sort of endemic disease that has so far prevented human life from reaching its full stature.... According to me this is a terrible mistake, and faith is not a virtue but a positive vice.... "Have faith," in the Christian sense, means "make yourself believe that there is a god without regard to evidence." Christian faith is a habit of flouting reason in forming and maintaining one's answer to the question whether there is a god. Its essence is the determination to believe that there is a god no matter

what the evidence may be.... Faith is a great vice, an example of obstinately refusing to listen to reason, something irrational and undesirable, a form of self-hypnotism (1976, pp. 116,118-119,120,121).

Unfortunately, even some supposedly "neutral" authorities have added to the conflict. Reputable dictionaries, for example, suggest that faith is a "firm belief in something for which there is no proof" (*Webster's Ninth New Collegiate*), "belief that does not rest on logical proof or material evidence" (*American Heritage*, fourth edition), "firm belief especially without logical proof" (*Oxford Illustrated American Dictionary*), or "belief without need of certain proof" (*Funk and Wagnall's Standard Desk Dictionary*). [Modern dictionaries, of course, are not the standard for definitions of biblical terms. As eminent logician Lionel Ruby pointed out in his widely used text, *Logic—An Introduction*, a dictionary is a historian, not a law-giver (1960, pp. 30-31). The **biblical** position on faith does not depend upon the **current** definition of an **English** word.]

False Views of Faith Offered by Believers

As incredible as it may seem, some in the religious community itself have been responsible for much of the current confusion in regard to the definition of biblical faith. Examples abound. Danish philosopher and theologian, Søren Kierkegaard (who is considered the father of modern existentialism), defended the viewpoint that although our human reasoning power repeatedly is drawn to the "Great Unknown," it nevertheless cannot penetrate that Unknown —which he referred to as "God." He therefore believed that the only way to have "faith" was to make a "blind leap" toward that Unknown (1936). Renowned German theologian Hans Kung, in his monumental work, *Does God Exist?*, followed a somewhat similar line of thinking when he wrote: "Even in faith, then, there is no certainty entirely free from doubt. In faith, we must commit ourselves to something uncertain" (1980, p. 61).

Popular televangelist Robert Schuller addressed the topic of biblical faith in one of his "Hour of Prayer" television programs by suggesting:

> Faith is a commitment to an unprovable assumption. The "bottom line" of all questions is: "Is there an intelligent, intervening God?" There are three possible answers to this question. (1) There is no God. Call me an atheist; (2) I won't say; I can't be sure. Call me an agnostic. (3) There is a God. Call me a theist. Can we be positively certain that any one of these answers is correct? The answer is No! Both the atheist and theist are making a commitment of faith. The atheist believes in nothing. The theist believes in something. But both are making a commitment to an unprovable assumption (1984).

In his "Introduction" to *The World and Literature of the Old Testament*, John T. Willis, professor of Bible at Abilene Christian University, wrote: "The Bible claims to be inspired of God (II Tim. 3:16). There is no way to prove or disprove this claim absolutely, although arguments have been advanced on both sides of the issue. It must be accepted by faith or rejected by unbelief" (1979, 1:11). The late J.D. Thomas, while chairman of the Bible department at Abilene Christian University, stated in volume one of his two-volume series on *Facts and Faith*: "As indicated earlier, there is not enough evidence to absolutely **prove** God, but there is adequate evidence to justify the assumption or the faith that God exists" (1965, p. 263, emp. in orig.). Nine years later, when he penned *Heaven's Window*, Thomas remarked:

> In all matters of religious epistemology we come to the question of distinguishing between absolutely provable knowledge and that which is faith-dependent to some degree or other. ...In other words, men of strong faith "act like" they have absolute knowledge, even though in this life they can never have more than a strong faith (1974, pp. 131,132).

In his book, *Dear Agnos*, Abilene Christian University history professor Arlie J. Hoover stated:

> [F]aith implies something less than knowledge.... [F]aith, by standing between knowledge and ignorance, certainty and credulity, in a sense partakes of the essence of both. It has some evidence, which relates it to knowledge, yet it has some uncertainty, because the evidence is indirect (1976, p. 27).

Donald England, distinguished professor of chemistry at Harding University in Searcy, Arkansas, suggested in his book, *A Scientist Examines Faith and Evidence*:

> The approach used in this text is presuppositional rather than dogmatic.... The importance of the Christian walk in faith is repeatedly emphasized over reliance on proofs, signs, or demonstrations that tend to exclude faith.... I do not attempt to prove, to the exclusion of faith, that the Bible is inspired or even that God exists...since proof by demonstration...would exclude faith (1983, pp. 13,17,22).

If these writers are correct, faith is: (a) something based on no proof at all; (b) something based on a little substantive proof; (c) a "probability proposition" that may, or may not, have anything to do with truth; (d) something that allows men to "act like" they know something when, in fact, they do not; or (e) something composed of a **small** amount of knowledge and a **big** dose of uncertainty. Is it any wonder, then, that there is so much confusion in today's world regarding the concept of biblical faith?

The Importance of Having a Correct View of Faith

Ultimately, improper concepts of faith damage or destroy the effectiveness of Christianity. There are a number of reasons why this is the case. First, unlike many other religions, Christianity always has been based in historical fact. From the historicity of Jesus Himself to the reality of His resurrection, Christianity has competed in the marketplace of ideas with factuality as its formidable foundation.

While it may be true to say that some religions flourish best in secrecy, such is not the case with Christianity. It is intended to be presented, and to be defended, in the swirling maelstrom that is the public eye. In addition, while some religions eschew open investigation and critical evaluation, Christianity welcomes both. And so it should, since of all the major religions based upon an individual rather than a mere ideology, Christianity is the only one that claims, and can document, an empty tomb for its Founder. As British author Graham Fisher observed:

> A faith which cannot withstand the searing heat of rational logic is not **true** faith at all, and, no matter how successfully one can build subsequent belief systems from its unqualified axioms, it will always be no more stable than a house of cards, ready to fall at the slightest wind or the mildest shaking of its foundations....
>
> The Christian faith is the one major belief-system which bares its soul to its inner-most depths and challenges sceptics to make a diagnosis....
>
> The rationale of Christianity is based solidly in an event, not an idea. An event can be put under the critical microscope of historical investigation and can be interpreted logically and rationally. It matters not a whit what we believe in our hearts, it is what our heads tell us, as a result of honest inquiry, which must count. But it matters a great deal how we react to the results of that investigation for if our investigation reveals that this dead man actually did rise from the dead then He was no ordinary man, nor were His teachings merely great human wisdom. His resurrection, if true, confirms the truth-claims made for Him as being true and makes His other words authoritative too (1990, pp. 13,16,17, emp. in orig.).

Or, as one writer put it: "Christianity is the religion of **knowledge** and **surety**" (Lewis, 1987, p. 47, emp. added). For someone then to turn and suggest that Christianity is based on an unproven (and unprovable) belief system nebulously termed "faith" is to rob Christianity of one of its most important constructs—verifiability that is rooted in historical fact.

Knowledge and truth are precious commodities. As a body of factual information and legitimate principles, knowledge is indispensable in human relationships. Truth, as knowledge justifiably believed, represents a fundamental reality of life that transcends both the provincial and the temporal. In their book, *Unshakable Foundations*, Geisler and Bocchino noted:

> Truth by its very nature is: noncontradictory—it does not violate the basic laws of logic; absolute—it does not depend upon any time, places, or conditions; discovered—it exists independently of the mind, we do not create it; descriptive—it is the agreement of the mind with reality; inescapable—to deny its existence is to affirm it (we are bound by it); and unchanging—it is the firm standard by which truth claims are measured (2001, p. 52, parenthetical comment in orig.).

He who possesses correct knowledge has within himself the potential to discern, and then act upon, truth. Knowledge frees from the shackles of ignorance; truth frees from the shackles of error. Indeed, knowledge and truth **are** precious commodities.

While almost anyone you ask will admit, **in theory**, that knowledge and truth are indispensable attributes of a sensible, everyday existence, **in practice** many people live out that daily existence as if knowledge and truth ultimately do not matter. Much of mankind lives according to an abstract, confusing, and largely inconsistent system of personal behavior. This is a bit odd, to say the least. In most matters, a man likely will insist upon complete **objectivity**. For example, in regard to his eating habits he might say, "I will not eat this food; it contains bacterial toxins that will kill me." In regard to matters of civil law, he might suggest, "That action is illegal; it violates my rights."

Yet when it comes to religion in general, and Christianity in particular, **subjectivity** rules the day. People can be so certain about their beliefs in the physical realm, but so nebulous about their beliefs in the spiritual realm. For example, on occasion when a person who believes in God is asked if God does, in fact, exist, he may say, "I **believe** He exists," or "I **hope** He exists," or "I **think** He exists." But rarely do you hear him say boldly, "I **know** He exists." Or, if a Christian is asked the question, "Do you know you are saved?," the response may go something like this: "I **believe** that I am," or "I **hope** that I am," or "I **think** that I am." But rarely do you hear someone confidently assert, "Yes, I **know** that I am saved."

This is indeed a sad state of affairs. We now have progressed to the point where in matters as mundane as food choices or legal wrangling, objectivity is an absolute requirement. Meanwhile, in the much more important area of spiritual matters, we not only expect, but in many cases insist upon, a subjectivity that we would not tolerate in any other sphere of our lives. It is as if the pluralistic postmodernism that has affected secular society (the "I'm OK, you're OK" or "Who am I to judge?" concept) finally has made its way into the spiritual community as well. Apparently, some among us either once knew but long since have forgotten, or never really understood in the first place, the proper relationship between truth and faith. Similarly, we either have forgotten, or no longer care about, the damage that an improper concept of truth and its relationship to faith can cause.

The time has come for Christians to embolden themselves once again with the same high regard for truth and faith that Jesus expressed when He stated: "And ye shall **know** the truth, and the truth shall make you free" (John 8:32, emp. added). Christianity is not an "I-hope-so/pie-in-the-sky/by-and-by" kind of religion based upon some esoteric, fairy-tale-like concept known as "faith." Rather, it is rooted and grounded in the provable existence of the one true God and the verifiable nature of the historical facts surrounding the life, death, and resurrection of His Son. When the apostle John wrote to comfort and reassure first-century Christians who found themselves in the midst of numerous trials and persecutions, he said: "These things have I written unto you, that ye may **know** that ye have eternal life, even unto you that believe on the name of the Son of God" (1 John 5:13, emp. added). Thus, according to both Jesus and John, a person not only can know something, but he can know that he knows it.

There are certain undeniable, critically important implications standing behind this kind of firm, confident declaration. Consider the following. If a person cannot **know** (with certainty) that God exists, then he cannot know (with certainty) that the Bible is His inspired Word. If a person cannot know that the Bible is the inspired Word of God, then he cannot know that Jesus is God's Son, since the Bible provides the evidentiary basis for such a claim. If a person cannot know that Christ is God's Son, then he cannot know that he is saved. Yet John specifically stated: "These things have I written unto you, that ye may **know** that ye have eternal life."

Christians are not agnostics! The agnostic suggests, "I **cannot know** whether God exists." Christians, on the other hand, **know** that God exists (see Psalm 46:10). Consider the alternative. Do Christians serve a God Who "may" or "may not" exist? Do Christians believe, and ask others to believe, the testimony of a Bible that "may" or "may not" be inspired? Do Christians place their faith in, trust, and obey a Christ Who "may" or "may not" be the Son of God? Hardly!

Even the casual reader will discern the close relationship among these vital issues. Faith in God's existence is foundational (Psalm 46:10; Hebrews 11:6), which is why I have marshaled the evidence for such a faith (Thompson, 1995a, 1995b, 2000). Faith in Christ's Sonship is pivotal to a person's salvation, which is why I have documented the facts that attend such a faith (Thompson, 1997, 1999b, 2000). Faith in the verbal, plenary inspiration of the Bible is critical, which is why I have gone to such lengths to establish the fact that faith in the Good Book as God's Word is not misplaced (Thompson, 1999a, 2000).

Second, we live in a society in which an examination of the evidence behind a claim has become practically an everyday occurrence. Whether we are purchasing an automobile or considering an advertiser's boasts about its products, we routinely investigate a veritable plethora of evidences that can prove, or disprove, what is being said. The Bible teaches that mankind is lost and in desperate need of salvation—salvation that comes only through Jesus Christ. More often than not, the person who accepts and obeys the biblical message undergoes a radical change in both his thinking and his lifestyle. Surely the grand nature of Christianity's claim is such that it invites and requires both investigation and verification. For someone to suggest that Christianity, or the life-altering changes it ushers in, is based on little more than an unproven assertion (which, in the end, might or might not be true) hardly could be viewed as a rational approach that would commend itself to intelligent people.

Third, surely people in the world who are not yet Christians, yet whom we hope to see become Christians, are smart enough to see through a ruse that asks them to "act as if" they know God exists, to "act as if" they know Jesus is His Son, or to "act as if" the Bible is His inspired Word when, in fact, they do not know any of those things at all. Further, if Christians simply "act like" they know, when in reality they do not, why are they not hypocrites? In his book, *Faith and Reason*, theistic philosopher Dick Sztanyo first explained the error of what he termed the "as if" hypothesis of faith by representing it diagramatically as seen below, and then offered these comments:

Those holding this position generally maintain that there is no possible way to know whether or not God exists. Thus, in the diagram, the vertical line represents an impenetrable "wall" that separates the intellect from God. As such, "faith" cannot possibly reach the object of its quest. "Real faith" is **acting as if** there really is an object of faith "out there" somewhere. Since it cannot be maintained that this "faith" is the

same as the faith possessed by the apostles, it becomes absurd to speak of restoring apostolic faith and practice (1996,
p. 26, emp. in orig.).

Furthermore, if the "as if" hypothesis of faith were correct, how
would the Christian—who eventually will be forced to admit that he
does not really know these things—be any different from the agnostic (who readily admits that he **cannot know** these things)?

Fourth, any idea which suggests that faith is based on mere "probability" is, at the same time, tacitly admitting that there is some probability, however minute, that Christianity just might be false. Theologian J.D. Thomas advocated the view that biblical faith is at best
a matter of probability when he suggested: "All persons live their
lives by proceeding on faith, which amounts to what they consider
a high degree of probability" (1965, p 262). He then went on to
quote Roy F. Osborne, who one year earlier had concluded:

> However, faith of any sort is based on **probability**. The sci-
> entist dotes on this in his experiments; the mathematician
> thinks he invented the idea. In a world of fallible beings, im-
> perfect senses, and partial experience, **absolute certainty
> is only a theoretical concept**.... I firmly believe that any
> earnest person, who goes to the Bible to study it carefully,
> finds staggering evidence that it could not have been written
> by man. On the positive side, he will discover evidence of the
> omniscience of the author. Add to this the moral quality and
> philosophical perfection of the writing, and the **probability**
> of God's being the author is great (1964, pp. 132,133, emp.
> added).

In addressing the idea that faith should be view as some sort of
probabilistic proposition, Sztanyo observed:

> At first glance, this view seems to be respectable because it
> appears non-dogmatic, while still claiming to tip the scales
> of probability toward theistic belief. Nevertheless, this par-
> ticular position is more dangerous than any of the others.
> This is not because the adherents of such a view are insin-
> cere, or because they lack psychological commitment to their
> belief.

To admit that Christianity is only probable is to admit the possibility that, in fact, it might be a hoax! Could you in your most irrational moment imagine even the slightest possibility of an apostle preaching the "God of probability" or the "God who may be"? ...I want to insist that there is not a single item in Christianity, upon which our souls' salvation depends, which is only probably true. In each case, the evidence supplied is sufficient to establish conclusive proof regarding the truth of the Christian faith (1996, pp. 26,14,16, emp. in orig.).

Sztanyo then suggested the following diagram:

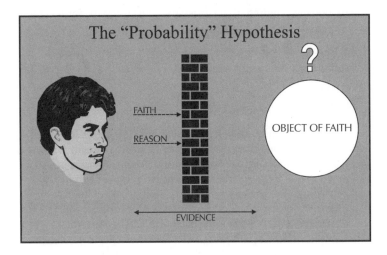

In the "as if" hypothesis, the question mark is placed on the subject side, but in this view, the question mark is placed on the object side. That is to say, if the object of faith only "probably" exists, then an impenetrable barrier prevents one from ever reaching the object of faith. After all, given this view, it is just as probable that **nothing** is on the other side of the barrier. At the same time, no action is required of the person holding such a belief (as in acting "as if"). Instead, the emphasis is placed upon the object's probability of existence, whether or not one ever **acts** at all. The only possibility of a worse position would be if one conceived of the "as if" theory having a question mark on **both** sides of the barrier!

One Christian logician, writing in a similar vein, commented:

> When someone affirms that such and such is probably the case, he is already admitting that he may be wrong, even though he may claim that his view is characterized by an extremely high degree of probability. Please note, the affirmation of a probability is at the same time an admission of the possibility of the contradictory! **That is, if I say that God probably exists (even though I call my view "faith"), I have admitted that it is possible that he does not. It doesn't matter in the least that I may say that it is an extremely high probability, for probability always remains short of certitude**. Thus, to classify "faith" as "extremely high probability" is to admit the possible correctness of the contradictory position.... It is not possible that God does not exist, and any position (on the doctrine of faith or on any other matter) which implies the possible non-existence of God is false (Deaver, 1984a, 101:673, emp. and parenthetical item in orig.).

The concept that suggests, as Arlie Hoover's statement (quoted at the beginning this chapter) does, that "faith, by standing between knowledge and ignorance, certainty and credulity, in a sense partakes of the essence of both" and "yet has some uncertainty, because the evidence is indirect," is completely at odds with biblical teaching on faith and therefore must be rejected. Faith is not a matter of ignorance, uncertainty, credulity, or probability. Those traits—each of which is intended to express some degree of doubt—are not connected in any way whatsoever with **biblical** faith. Nineteenth-century apologist Richard Whately addressed this problem when he wrote:

> The faith which the Christian Scriptures speak of and command is the very contrary of that blind sort of belief and trust which does not rest on any good reason. This last is more properly called credulity than faith. When a man believes without evidence, or against evidence, he is what we rightly call credulous. But he is never commended for this; on the contrary, we often find in Scripture mention made of persons who are reproached for their unbelief or want of faith, precisely on account of their showing this kind of credulity; that is, not

judging fairly according to the evidence, but resolving to believe only what was agreeable to their prejudices, and to trust any one who flattered those prejudices (1856, p. 196).

What, then, is biblical faith? How does it relate to "belief"? What part does sincerity play in relation to faith? And what is faith's proper relationship to reason, knowledge, evidence, and testimony?

Faith's Relationship to Belief, Feelings, and Sincerity

It is not uncommon to hear someone say, in regard to a particular belief that obviously cannot be proved, "It's just a matter of faith." Or, if someone is being advised about a specific course of action, the recommendation from friends and associates might be, "Just launch out on faith." How many times have we heard the comment that a particular belief or action is merely "a leap of faith"? Certainly, it is true that the word "faith" is used frequently in such instances. And each of these statements may well express a certain "belief." However, such a usage is neither representative of nor consistent with **biblical** faith. What is the relationship between belief and biblical faith? And what part do a person's feelings and sincerity play in building and sustaining biblical faith?

Faith and Belief

Is faith belief? Yes, faith is a type of belief. The issue, however, centers on the **kind** of belief that is biblical faith. Belief refers primarily to a judgment that something is true. But belief may be either weak or strong. If I say, "I believe it may rain tomorrow," that is an example of a weak belief. It is an opinion I hold that, while I hope is true, and thus believe to be true, nevertheless is one that I cannot prove. In an article addressing this concept, Richard England observed:

> Opinion is what one considers to be true due to one's own intuition or inward feelings based on personal fears, likes and dislikes, general attitudes and desires, or just plain guesses.

> No specific statements, experiences or arguments determine an opinion. Opinions may well be correct, or they may be incorrect. In matters of significance, what one holds as personal opinion is unimportant and makes little or no difference (2000, 142[12]:36).

However, if I say, "I believe the guilty verdict in the criminal's trial is correct and just," that is an example of a strong belief because I am able to present factual reasons for my belief, based upon available evidence. In addressing the idea of "weak" versus "strong" beliefs, philosopher David Lipe stated that "...the difference in these two types of belief turns on the **causes** of the beliefs" (n.d., p. 3, emp. added). In his text, *Critique of Religion and Philosophy*, well-known philosopher Walter Kaufmann listed seven causes of belief, the first of which was: "Arguments have been offered in its support" (1958, pp. 132ff.). Thus, strong belief is a rational act based upon adequate evidence, whereas weak belief is produced by such things as emotion, vested interest, etc. (see Lipe, p. 4).

Biblical faith is a strong belief based upon adequate, credible evidence. Although the word "faith" is used only twice in the text of the King James Version of the Old Testament (Deuteronomy 32:20 and Habakkuk 2:4), the idea of "faith" is presented throughout the text via the use of words such as "trust" (Psalm 4:5; Isaiah 26:4), "believe" (2 Chronicles 20:20), and "fear of God" (Genesis 20:11; Psalm 111:10; Ecclesiastes 12:13). According to *The Theological Wordbook of the Old Testament*, the verb form of the Hebrew term from which the English word "faith" derives is *aman*, which means to confirm, support, uphold, be established, or be faithful. The noun form (*emuna*) signifies firmness, fidelity, steadiness (see Harris, et al., 1981, 1:51).

Within the New Testament, the Greek word for "faith" is *pistis* (which is the word used in the Septuagint to translate *aman* and its varied forms into Greek). A study of the etymology of the word indicates that likely the original word was *pistos*, a verbal adjective meaning "trusting" or "worthy of trust." As Tim Ayers has noted:

Very early it appears that *pistos* included the idea of obedience, the action that proves the trust or confidence placed in men. The word was used to refer to the reliability of parties in agreements, contracts, marriage, *et cetera.*

Later, in classical Greek, *pistis* was used to speak of trust placed in other people or the gods. It also referred to credibility, credit in business, guarantee, proof, or something entrusted. The verb form *pisteuo* meant to trust something or someone. When referring to people, *pisteuo* included the idea of obedience.... In the New Testament, the noun, verb, and adjective forms of *pistis* occur over 300 times. The idea of faith is prevalent (2000, pp. 164-165).

The noun form, *pistis*, is defined primarily as: (a) "firm persuasion, a conviction based upon hearing...used in the New Testament always of faith in God or Christ, or things spiritual" (Vine, 1940, 2: 71); (b) "faithfulness, reliability, trust, confidence, faith, body of faith or belief, doctrine" (Arndt and Gingrich, 1957, pp. 668-669); or (c) "faith, confidence, fidelity, or faithfulness" (Moulton and Milligan, 1976, p. 515). In his *Greek-English Lexicon of the New Testament*, J.H. Thayer defined *pistis* as:

...conviction of the truth of anything believed...; in the N.T. of a conviction or belief respecting man's relationship to God and divine things, generally with the included idea of trust and holy fervor born of faith and conjoined with it.... [W]hen it related to God, *pistis* is the conviction that God exists and is the creator and ruler of all things, the provider and bestower of eternal salvation through Christ.... [I]n reference to Christ, it denotes a strong and welcome conviction of belief that Jesus is the Messiah, through whom we obtain eternal salvation in the kingdom of God (1958, pp. 512-513).

The verb form, *pisteuo*, is defined as: "to be persuaded of, and hence, to place confidence in, to trust...reliance upon, not mere credence" (Vine, 1:116). In fact, in the Bible *pistis* is used most often in the sense of trust or confidence. Sometimes the **object** of faith is included, as in, for example: (a) God (Mark 11:22; 1 Thessalonians 1:8; Hebrews 6:1; 1 Peter 1:21); (b) Christ (Acts 20:21;

26:18; Romans 3:22; Galatians 2:16; 3:22,26; Ephesians 1:15; 3:12; Philippians 3:9; Colossians 1:4; 2:5; 1 Timothy 3:13; 2 Timothy 3:15; Philemon 5); (c) the gospel message (Philippians 1:27); (d) the operation of God (Colossians 2:12); or (e) the Truth (2 Thessalonians 2:13).

The term "faith" also is used in other ways. Jesus spoke of "faith as a grain of mustard seed" (Matthew 17:20; Luke 17:6), indicating that faith was intended to be dynamic and to grow, not to remain static or to stagnate (which fits perfectly with the disciples' request that Jesus "increase" their faith—Luke 17:5). Christ also spoke of "having faith and doubting not" (Matthew 21:21), and indicated that He considered faith (along with judgment and mercy), as among the "weightier matters of the law" (Matthew 23:23). Prior to His crucifixion and subsequent death, Christ remarked to Peter: "I have prayed for thee, that thy faith fail not" (Luke 22:32). And in Acts, Luke used *pistis* to describe Stephen when he referred to him as "a man full of faith" (6:5,8), and to Barnabas as one who was "full of the Holy Spirit and of faith" (11:24).

On occasion, the Greek text places the direct object ("the") with *pistis* to refer to the total Christian message, thus becoming "the faith," as in: (a) Acts 6:7—"a great company of priests were obedient to the faith"; (b) Acts 14:22—Paul and Barnabas urging the new churches to "continue in the faith"; (c) Acts 24:24—Felix coming to hear Paul "concerning the faith"; (d) etc. (e.g., Romans 3:27; 1 Corinthians 6:13; 2 Corinthians 13:5; Galatians 1:23; Colossians 1:23; 2:7; 1 Timothy 3:9; 4:1; 5:8; 6:10,21; James 2:1; Jude 3).

In assessing the import and content of *pistis*, biblical language scholar Hugo McCord noted:

> On the human side, faith (*pistis*) is the greatest word in the New Testament. It is that which stands under (*hupostasis*) the things hoped for (as, heaven). It is the proof, the sure persuasion (*elenchos*) of things not visible (as, God—He. 11:1). By it human beings are able to go beyond empirical knowledge to faith-knowledge, and have an assurance that is as

> certain and reliable as sense perception. A deduction from things that are made (*poiemata*) leads one into faith-knowledge of an eternal power and deity that is so sure men who refuse to entertain it are without excuse (Ro. 1:20) [1983, p. 211, parenthetical items in orig.].

This is why Peter commanded Christians to "be ready always to give answer to every man that asketh you a reason concerning the hope that is in you, yet with meekness and fear" (1 Peter 3:15). Such a defense corresponds directly to what Walter Kaufmann would label a **cause for belief** because "arguments have been offered in its support."

Faith, Feelings, and Sincerity

But what part do feelings and sincerity play in the role of biblical faith? Certainly there can be no doubt that we live in an age in which feelings and emotions often are elevated above the teachings contained in the Word of God. Many people desperately seek a "better felt than told" type of religion. The simple fact remains, however, that **where there is no Word from God, there can be no faith** since "faith cometh by hearing, and hearing by the word of God" (Romans 10:17). Furthermore, personal feelings and emotions are not a reliable spiritual guide. As David Parks noted:

> When Samson violated his oath to God and lost his strength, he boasted to Delilah, " 'I will go out as before, at other times, and shake myself free!' But he did not know that the Lord had departed from him" (Judges 16:20). Samson felt that God was still with him when, in fact, God had departed.

> In another case, Jacob apparently felt that when he left his father's tent, he had left God behind. After dreaming of what is commonly called "Jacob's ladder," he awoke and exclaimed, "Surely the Lord is in this place, and I did not know it" (Genesis 28:16). Jacob's experience with his feelings was just the opposite of Samson's. Samson felt God was with him; God was not. Jacob thought God was not with him; God was. In both cases, their feelings were unreliable guides.

25

Jacob felt deeply and sincerely that his son Joseph was dead (Genesis 37:34). His feelings were an unreliable guide. Twenty-one years later he discovered that Joseph was alive and prospering in Egypt (45:26-27).

Hebrews 11 is filled with examples of great men and women of faith. In each example faith required them to ignore their feelings and follow the Lord's word. Faith comes from the Word of God, not our feelings (Romans 10:17) [2000, 142 [11]:19].

While biblical faith may (and often does) generate within a person certain feelings and/or emotions, the reverse is not true. That is to say, faith itself—since it is evidence-based/knowledge-based—is neither generated, nor increased, by mere feelings or emotions. The late Guy N. Woods observed:

The disposition to regard faith as a form of emotionalism has long been with us, and in former days the wide swings of subjectivism such a concept inevitably produces was considered normal and expected.... Feelings were thus suffered to take the place of facts and that which resulted, though often styled faith, was very far from it. Genuine faith derives from facts presented to the mind and from which proper and correct deductions are then drawn (John 20:30-31). Feelings which necessarily follow are the effect, not the cause, of faith (1994, 136:31).

In his book, *Surprised by Faith*, Don Bierle discussed by way of analogy the relevance (or irrelevance, as the case may be) of feelings and emotions in regard to biblical faith.

Suppose that I was asked if I believed a certain chair could hold me. Since other people were sitting on similar chairs, and because the chair looked perfectly normal, I was confident that it would. Being impatient with further questioning on the matter, I exclaim emphatically, "I have no doubt in my mind the chair will hold me!" However, if someone slipped in earlier and cut the legs through so that the least touch would topple it, my confidence and sincerity would be of no avail. My faith is only as good as the object in which I place it. If the chair is good, my faith will be good. But if the chair is bad, no matter how sincere I am, I am destined for a fall (1992, p. 66).

The point is well taken. Faith is only as good as the object in which it is placed. A "faith" that is based solely on ever-changing human emotions has shifting sands as its foundation. On the other hand, a faith that is based on evidence, and the knowledge that accrues as a result of that evidence, has bedrock as its foundation. Feelings may wax and wane; evidence does not.

Nor is sincerity alone to be equated with biblical faith. Yes, a person who desires to build and sustain a rock-solid faith would **want** to be sincere in every aspect of that faith. And again, while faith may (and often does) generate within a person a certain sincerity, the reverse is not true. Faith itself—since it is evidence-based/knowledge-based—is neither generated, nor increased, by sincerity. As Bierle went on to observe: "Faith is not the same as sincerity, nor does sincerity make faith genuine" (1992, p. 66).

An Old Testament story is illustrative of this point. Consider the case, recounted in 2 Samuel 6, of Uzzah. The Israelites had won back the Ark of the Covenant from the evil Philistines who had captured it during an earlier battle. King David commanded that the Ark be placed on an oxcart (driven by Uzzah's brother, Ahio) in order to be moved to Jerusalem. Uzzah, the text indicates, was walking beside the Ark when "the oxen stumbled" (6:6a). Uzzah—no doubt believing that the precious cargo was about to tumble from its perch on the cart and be damaged or destroyed—reached up to steady the Ark (6:6b). But Jehovah had commanded that the Israelites were not to touch the holy things of God (Numbers 4:15). And so, the moment Uzzah touched the Ark, God struck him dead (6:7).

Was Uzzah sincere in what he did? Unquestionably. And would he, personally, have considered his action on that fateful day to be one sincerely "borne of faith"? Undoubtedly. But neither his sincerity, nor the "faith" he had perilously constructed upon it, counted for anything or was able to save him from God's wrath. The simple fact is that Uzzah had ignored the Word of God on the subject—which, by definition, ensured that his action was **not** one "borne of faith" (cf. Romans 10:17), regardless of how well-intentioned or how sincere Uzzah may have been. It is not by accident that the Bible specifically states: "God smote him there for his **error**" (6:7). Faith—biblical faith—is not merely **sincere**, but also **obedient** (a topic on which I will have more to say in chapter 2).

And so, while faith may affect the emotions in a positive fashion, and even may simultaneously increase a person's desire to be sincere, faith itself is neither the end result of, nor sustained by, personal feelings and/or declarations of sincerity. Something more must be involved. That "something" is reason coupled with knowledge.

Faith and Reason

"Reason," suggested atheistic philosopher Ayn Rand, "is the faculty that identifies and integrates the material provided by man's senses" (1964, p. 13). Well-known infidel George H. Smith offered the following definition:

> Reason is the faculty by which man acquires knowledge; rational demonstration is the process by which man verifies his knowledge claims. A belief based on reason is a belief that has been examined for evidence, internal coherence, and consistency with previously established knowledge. There can be no propositions beyond the "limits of reason." To advocate that a belief be accepted without reason is to advocate that a belief be accepted without thought and without verification (1979, p. 110).

Theists Norman Geisler and P.D. Feinberg referred to reason as "the natural ability of the human mind to discover truth" (1980, p. 255). Simply put, then, reason is related directly to truth. It is man's way of discovering, understanding, and knowing truth via his mind and senses.

The **object** of reason refers to all that reason can know, which includes all truths that can be: (a) understood by reason; (b) discovered by reason to be true; and (c) proved logically to be correct. In their *Handbook of Christian Apologetics*, Kreeft and Tacelli offered the following examples. "[W]e can understand what a star is made of by human reason alone.... [W]e can discover that the planet Pluto exists by human reason alone.... [W]e can prove the Pythagorean theorem in geometry by human reason alone..." (1994, p. 32). But according to Kreeft and Tacelli, "the **act** of reason, as distinct from the **object** of reason, means all the subjective, personal acts of the mind by which we (a) understand, (b) discover, or (c) prove **any** truth" (p. 32, emp. added).

Theists teach that there are at least two different categories of truths: (1) truths of reason, but not faith; and (b) truths of both reason and faith. Truths of reason but not faith would include such things as those discovered through the empirical sciences (e.g., the composition of a star, or the existence of a planet). Truths of both reason and faith would include those things revealed by God but also understandable, discoverable, and provable by human reason (e.g., the existence of God, objective moral law, etc.). [Some theists (who accept that reason deals with those things identified solely by man's senses) contend that there exists a third kind of truth—truth of faith and not of reason (examples of which, they believe, would be the existence of the Trinity or Christ's atoning death for human sins).]

One of the foundational laws of human thought is the Law of Rationality, which demands that we draw only such conclusions as are warranted by adequate evidence. Agnostic philosopher Bertrand Russell stated it this way: "Give to any hypothesis that is worth your while to consider just that degree of confidence which the evidence warrants" (1945, p. 816). The theist's position is that biblical faith adheres firmly to the Law of Rationality and seeks conclusions that have a confidence warranted by the available evidence.

Atheism, skepticism, and infidelity, of course, would disagree vehemently with such an assessment. The adherents of those dogmas have long believed that **any** kind of "faith," by definition, is opposed to reason and thus is irrational. For example, in his widely circulated book, *Atheism: The Case Against God*, George H. Smith expended a great deal of energy and space in an attempt to prove to the reader that faith—especially "biblical" faith—is an "anti-reason" proposition from start to finish. He wrote:

> The conflicts between science and theology, or between philosophy and theology, are offshoots of a more basic conflict, that between reason and theology. Anyone who advocates theism—the belief in the supernatural—simultaneously advocates irrationalism—the belief in the unknowable.... The conflict between Christian theism and atheism is fundamentally a conflict between **faith** and **reason**. This in epistemological terms, is the essence of the controversy. Reason and faith are opposites, two mutually exclusive terms: there is no reconciliation or common ground. Faith is belief without, or in spite of, reason (1979, pp. 89,98, emp. in orig.)

Smith then lamented:

> I am not merely arguing, as a matter of historical fact, that all attempts to reconcile reason and faith have failed. My position is stronger than this. I am asserting that all such efforts must fail, that **it is logically impossible to reconcile reason and faith**. The concept of faith itself carries a "built-in" deprecation of reason; and without this anti-reason element, the concept of faith is rendered meaningless.... [A]ll defenses of faith as a means of acquiring knowledge rely upon an (implicit or explicit) deprecation of reason, such as by proclaiming the limits of reason or its undesirability in certain areas. Nor can this be otherwise. The limiting of reason is a necessary ingredient for the concept of faith; it is what makes the concept of faith **possible**.... Faith is required only if reason is inadequate; if reason is not deficient in some respect, the concept of faith becomes vacuous. The Christian creates the need for faith by denying the efficacy of reason. Without this element of denial, faith is stripped of its function; there are no gaps of knowledge for it to fill.... **The entire notion of faith rests upon and presupposes the inadequacy of reason**. This is why reason and faith are incompatible. Faith depends for its survival on the unknowable, the incomprehensible, that which reason cannot grasp. Faith cannot live in a natural, knowable universe.... A man committed

to reason, a man committed to the unswerving use of rational guidelines in all spheres of existence, has no use for the concept of faith. He can adopt faith only at the expense of reason (pp. 101,103,104,108, emp. and parenthetical item in orig.).

While all of this would be bad enough, the fact is that the situation has grown worse as a result of similar (if not identical!) statements made by some within the religious community. Liberal theologian Emil Brunner wrote, for example:

> Revelation, as the Christian faith understands it, is indeed, by its very nature, something that lies beyond all rational arguments; the argument which it certainly claims in the support does not lie in the sphere of rational knowledge, but in the sphere of that divine truth which can be attained only through divine self-communication, and not through human research of any kind (1946, p. 206).

Writer Arnold Toynbee suggested: "We must recognize the truth that it is a mistake to try to formulate religion in intellectual terms" (1956, p. 82). Adding to the confusion is this statement from J.D. Thomas in volume one of his *Facts and Faith* series:

> The necessary limitation to objectivity required in a faith system is, simply, that if faith is to be the ground or basis of acceptance with God, there cannot be a complete objectivity or absolute and empirical proof of all the facts involved. If Christianity and all its demands could be **proved**, there would be no need for faith. We would prove it to all the atheists and skeptics, and they would accept it because of being clearly forced to—in which case there would be no element of faith or trust in Christ as a sin-offering, and the entire system would be changed. By its nature, Christianity is a faith system, and for reasons best known to God, it must be.... Whether man ever rationally understands why Christianity must be a faith system, he must accept it as that and evaluate it on that basis (1965, p. 270, emp. in orig.).

What, then, is the truth of the matter? Are all of these writers correct? Is it a mistake to "formulate religion in intellectual terms"? Must man—whether or not he ever "rationally understands" Christianity

—simply accept it "by faith"? Does Christianity deprecate reason and foment revolt against rationality? Are faith and reason incompatible?

The answer to each of these questions is a resounding "No!" It is not a mistake to consider the claims of Christianity in the intellectual arena. No man or woman has to abandon "rational understanding" in order to believe in and accept Christianity's tenets. The Christian religion does not deprecate, belittle, or denigrate rational thought. And faith and reason most certainly are not incompatible. Woods wrote: "Rather than to say, 'If reason establishes the way, man has no need for faith,' it should be said, 'Reason enables one by the use of faculties divinely given—a logical and intelligent mind—to arrive at faith'" (1994, 136:31). I agree wholeheartedly with such an assessment. Reason is the capacity for logical thought. And as such, it is in no way opposed to faith, which is itself dependent upon logical thought. While faith and reason each may be distinct, they are not necessarily opposites. In his book, *Christ and the Cosmos*, E.H. Andrews explained the matter as follows.

> Another way to express this same point is to say that faith and reason belong to different "dimensions"; they are not of the same kind, and cannot therefore be opposites. If I were to tell you that "late" is the opposite of "short," you would accuse me of being illogical if not something worse. "Late," you might point out, is an adjective relating to time, whereas "short" belongs to the realm of space. Space and time are different dimensions. Only things of the same kind, belonging to the same dimension, can properly be compared or contrasted, related or opposed. Similarly, faith and reason belong to different dimensions and can no more be opposed to each other than can "late" and "short."
>
> Faith...is a **means of access** to the unseen world around us. As reason acts upon sense data to interpret the material cosmos, so reason acts upon the data of faith to comprehend the spiritual universe and God himself.... Faith and reason, therefore, work **together** to produce understanding, just as sight and reason do in matters concerning the material world. They cannot be opposed (1986, p. 15-16, emp. in orig.).

While it is true that the Bible (and Christianity) emphasize building and sustaining faith, it is not true that such an emphasis occurs at the expense of either reason or rational thought. In fact, within the pages of the Bible, faith and reason are interconnected. I will have much more to say about this in the sections that follow, but at this point, consider at the very least Paul's statement about the Christians in Berea: "Now these were more noble than those in Thessalonica, in that they received the word with all readiness of mind, **examining the Scriptures daily, whether these things were so**" (Acts 17:11). The faith of the Bereans was not divorced from reason. Whether or not they knew they were doing so, each and every day they used the Law of Rationality to draw only such conclusions as were warranted by adequate evidence—and for that they drew an apostolic commendation! The implication for other Bible believers is inescapable: the Lord expects us to use our God-given abilities of reason and rational thought to examine evidence so that we may "prove all things" (1 Thessalonians 5:21a), "try the Spirits" (1 John 4:1), and "hold fast to that which is good" (1 Thessalonians 5:21b). As Warren C. Young observed in his volume, *A Christian Approach to Philosophy*, "Deep indeed are the pitfalls into which the religious man may fall if he neglects the function of the rational faculty" (1954, p. 207). Deep pitfalls indeed!

Faith and reason, if used properly, will arrive at identical truth. As Winfried Corduan pointed out:

> [T]he path of knowing faith does not preclude a second path based on reason. When I was a child, my father told me that water consisted of oxygen and hydrogen. I believed him, for I respected his authority. However, that faith in him did not prevent me from taking a course in chemistry in college in which I carried out an experiment of producing water by combining oxygen and hydrogen. I still accept the same belief as true, but on different grounds—I first knew it by faith, now I know it by reason. The same logic may apply to our knowledge about God. Many truths are accessible to us only on the basis of faith in God's revelation including the facts

> concerning the plan of salvation. Nevertheless, there are also truths that we can know on the basis of reason as well as by faith.... There is nothing in the nature of knowing faith to preclude our accepting some truths on the basis of reason (1993, pp. 20-21).

Reason is the mental activity used in the search for truth, and neither philosophical nor theological systems avoid its use—which makes sense, considering that both are supposed to be actively involved in a search for truth. When we read in John 18:38 that Pilate asked Jesus, "What is truth?," the context makes it fairly clear that in all likelihood he had no real interest in receiving a correct answer. But that same accusation hardly can be leveled at Christian theists who base their present (and future!) lives on locating, understanding, and living by truth. When the writer of Proverbs urged us to "buy the truth, and sell it not; yea, wisdom, and instruction, and understanding" (23:23), it was excellent advice. And we have tried to take it to heart.

Consider, for example, the Universe. It exists, and reason (e.g., the Law of Cause and Effect) says that it must have an adequate antecedent cause. It is reasonable, then, to believe that this intricately designed Universe had a Designer. The choice is between matter only and more than matter as the fundamental explanation for the existence and orderliness of the Universe. The difference, therefore, between the two models is the difference between: (a) time, chance, and the inherent properties of matter; or (b) design, creation, and the irreducible properties of organization. In fact, when it comes to any particular case, there are again only two explanations for the origin of the order that characterizes the Universe and life in the Universe: either the order was imposed on matter, or it resides within matter. However, if it is suggested that the order resides within matter, we respond by stating that we certainly have not seen the evidence of such. The evidence that we do possess speaks clearly to the existence of a non-contingent, eternal, self-existent Mind that created this Universe and everything within it.

Atheists, agnostics, skeptics, and infidels expect us to believe that this highly ordered, well-designed Universe (and the complicated life it contains) "just happened." But such a suggestion is unreasonable, irrational, unwarranted, and unsupported by the facts at hand. The cause simply is not adequate to produce the effect. Every material effect must have an adequate antecedent cause. The Universe is here; intelligent life is here; morality is here; love is here. What is their adequate antecedent cause? Since the effect never can precede, or be greater than the cause, it is reasonable to suggest that the Cause of life must be a living Intelligence that Itself is both moral and loving. When the Bible records, "In the beginning, God," it makes known to us just such a First Cause.

In a similar fashion, it is reasonable to believe that the Bible is God's Word. There is no other book like it on the planet. Evidence to substantiate the Bible's claims of its own inspiration can be drawn from both external and internal sources. External evidences for inspiration include such things as historical documentation of biblical people, places, and events, or archaeological artifacts that corroborate biblical statements or circumstances. Internal evidences are part of the warp and woof of the actual biblical fabric itself. These are self-authenticating phenomena from within the Sacred Volume that bear singular testimony to the fact that the very existence of the Holy Scriptures cannot be explained in any other way except to acknowledge that they are the result of an overriding, superintending, guiding Mind. The Bible's unity, predictive prophecy, and scientific foreknowledge (to list just three examples) are unparalleled in human history—as one would expect, considering their divine source.

And the recognition of Jesus Christ as the miracle-working, resurrected-from-the-dead Son of God not only is warranted by the evidence at hand, but is historically documentable. As I stated earlier, of all the world's religions based on a man rather that just a mere "ideology," Christianity is the only one that claims, and can verify, an empty tomb for its Founder. Thousands of people go annually to the graves of the founders of the Buddhist and Muslim religions to pay homage. Yet Christians do not routinely make pilgrimages to pay homage at the grave of Jesus Christ—for the simple fact that **the tomb is empty**.

The Jews of the first century inquired, "What happened to the body?" And skeptics ever since have been pressed with the urgency of the same question. In agreement with Old Testament prophecy, and just as He had promised, Christ came forth from the tomb three days after His brutal crucifixion (Matthew 16:21; 27:63; 28:1-8). His resurrection even was confirmed (albeit inadvertently) by the Roman soldiers who had been appointed to guard His tomb. In the end, those soldiers had to be bribed to change their story so that the Jewish leaders would not lose credibility, and in order to prevent the Jewish people from recognizing their true Messiah (Matthew 28: 11-15). It is a matter of history that Christ's tomb was empty on that Sunday morning 2,000 years ago. If Jesus was not raised from the dead, how came His guarded and sealed tomb to be empty? What happened to the body?

That Christ had been raised from the dead was witnessed by many different types of people: the soldiers who guarded His tomb; the women who came early in the morning to anoint His body with spices; eleven apostles; and more than 500 other witnesses (1 Corinthians 15:4-8). When they saw the living, breathing Jesus—days after His death—they had insurmountable proof that He was Who He claimed to be all along! Even His detractors could not deny (successfully) the fact, and significance, of the empty tomb.

For those who accept, and act upon, the bountiful evidence for Christ's deity that is provided by the resurrection, life is meaningful, rich, and full (see Paul's discussion in 1 Corinthians 15). For those who reject the resurrection, the vacant tomb will stand forever as eternity's greatest mystery, and one day will serve as their final, silent judge.

Is faith opposed to reason? Hardly! Reason is faith's silent-yet-stalwart partner.

Faith and Knowledge

What, then, is the connection between faith and knowledge? Or is there one? It is possible for a person both to "know" and to "have faith" at the same time, or is it purely an either/or proposition? Some have suggested that having faith automatically rules out possessing knowledge. Flannery O'Connor, a well-known Catholic author, remarked: "Where you have absolute solutions...you have no need of faith. **Faith is what you have in the absence of knowledge**" (1979, p. 477, emp. added). In his book, *Heaven's Window*, J.D. Thomas wrote in agreement when he said: "Scientific knowledge we **know**, and things seen we know, but faith is the assurance of what we accept that we do not yet know..." (1974, p. 137, emp. in orig.). Sadly, the idea that one has **either** faith **or** knowledge—**but not both**—is quite common within the religious community. In his sorely mistitled book, *The Certainty of Faith*, Herman Bavinck asserted that while "the convictions of faith are the deepest, the most intimate, the dearest, and at the same time the most tenacious of all," it nevertheless is the case that "scientific certainty is actually more universal and stronger than the certainty acquired by faith" because "scientific certainty rests on rational and therefore more universal ground than" faith (1980, pp. 29,24).

What is the truth of the matter? Can faith and knowledge co-exist, or must one be viewed as the antithesis of the other? In addressing the proper relationship between the two, Guy N. Woods wrote:

> More recently, a much more sophisticated form of subjectivism has appeared wherein faith and knowledge are compartmentalized, put in sharp contrast, and each made to exclude the other. The allegation is that a proposition which one holds by faith one cannot know by deduction. This conclusion is reached by taking one definition of the word "know," putting it in opposition to the word "faith," and thus making them mutually exclusive. To do this is to err with reference to both faith and to knowledge! (1994, 136:31).

Pitting knowledge against faith, or faith against knowledge, is indeed "to err." Knowledge and faith are neither diametrically opposed nor mutually exclusive. In fact, faith is dependent upon knowledge. Oddly, nine years before he wrote *Heaven's Window*, J.D. Thomas published *Facts and Faith* (volume one), in which he correctly noted:

> In the same way that **factual knowledge is necessary as a pre-condition of faith**, so also is some degree of reason. Both knowledge and reason have to do with the intellect— the former being the content or raw material for the intellectual process, while reason provides the machinery for identifying, classifying and critically evaluating such material, and reaching a conclusion about it.... **Both knowledge and reason must precede commitment for valid faith** (1965, p. 260, emp. added).

What caused Dr. Thomas to abandon that position almost a decade later, I do not know. But this I do know: his position in 1965 was correct, while his position in 1974 was not. Knowledge is indeed a "pre-condition" of faith. While Christianity is seen properly as a religion of faith, it likewise must be admitted that it is a religion of knowledge. The former cannot exist without the latter. As Dave Miller put it:

> The faith spoken of in the Bible is a faith that is preceded by knowledge. One cannot **biblically** have faith in God until he comes to a knowledge of God. Thus, faith is not accepting what one cannot prove. Faith cannot outrun knowledge—for it is dependent upon knowledge (1988, 8[9]:10, emp. in orig.).

The Lord Himself hardly could have been clearer in his assessment of the part that knowledge has to play in establishing faith when He said: "Ye shall **know** the truth, and the truth shall make you free" (John 8:32). If knowledge relates to the truth (John 8:32), then faith relates no less to Him Who is the truth (John 14:1, 6). Both faith (John 16:27-30) and knowledge (John 7:17) realize that He and His teaching are from the Father. The apostle Peter's desire was that Christians "grow in the grace and **knowledge** of our Lord Jesus Christ" (2 Peter 3:18). Peter's fellow apostle, Paul, expressed "the desire that ye might be filled with the **knowledge** of his will in all wisdom and spiritual understanding" (Colossians 1:9). God's desire is that "all men be saved and come unto the **knowledge** of the truth" (1 Timothy 2:4). Paul's statement, "I **know** him whom I have believed..." (2 Timothy 1:12) is beyond all comprehension unless one understands the correct relationship between faith and knowledge. Furthermore, not only can men **know** the truth, but they can **know** that they know it, as the apostle John emphasized repeatedly. John stated that we can **know** the truth (1 John 2:21). Similarly, he noted that we can "know that we know" Jesus and "**know** that we are in him" as we keep His commandments or His word (1 John 2:3,5). Also, we can "**know** that we are of the truth" (1 John 3:14,19). Thus, John summed up this sentiment by saying simply, "We **know** that we are of God" (1 John 5:19; cf. John 7:16-17).

Faith (i.e., belief) does not somehow preclude knowledge. In fact, in the Scriptures "believing" something often is the same as "knowing" it. As Woods pointed out:

> The word "know" is often used in the sacred writings to denote that disposition ordinarily spoken of as "believing." "But as for me I know that my Redeemer liveth, and at last He will stand upon the earth" (Job 19:25). This Job knew! That is, the confidence he felt in the truth expressed was such that he could and did say that he knew it. He had no sensory evidence of it. He had neither seen, tasted, smelled, felt nor heard that which he affirmed. Yet, he knew it (cf. 2 Corinthians 5:1; 2 Timothy 1:12). Such is common biblical usage (1994, 136:31).

Isaiah used the terms "know" and "believe" synonymously with reference to God Himself: "Ye are my witnesses, saith Jehovah, and my servant whom I have chosen; that ye may **know** and **believe** me, and understand that I am he: before me there was no God formed, neither shall there be after me. I, even I, am Jehovah; and besides me there is no saviour" (Isaiah 43:10-11). On one occasion, when Jesus was having a conversation with the Jews about His status as the Son of God, He said to them: "Except ye **believe** that

I am he, ye shall die in your sins" (John 8:24). Yet in that same context, He stated that eventually those same Jews could "**know** that I am he, and that I do nothing of myself, but as the Father taught me" (8:28). The Lord also used faith and knowledge synonymously in John 17:21,23:

> That they may all be one; even as thou, Father, art in me, and I in thee, that they also may be in us: that the world may **believe** that thou didst send me. And the glory which thou hast given me I have given unto them; that they may be one, even as we are one; I in them, and thou in me, that they may be perfected into one; that the world may **know** that thou didst send me, and lovedst them, even as thou lovedst me.

He further advised the Jews: "If I do not the works of my Father, believe me not. But if I do, though ye believe not me, believe the works: that ye may **know**, and **believe**, that the Father is in me, and I in him" (John 10:37-38). From Christ's vantage point, there was no distinction between faith and knowledge.

In John 6:69, Peter said to the Lord: "And we have **believed** and **know** that thou art the Holy One of God." Here the word "know" is a form of *ginosko*, which means "to come to know, recognize, understand, or understand completely" (Vine, 1940, 2:297). Writing in 2 Timothy 1:12, Paul said "I **know** him whom I have **believed**." The Samaritans told the woman who brought Christ to them, "Now we **believe**, not because of thy speaking; for we have heard for ourselves, and **know** that this is indeed the Savior of the world" (John 4:42). The word translated "know" is a form of the Greek *oida*, which suggests "fulness of knowledge" (Vine, 2:298). Paul wrote to Timothy that

> in later times some shall fall away from the faith, giving heed to seducing spirits and doctrines of demons, through the hypocrisy of men that speak lies, branded in their own conscience as with a hot iron; forbidding to marry, and commanding to abstain from meats, which God created to be received with thanksgiving by them that **believe** and **know** the truth (1 Timothy 4:3).

In 1 John 4:16, the apostle wrote: "And we **know** and have **believed** the love which God hath in us."

Clearly, faith and knowledge are neither mutually exclusive nor diametrically opposed. These scriptures teach that for faith to be a rock-solid, truly biblical faith, it must be founded on fact. In 1 Timothy 4:3, for example, the word "know" is a form of *epiginosko*, which denotes "to observe fully, fully perceive, notice attentively, discern, recognize" (Vine, 2:99). J. Gresham Machen, one of America's most distinguished Greek scholars, spoke forcefully and critically about those who attempted to separate knowledge from faith, or who equated faith with ignorance.

> If the growth of ignorance is lamentable in secular education, it is tenfold worse in the sphere of the Christian religion and in the sphere of the Bible.... What is called faith after the subtraction of that element [knowledge—BT] is not faith at all. ...All faith involves knowledge and issues in knowledge (1946, pp. 21,41).

Consider, for example, the faith of Abraham. What kind of faith would the ancient patriarch have possessed in a God he did not **know**? If God had not spoken to Abraham, and Abraham did not have a subsequent knowledge of God, how could he have trusted Him? Interestingly, Abraham is said to have had faith only after he came to a knowledge of God's promises and thus was fully persuaded that God could, and would, do what He had pledged (Romans 4:20-21). In discussing this point, Winford Claiborne commented:

> Abraham's trust in God rested on God's previous dealings with Abraham. God had never failed to abide by his promises to Abraham. Abraham **knew** he could rely on God to fulfill exactly what he had promised him. Abraham's faith was built on a **solid foundation**—a foundation of God's faithfulness (1994, 25[2]:36, emp. added).

In the Bible, neither faith and knowledge, nor faith and reason, is set in contradistinction. The two concepts may be **distinct**, but that does not mean they must, by necessity, be **separate.** As Dick Sztanyo has noted:

It is fundamental that we learn to distinguish without separation! The fact that terms are distinct, or that various things must be understood differently, doe not imply that these terms or things are **separated** in reality. For instance, the soul and body must be distinguished, but not separated. The body has size, volume, shape, color, mass, appendages, etc., whereas the soul has none of these qualities. Do we argue, since this is so, that the body and soul must be completely separated one from the other? In a similar way, "faith" and "knowledge" differ in certain respects from one another, but it does not follow that they are to be separated.... In brief, one must **know** (or **understand**) **what** to believe before the belief is possible at all. This is true of even the most rudimentary beliefs men may hold. Thus, knowledge is **always** prior to belief (1986, pp. 206,205, emp. in orig.).

On occasion, faith may be contrasted with a **means** of obtaining knowledge (e.g., sight—see additional comments below on this point), but faith never is contrasted with knowledge (or, for that matter, with reason). In addition, at times faith and knowledge may have the same object. The Scriptures make it clear that the following can be both **known** and **believed**: (a) God (Isaiah 43:10); (b) the truth (1 Timothy 4:3); and (c) Christ's deity (cf. John 11:27 and 20:31, where the fact that He is the Christ is an object of faith, with John 6:69 and 4:42, where His deity also is an object of **both** faith **and** knowledge). I repeat: knowledge always precedes faith, and where there is no knowledge there can be no biblical faith.

In Hebrews 11, we find the "Hall of Fame of Faith," wherein each person acted out of obedient faith to God's commands. We are told that "by faith Abel **offered** unto God a more excellent sacrifice than Cain..." (11:7), "by faith Noah...**prepared** an ark to the saving of his house..." (11:7), and that "by faith Moses, kept the passover and the sprinkling of the blood, that the destroyer of the firstborn should not touch them" (11:28). What does the phrase "by faith" mean in these verses? Did these "heroes of faith" have no personal knowledge of **what** they were doing, or **why** they were doing it? Hardly!

In each of these instances, the people involved acted because they possessed **knowledge** upon which to base their faith. Cain and Abel obviously had been instructed on what would be a "more excellent" sacrifice. Noah had the dimensions of the ark set before him by God. Moses had been instructed by God Himself regarding what the Israelites were to do in order to save themselves from the death that was to befall their Egyptian captors. None of these individuals acted out of ignorance; rather, they acted from faith that had been produced by, and that was based on, knowledge.

It is true, of course, that at times the Bible records instances of men who had a "weak" or a "little" faith. But such was due to a lack of **trust** on their part, not a lack of **knowledge**. Peter provides the perfect example of this very point. When he began to walk on the water, but began to falter and sink, his problem was not a lack of knowledge, but a lack of trust (Matthew 14:24-37). One hardly could argue that Peter was ignorant of the divine power of Christ, for He had seen Him walking on the water just seconds earlier. Furthermore, when the entire affair was over, the apostles worshipped Christ and confessed Him as the Son of God (14:33). Thus, it was trust that Peter lacked, not knowledge.

It also is true, of course, that there are several different means by which a person may come to "know" something. First, there is **empirical** (or experiential) **knowledge**, which derives from the five senses (hearing, seeing, smelling, touching, tasting). Christ placed His imprimatur on this type of knowledge when He said to the multitudes in Luke 12:54-56:

> When ye see a cloud rising in the west, straightway ye say, "There cometh a shower"; and so it cometh to pass. And when ye see a south wind blowing, ye say, "There will be a scorching heat"; and it cometh to pass. Ye hypocrites, ye know how to interpret the face of the earth and the heaven; but how is it that ye know not how to interpret this time?

Second, there is **deduction**, which is "the marshaling of evidence in such a way that conclusive results can be obtained" (Sztanyo, 1996, p. 9). The Lord used an example of deduction in Mark 3:4ff. when

He asked the Pharisees: "Is it lawful on the sabbath day to do good, or to do harm, to save a life, or to kill?" The Pharisees, of course, were unable to answer Him, which is why the text goes on to say: "But they held their peace." There are numerous other examples of the use of deduction within the Bible. The writer of Hebrews remarked: "Through faith we understand" (11:3). The word translated "understand" is a form of the Greek *noeo*, which means "to perceive with the mind" (Vine, 1940, 4:168).

Third, there is **credible testimony** (see my discussion on this point in chapter 2), which is testimony from witnesses who either are known to be trustworthy, or whose testimony cannot be doubted in a justifiable fashion (cf. John 20:25-31; 1 Peter 1:8-11; 1 Corinthians 15:1-8; et al.).

Fourth, there is **intuition** (see as an example Matthew 12:24-28, where Christ responded to the Pharisees' accusation that His works were the result of the devil). In commenting on intuition as a means of knowing, Sztanyo wrote that it

> ...must be distinguished from a mere hunch or guess (the usual modern understanding of this word). By intuition, I mean a knowledge that does not depend in any way on sense perception or empirical experience. It is evident immediately, even though it may require some effort to grasp. The passage alluded to above [Matthew 12:24-28—BT] is an example in Scripture of such. It is intuitively absurd to suppose that Jesus would cast out Satan's coworkers by using Satanic power. Other examples include the metaphysical **principle of noncontradiction** ("a thing cannot both exist and not exist at the same time and in the same sense"), and the logical **law of contradiction** (derived from the metaphysical principle) which states that "contradictory statements cannot both be true." These principles are known immediately and with absolute certainty. Any attempt to deny them, in fact, presupposes them (i.e., if you deny either principle, then your denial is either true or false; it cannot be both true and false). And this knowledge does not depend upon even a single empirical observation. For instance, these principles hold true for the Universe as a whole, and even for God Himself. I know

> with certainty that God cannot both exist and not exist at the same time and in the same sense. He either exists or He does not. Empirical observation is worthless here. Yet this is a legitimate pathway to knowledge (1996, pp. 9-10, parenthetical comments in orig.).

This point deserves some elaboration. There are propositions that may be known with absolute certainty that are not, and never will be, subject to sensory perception. Consider, as an example, the following: (1) "Justice cannot be attributed to impersonal beings"; (2) "Moral virtue presupposes individual freedom"; (3) "Every judgment makes a claim to be either true or false"; (4) "Responsibility presupposes individual freedom"; (5) "Every change presupposes a sufficient cause"; (6) "Every value demands an adequate response to the part of the person to whom it is revealed"; (7) "Love implies interest in the happiness of the beloved" (see Sztanyo, 1986, p. 209).

Fifth, there is **metaphysical deduction**, a term that Sztanyo coined

> to refer to a deduction made **from** things that can be observed **to** things that potentially may never be seen (see Luke 17:20-21 and Hebrews 11:3). Robinson Crusoe (so the story goes) was marooned on an island. While walking on a beach, he discovered a footprint in the sand that clearly was not his own. He deduced accurately: (1) that there was another being on the island; and (2) that this other being was a human being. If he had never seen "Friday" face to face, the certainty of his knowledge nevertheless was not jeopardized. This same concept relates to the arguments for God's existence. God has left His "footprints," as it were, throughout the Universe (note Acts 14:17: "Yet he left not himself without witness"). Naturally, each person is responsible for reasoning properly and for drawing correct conclusions from the available evidence (Romans 1:19-22; Psalm 19:1-6; Hebrews 3:4; et al.) [1996, p. 10, emp. and parenthetical comment in orig.].

There is nothing, in or out of Scripture, to suggest that only one of these ways of arriving at knowledge results in "proof," while every other means is denied such a status. One may prove his case using any, or all, of these legitimate means of coming to knowledge (so long as the limits of each method are understood). Other factors may come into play as well. For example, the context into which a knowledge base is placed is important. In his book, *The Case for Faith*, Lee Strobel remarked:

> The point is that we certainly do have sufficient evidence about God upon which to act. And in the end, **that's** the issue. Faith is about a choice, a step of the will, a decision to want to know God personally. It's saying, "I believe—help my unbelief!" (2000, p. 255).

As Dave Miller correctly observed:

> Nevertheless, there are always those who, for one reason or another, refuse to accept the law of rationality and avoid the warranted conclusions—like those who side-stepped the proof which Christ presented by attributing it to Satan (Matt. 12:24). Christ countered such an erroneous conclusion by pointing out their faulty reasoning and the false implications of their argument (Matt. 12:25-27). The proof which the apostles presented was equally conclusive, though unacceptable to many (Acts 4:16) [1988, 8[9]:11].

Knowledge, regardless of the method by which it is obtained, must be received into an honest heart in order to accomplish any good. As the old saying suggests, "a man convinced against his will, is of the same opinion still."

It also is important, in this context, to understand that when Christians state that it is possible to "know something with absolute certainty," it is not the same thing as claiming that a person possesses "perfect knowledge." There is a vast difference between the two. As Geisler and Bocchino stated in their book, *Unshakable Foundations*:

> Since we are finite beings and cannot see all of reality at once, our view of reality is necessarily limited by our finitude. Even so, we believe that we can have **sufficient knowledge of reality** to find the answers to some of the most important questions in life without having an **exhaustive knowledge** of reality (2001, p. 52, emp. added).

For a person to say that **some** things can be known with certainty (e.g., his or her own existence, the existence of God, the inspiration of the Bible, etc.) does not commit that person to the position that **all** things may be known with absolute certainty! This difference needs to be recognized and appreciated.

CHAPTER 2

BIBLICAL FAITH—
DEFINING AND
SUSTAINING IT [PART II]

Faith and Evidence

Atheists, infidels, and skeptics have long accused Christians of holding to the irrational and illogical position that faith is little more than "belief without evidence" (or, even worse, belief **against** the evidence!). Earlier I quoted atheistic writer Richard Robinson who, in his book, *An Atheist's Values*, wrote:

> "Have faith," in the Christian sense, means "make yourself belief that there is a god **without regard to evidence**." Christian faith is a habit of flouting reason in forming and maintaining one's answer to the question whether there is a god (1964, pp. 119-120, emp. added).

British atheist Antony Flew combined Christians' so-called "belief without evidence" with their attempts to instill faith in their children, and drew the conclusion that such a feat amounts to "a moral outrage."

> Campaigns for proselytization must become...perfectly preposterous if there...is no good reason to believe the doctrines

to be preached.... If matters of faith have no sort of claim to constitute knowledge...then the religious indoctrination of children is immediately exposed as a moral outrage (1966, p. 159).

[How an atheist could call **anything** a "moral outrage"—and yet still claim to be an atheist—is utterly incomprehensible. By what objective standard may an atheist consistently label something or someone either "moral" or "immoral," since atheism and its cosmogony of organic evolution are completely dependent upon morals and ethics being, by definition, situational?] In his *Atheist Debater's Handbook*, B.C. Johnson commented:

The theist argues that we have to rely on some faith in our everyday lives and then using this statement as a springboard, he leaps to the conclusion that faith in anything is somehow justified—fairies, leprechauns, walking on air, and God. But the fact remains that **we do not have good reason for believing any of these things** (1981, pp. 95-96, emp. added).

Do Christians "believe without evidence"? Do we not have "any good reason for believing" what we believe? Is our proselytization of our own children, and others whom we may influence to believe as we do, "a moral outrage" due to the fact that Christianity "has no sort of claim to constitute knowledge"?

The answer to each of these questions, and others like them that have been posed by infidelity throughout the ages, is a resounding "No!" Christians do not believe in God "without evidence." Nor is faith believing the unbelievable or thinking the unthinkable. As James F. Ross noted in his *Introduction to the Philosophy of Religion*, to argue that faith rests upon "inadequate evidence" or that faith "is the habit of the irrational or the nonrational" is "entirely unfaithful to the Scriptural and traditional teaching of Judaism and Christianity" (1969, pp. 84-85). The fact is that we believe **because** of the evidence, **not in spite of it**! In his book on the relationship between faith and knowledge, *Faith and Reason*, Dick Sztanyo remarked:

> Biblical faith is built upon a prior understanding (knowledge) of what is to be believed.... Any conception of faith that severs it from its objective, epistemological base (foundation of knowledge) is at variance with biblical teaching! Biblically speaking, one does not believe that God is (or any other items to be accepted "by faith"): (1) against the evidence; (2) without evidence; and/or (3) beyond the evidence. Rather, one believes on the basis of evidence sufficient to establish the conclusion (1996, p. 8, emp. and parenthetical items in orig.).

Faith, because it is related directly to knowledge, is based on credible evidence. Further, knowledge is critical in making faith active. Steve Kumar concluded: "Faith which lacks knowledge and evidence cannot win obedience" (1990, p. 49). In regard to what he termed "rational" belief, Sztanyo observed:

> This evidence enlightens the intellect which then makes a volitional commitment not only possible (since I now know **what** to believe) but also rational (i.e., **I know** what to believe)! Thus, **faith is a volitional commitment of an informed intellect**! Knowledge without commitment is disbelief (John 8:30-46; 12:42,43; James 2:19); commitment without knowledge is irrationality! Neither is a genuine option for a Christian (p. 29, emp. and parenthetical items in orig.).

From a logical standpoint, any view of faith that lacks objective evidence is unworthy of the name "faith." If faith is not objective, then how do we know that we "have faith" in the first place? Gordon H. Clark asked: "If there is no objective truth, if the How supersedes the What, then can truth be distinguished from fancy?" (1961, p. 75). Edward John Carnell, in his text, *The Case for Biblical Christianity*, addressed this same point when he commented: "While faith may involve a cordial commitment of the whole man to Jesus Christ, it is a passion which is drawn out by **objectively measurable evidences**" (1969, p. 56, emp. added).

It is those "objectively measurable evidences" that we as Christians are commanded to use to **prove** our case "to every man that asketh a reason concerning the hope" that we possess (1 Peter

3:15). Whether God exists, and what He is like, are issues to be settled by an appeal to credible evidence. In the Old Testament, Isaiah presented a clear challenge to those who dared argue against God's existence when he said: "'Produce your cause,' saith Jehovah; 'bring forth your strong reasons'" (Isaiah 41:21). When Isaiah challenged (and defeated) his detractors, he used the evidence from predictive prophecy—a clear proof of an omniscient Being—to do so. He declared: "Let them bring forth, and declare unto us what shall happen: declare ye the former things, what they are, that we may consider them, and know the latter end of them; or show us things to come" (41:22). The very thing the false gods of the pagans could **not** do (41:22-24), God **could** do (see Isaiah 42:8-9).

Proving such things as the existence of God and the legitimacy of Christianity is not an **option**; it is an **obligation**! Paul commanded: "Prove all things [literally, "put all things to the test"]; hold fast to that which is good" (1 Thessalonians 5:21). When the apostle wrote to the first-century Christians in Philippi, he spoke of his "defense and confirmation of the gospel" (Philippians 1:7). An example of Paul's defense of God's existence—and his use of reason, knowledge, and evidence in the presentation of that defense—can be seen in Romans 1:20-22 where he wrote:

> For the invisible things of him since the creation of the world are clearly seen, being perceived through the things that are made, even his everlasting power and divinity; that they may be without excuse: because that, knowing God, they glorified him not as God, neither gave thanks; but became vain in their reasonings, and their senseless heart was darkened. Professing themselves to be wise, they became fools.

An additional example of his defense (this time of the Christian system) can be seen in his powerful sermon presented on Mars Hill (Acts 17). And later, when he wrote his first epistle to the Christians at Corinth, he specifically linked the truthfulness and efficacy of the Christian faith to the fact of, and evidence for, Christ's resurrection

(1 Corinthians 15). In his book, *A Christian Approach to Philosophy*, Warren C. Young addressed this point:

> The Biblical pattern for the defense of the faith is well illustrated in the book of Acts. The apostles preached a message which arose out of their personal experience with Christ. Invariably the question arose, What evidence have you to show that your so-called experience is more than fanaticism? In each case they pointed to the fact of the living Lord. The resurrection was presented as the supreme evidence for the hope that was within them (1954, p. 208).

Bierle correctly noted:

> The significance of knowledge to a valid faith must be understood. The object of Christian faith is the person of Jesus. If he is not who he claims to be, the incarnate Son of God, then no amount of sincerity, confidence, and religious experience can make it legitimate. This is precisely the conclusion of the apostle Paul to the people at Corinth. He said that "if Christ has not been raised [from the dead], then our preaching is vain, your faith also is vain, your faith is worthless...."

> The apostle Paul is right. I can only put faith in Jesus if I **know** about him. And only if that knowledge indicates reasonable certainty of His deity will my faith in Him be any good. I cannot even get started into the area of personal faith **without using my mind and interacting with the evidence**. This first component of faith as taught in the Bible is certainly more attractive than the anti-intellectual caricature of it... (1992, pp. 66-67, emp. added, bracketed material in orig.).

Earlier in the book of Acts, we are told that Apollos "powerfully confuted the Jews, and that publicly, showing by the scriptures that Jesus was the Christ" (Acts 18:28). Apollos compelled the Jews to "interact with the evidence," and in so doing "powerfully confuted them." That was not done via an irrational, nebulous concept called "faith." Rather, it was done with irrefutable evidence. When John the Baptist, while in prison, heard about the works of Christ (Matthew 11:2-6), he sent his disciples to inquire: " 'Art thou he that cometh, or look we for another?' And Jesus answered and said unto

them, 'Go and tell John the things which ye hear and see: the blind
receive their sight, and the lame walk, the lepers are cleansed, and
the deaf hear, and the dead are raised up, and the poor have good
tidings preached to them' " (Matthew 11:3-5). Christ's point was this:
look at the evidence, and make up your own mind—which is exactly what John and his disciples did!

The fact is, neither Isaiah, nor Christ, nor Paul, nor Apollos, nor
any of the other Bible characters, ever saw faith as anything but ev-
idence-based/knowledge-based. Nor should we today view biblical faith any differently.

In discussing the type, and strength, of the evidence upon which
Christianity is built, Dave Miller wrote:

> The Bible insists that evidence is abundantly available for
> those who will engage in unprejudiced, rational inquiry. The
> resurrection claim, for example, was substantiated by "many
> infallible proofs," including verification through the observa-
> tion of more than 500 persons at once (Acts 1:3; 1 Cor. 15:
> 5-8). Many proofs were made available in order to pave the
> way for faith (John 20:30,31). Peter offered at least four lines
> of evidence to those gathered in Jerusalem before he con-
> cluded his argument with "therefore..." (Acts 2:14-36). The
> acquisition of knowledge through empirical evidence was un-
> deniable, for Peter concluded, "as ye yourselves also know..."
> (Acts 2:22). John referred to the auditory, visual and tactile
> perceptions which provided further empirical verification (1
> John 1:1,2). Christ offered "works" to corroborate his claims
> so that even his enemies did not have to rely merely on his
> words—if they would but honestly reason to the only logical
> conclusion (John 10:24,25,38). The proof was of such a
> magnitude that one Pharisee, a ruler of the Jews, even ad-
> mitted: "We know that thou art a teacher come from God;
> for no man can do these miracles that thou does, except God
> be with him" (John 3:2) [1988, 8[9]:10-11].

Thus, as Young went on to note: "...true belief must always be based
on some cognitive content" (1954, p. 206). That "cognitive content" derives from the available evidence, not from some "better-
felt-than-told" type of religious mumbo-jumbo.

Faith and Credible Testimony

While it is true that a portion of the evidence that builds and sustains faith derives from experiential knowledge, it also is true that a portion of the evidence does not. The fact of the matter is that a sizable portion of the evidence that we use to build and sustain a legitimate, personal faith derives from credible testimony. Skeptics, of course, have suggested that reliance upon the testimony of another person does **not** result in reliable knowledge. Thomas Paine wrote in *The Age of Reason*:

> No one will deny or dispute the power of the Almighty to make such a communication, if he pleases. But admitting, for the sake of a case, that something has been revealed to a certain person, and not revealed to any other person, it is revelation to that person only. When he tells it to a second person, a second to a third, a third to a fourth, and so on, it ceases to be a revelation to all those persons. It is revelation to the first person only, and **hearsay** to every other, and consequently they are not obliged to believe it (1794, pp. 8-9, emp. in orig.).

Paine's assessment, however, is completely incorrect, as an examination of both historical and biblical cases will attest. Is testimony, by necessity, diluted or destroyed simply because it has been passed from generation to generation? Not at all. As J.D. Thomas noted, one source

> ...through which valid knowledge is considered to come is by or from an **authority**, who is qualified to know, and who testifies or reveals his knowledge to others who in turn accept his testimony by faith. This chain of knowledge, revelation and faith, is the way that the most of the knowledge that each one of us possesses has come to us. Our knowledge about George Washington, Napoleon, and Alexander the Great is dependent upon the testimony of their contemporaries and the historians who have brought it on down to us. Even much of our knowledge of current events is dependent upon authority, testimony, and faith—events like wars, scientific achievements and activities of people whom we do not know personally are accepted as having happened through the testimony of those whom we count to be competent authorities.

> Testimony or revelation is a valid and legitimate source of obtaining accurate knowledge. If we accept that Jesus Christ was literally raised from the dead we do so because of the testimony of eyewitnesses, who thus, because of their empirical knowledge, are competent authorities and qualified to thus testify. The knowledge that is learned through such an avenue can be just as true for us today as for the original eyewitnesses. Had we witnessed the resurrection ourselves, the fact that it happened would not be any truer than if we accept the testimony of the authorities who saw it. This means simply that certain truth or certain knowledge can come through the avenue of testimony and faith just as well as it can come by our own sense experience. Its validity is not weakened merely because it came through testimony (1965, pp. 254-255, emp. in orig.).

Indeed, we **know** that historical characters such as George Washington, Napoleon, and Alexander the Great lived, even though no one still living has seen them. We **know** that Plato, Aristotle, and Socrates lived, even though no one for many generations ever set eyes on them. We **know** of numerous other people and events in the same manner, as a direct result of credible testimony passed faithfully from age to age. Were we to take Paine's assessment at face value, we would lose all knowledge of people and events beyond the lifetimes of the actual eyewitnesses that saw those actual people or events.

Further, biblical information provides a good test case for the accuracy of information passed from one person to another. In Mark 16, the account is recorded of Mary Magdalene having seen the Lord after His resurrection. She immediately went and told other disciples who, the text indicates, "disbelieved" (Mark 16:11). Later, Jesus appeared to two men walking in the country. They, too, returned to the disciples and reported that the Lord was alive, but of the disciples it is said that "neither believed they them" (Mark 16:13). Were these disciples justified in rejecting the report of the Lord's resurrection merely because they had not been eyewitnesses themselves? Was their disbelief somehow to be considered evidence of "intellectual integrity" on their part? Were they correct in, and to be commended for, their rejection of two different reports that originated with trustworthy eyewitnesses?

No, the disciples were not justified in their disbelief. Nor was that disbelief evidence of intellectual integrity on their part. Later, when the Lord appeared to them, He made it clear that He did not appreciate either their skepticism or their failure to accept credible testimony, since He "upbraided them with their unbelief and hardness of heart, because they believed not them that had seen him after he was risen" (Mark 16:14). Thus, the Lord verified the principle that Thomas Paine attempted to refute. If Mary Magdalene had expressed accurately to the disciples what she had seen, and they in turn expressed accurately what they had been told, would this not constitute valid evidence-based testimony of the sort that would warrant genuine faith in the resurrection? Facts must be reported before they can be believed. In Acts 18, the circumstances are provided in which "many of the Corinthians, hearing, believed...." What did they hear that caused them to believe? It was the testimony given by Paul. At times, faith can be described as knowledge based upon credible testimony. As Dr. Thomas observed: "Man's faculty of reason, however, when considered as the capacity to evaluate revealed testimony, does not militate against faith but is actually necessary to it" (1965, p. 261).

Another biblical instance that documents the legitimate faith-building nature of reliable testimony can be found in the case involving the refusal of one of Christ's apostles to believe in His resurrection without empirical evidence. The text in John 20:24-29 reads as follows:

> Thomas, one of the twelve, called Didymus, was not with them when Jesus came. The other disciples therefore said unto him, "We have seen the Lord." But he said unto them, "Except I shall see in his hands the print of the nails, and put my hand into his side, I will not believe." And after eight days again his disciples were within, and Thomas with them.

> Jesus cometh, the doors being shut, and stood in the midst, and said, "Peace be unto you." Then saith he to Thomas, "Reach hither thy finger, and see my hands; and reach hither thy hand, and put it into my side: and be not faithless, but believing." Thomas answered and said unto him, "My Lord and my God." Jesus saith unto him, "Because thou hast seen me, thou hast believed: blessed are they that have not seen, and yet have believed."

While Thomas is to be commended for the fact that he wanted evidence adequate to the task of building and sustaining his faith, at the same time he is **not** to be commended for refusing to accept one of the legitimate avenues of obtaining that evidence—credible testimony. As J.D. Thomas went on to explain:

> Especially interesting, however, is Jesus' reply to Thomas, in that He declared that valid testimony given by a competent authority was adequate knowledge upon which to erect a valid faith. Empirical evidence is not required—that given by eyewitnesses is sufficient for the faith which brings blessedness. This means that those of us who live in later generations and who are forced to accept the testimony of eyewitnesses can have as valid a faith as anyone (1965, pp. 274-275).

Notice that Christ said to Thomas: "Blessed are they that have **not seen**, and yet **have believed**" (John 20:29b). Christ's point was that while Thomas could build and sustain his faith via firsthand, empirical evidence, there would be some who would be required to build and sustain their faith on the basis of credible testimony that came long after the actual events to which their testimony referred. The people of whom Christ spoke never would have the opportunity to witness, from a first-person perspective, the kinds of things Thomas had seen. Yet that did not mean that they would possess a faith that was any less valid. Their faith would not be diminished by a lack of empirical evidence, since credible testimony from reliable eyewitnesses could serve just as well to establish the veracity of Christ's life, death, and resurrection. Regarding this point, Mark Lewis wrote:

We obtain knowledge by either our senses, or by testimony. The keyboard before me, the screen into which I am looking, the books on my table—I know they are there by sensory evidence, i.e., feeling, seeing, tasting, hearing, or smelling. One or more of these I now use regarding my computer, books, etc. around me. I know they are here; it is not a matter of opinion with me, it is a matter of knowledge. However, I know, just as surely as these books, etc. are before me now, that the city of Kiev in Russia exists. I have never been there to see it or touch any building or to smell peculiar smells and so forth: but no rational person can deny it exists. How do I know Kiev exists when I have no sensory evidence on which to base my judgment? I know by faith, by the testimony of others who have been there and recorded its existence. And, as our proposition states, this is exactly the way we obtain the vast, huge majority of our knowledge. Newspapers, magazines, TV, books, word of mouth—these avenues supply most of our enlightenment. As we grow up in school, we study history, geography, science, various disciplines, all of which frequently use some form of testimony to provide knowledge to the student, so that the system—fact, testimony, confirmation, faith—is the constant, unchanging order of things. And before there can be any faith, there must be facts; but before we can know the facts, they must be reported (testimony); but before they can be believed, there must be confirmation —then faith is produced. Again, this is the constant, never-changing order. Let us see how it works in example.

I report to you that Napoleon Bonaparte died on the island of St. Helena, off the African coast. So we have here the circumstances.

Fact—Bonaparte's death on St. Helena

Testimony—I report it to you

Confirmation—in this case, your confidence in me

Faith—your belief, acceptance of the fact, to the point that you could go and report your knowledge of that event

Now, I do not have any sensory knowledge of where Bonaparte died; I was not there, did not seen him succumb (it was in 1821!).... I know the place of the emperor's death by faith. Yet I do know it! I know the place of Bonaparte's demise just as surely as I know a red Bible sits before me right now....

Frequently, however, affairs may be more complex, and simple testimony may not be sufficient to produce faith: more confirmation is required. There are few statements in our language more often repeated than "I find that hard to believe." Someone might say, regarding our above example, "Ah, but I thought Napoleon died on Elba." You might be suspicious of my report; you do not believe; you require further confirmation. Thus, I bring to you several history books and give you the evidence. You are confirmed, you believe, you now know the place of Napoleon's death. This circumstance is not unusual.... The point here is that some facts require stronger confirmation than others. But our major proposition has been proven, i.e., that most of our knowledge, I would suspicion well over 90%, comes by faith, by the acceptance of some form of testimony, whether it be oral, written, physical, or logical. This is so crucial, so fundamental, and yet how few people really understand it (1987, pp. 48-50, parenthetical items in orig.).

Indeed, so few people do seem to "really understand" how much of our everyday knowledge is derived from credible testimony. That testimony forms an important part of the "many infallible proofs" that substantiate a person's faith. Without such testimony, and our legitimate acceptance of it, we would be left to drift aimlessly in a sea of doubt and despair, never cognizant of the things we need to know to live "soberly, righteously, and godly in this present world" (Titus 2:12).

Faith and Sight

In chapter 1, I quoted theologian Paul Tillich, who introduced his book *Dynamics of Faith* with this sentence: "There is hardly a word in the religious language, both theological and popular, which is subjected to more misunderstandings, distortions and questionable definitions than the word 'faith'" (1957). There is no doubt in my mind that many of those "misunderstandings, distortions and questionable definitions" have arisen from an abuse of Paul's statement in 2 Corinthians 5:7 where the apostle remarked that "we walk by faith, not by sight." I therefore believe that an examination of this passage, and the apostle's intent considering both the immediate and remote contexts, is critical to our study of biblical faith.

Paul's point in 2 Corinthians 5:7 is both amplified and clarified by his statement in verse 16 of that same chapter: "Wherefore we henceforth know no man after the flesh: even though we have known Christ after the flesh, **yet now we know him so no more.**" In other words, Jesus **had** been here in the flesh in the past, and hence could be known. But at the time Paul wrote 2 Corinthians 5:16, the situation had changed because Christ no longer was on the Earth—which is why the apostle reiterated the point that "**now** we know him no more." Of course, Christ still could be known (cf. 2 Timothy 1:12), but not "after the flesh." Had Paul written 2 Corinthians several years earlier while Christ still was alive and living in the Middle East, these passages (5:7; 5:16) never would have been included among his remarks. But since they were written at some point **after** Christ's ascension, Paul therefore was compelled to make the comparison he did in 2 Corinthians 5:7.

His point, quite simply, was this. There was a time when faith and sight went together. That is to say, at one time in history, men walked by faith **because of sight**. This was true, for example, of Thomas when Christ said to him after His resurrection, "Because thou hast **seen** me, thou hast **believed**" (John 20:29a, emp. added). The Samaritans, mentioned earlier, believed on the Lord, at least in part, because they had **seen** Him (John 4:41). This was true of many first-century Christians who were fortunate enough to see, from a first-person perspective, such things as Christ's miracles, death, and resurrection, or the marvelous wonders and signs performed by the apostles after His ascension. As one writer put it:

> Others during the Lord's ministry came to believe on him because of the things which they saw and heard. Some saw the dead raised. Some were amazed at his teaching and preaching. And because of such things, they understood the truth of the claims that he made. Later, others were impressed by the miracles which were performed during the days of the early church. And some of these obeyed the gospel (Deaver, 1984b, 101:690).

During the early years of the church, many believed because of the miracles they saw—the result being that strong faith was produced by such events. Many came in obedience to the Lord because of what they **heard** and **saw**. Luke, writing in Acts 6:6, commented on this very fact when he wrote: "The word of God was continuing to spread. The group of followers in Jerusalem increased, and a great number of the Jewish priests believed and obeyed" (New Century Version; cf. Acts 2:41-47).

However, as I stated earlier, at times faith may be contrasted with a **means** of obtaining knowledge (e.g., sight), **but faith never is contrasted with knowledge itself**. Paul's intent in 2 Corinthians 5:7—that "we walk by faith, not by sight"—was not to contrast faith and knowledge, but instead to contrast faith **produced by sight** with faith **produced by other means of gaining knowledge** (e.g., credible testimony, deduction, etc.).

To illustrate this point, notice what else Christ said to Thomas in their conversation. "Blessed are they that have not seen, and yet have believed" (John 20:29b). Christ's point was that while Thomas had faith **with** sight, there would be some who would possess just as genuine a faith **without** sight. That is to say, such people never would have the opportunity to witness, from a first-person perspective, the things that Thomas and those around him had seen. Yet according to Jesus, that did not mean that they would possess a less-valid faith than those who had witnessed such events. Their faith would not be diminished by lack of sight, since there were other legitimate means of knowing. Today, Christians can have a genuine, rock-solid faith **without** sight, thanks to such things as credible testimony from reliable eyewitnesses and other means of knowledge that are not necessarily dependent upon having personally seen something firsthand. In fact, that was Peter's exact point of emphasis when he wrote of Christ, "whom not having seen ye love; on whom, **though now ye see him not, yet believing**, ye rejoice greatly with joy unspeakable and full of glory: **receiving the end**

of your faith, even the salvation of your souls." All of us believe in people, places, and events that we never have seen personally, and that no one of our generation has seen firsthand. Yet that does not diminish the factuality of those people, places, or events. Nor does it diminish the faith routinely produced via credible testimony from people of the past who **did** witness such things. Truly, one may "walk by faith, not by sight," yet still possess knowledge (i.e., truth justifiably believed).

In addition, the passage in John 20:29 ("Because thou hast seen me, thou hast believed") helps us understand the statement found in Hebrews 11:1 in a much clearer fashion. The writer of Hebrews observed: "Now faith is the substance of things hoped for, the evidence of things not seen" (KJV/NKJV). The Bible's critics, of course, have objected strenuously to this passage. As atheist Richard Robinson lamented:

> When we investigate what Christians mean by their peculiar use of the word **faith**, I think we come to the remarkable conclusion that all their accounts of it are either unintelligible or false. Their most famous account is that in Hebrews 11:1: "Faith is the substance of things hoped for, the evidence of things not seen." This is obviously unintelligible (1976, pp. 120-121, emp. in orig.).

Such a charge, however, is based on the critic's bias against the text, not on the fact that the text itself is incomprehensible or unintelligible. Consider the following. The Greek word translated "substance" is *hupostasis*, and means that which stands under, the foundation, that which produces confidence. The Greek word for "evidence" is *elengchos*, and signifies proof, proving, and hence inner conviction (Arndt and Gingrich, 1957, p. 248). Thus, faith is seen as that which undergirds the Christian system and provides proof that allows for inner conviction. Nothing at all "unintelligible" about that, is there? Both terms are indicative of the fact that faith must be founded on fact or it is not faith at all. Or, as Winford Claiborne put it: "If confidence and proof have no foundation, we are guilty of merely wishing or dreaming. And wishing does not make it so" (1994, 25[2]:35). [One almost is tempted to suggest, in regard to the atheist's view of Hebrews 11:1 being unintelligible, that "wishing does not make it so."]

One of the best expositions of Hebrews 11:1 that I have ever seen was presented in a sermon delivered on June 25, 1893 in Louisville, Kentucky by the inimitable Restoration preacher J.W. McGarvey. As McGarvey began his lesson, he explained to the audience:

> I have been puzzled a good deal in former years over this verse, and the proper rendering of it, and in searching about through various learned works for something that would be clear and satisfactory, I fell upon a translation of it in Robinson's great Lexicon of the Greek New Testament. Edward Robinson was probably the most learned philologist that the Presbyterian Church of America has ever produced, and he translates the verse, "Faith is confidence as to things hoped for; conviction as to things not seen." Now that is as clear as a bell. Faith is thus defined as having relation to two classes of objects: things hoped for, and things unseen. But the latter class includes the former. All the things that we hope for are unseen. That which you see and have in your presence is not an object of hope, but, whilst the things not seen include the things hoped for, faith contains different elements with reference to these two classes of objects.
>
> With reference to the things that are unseen—and that expression includes everything in the past, the present, and the future, that is not an object of sight or knowledge—with reference to them, faith is conviction, and that means that when we have faith about them, we are **convinced** in regard to them. Now many of those things in the future that are unseen, are objects of hope; those in the past are not. We do not hope for what is past. And when this unseen thing on which faith rests is an object of hope, then that other element of faith comes in—**confidence** as to things hoped for (1958, p. 84, emp. added).

McGarvey then proceeded to provide his audience with a number of examples from the Divine Record that illustrated the point he was trying to make about faith being a "conviction" that provided a "confidence."

"By faith Enoch was translated so that he was not found" when they hunted for him. Here our author, seeing that nothing is said in the history of Enoch in the Old Testament about his having any faith, feels the necessity of proving that he had; so he proceeds to say that "before his translation he had testimony that he was well pleasing to God; but without faith it is impossible to please God, seeing that if a man comes to God, he must believe that He is, and that He is the rewarder of them that diligently seek Him." In these words, the apostle brings out the two elements of Enoch's faith. He believed that God is—the **conviction** of an unseen thing. He believed that God is the rewarder of them that diligently seek Him—**confidence** as to a hoped for reward. And, under that confidence, he walked with God and pleased Him....

"By faith Noah, being warned of God of things not seen as yet" (here he brings in the very terms of his definition, referring to the unseen flood yet in the future), "moved with godly fear, prepared an ark to the saving of his family." Here was **conviction** as to an unseen disaster that was to sweep over the earth, threatening the life of every human being, and here was **confidence** in the hoped-for deliverance of his own family under the promise that God had made....

The next example is Abraham.... "By faith, Abraham, when he was called to go out into a country that he should afterward receive for an inheritance, obeyed and went out, not knowing whither he went." Was not that a strange journey? He left his native land and kindred, and went off on a journey, he did not know how long, did not know how far, to receive a land for an inheritance; and he did not know where the land was. There was **conviction** as to an unseen and an unknown country, and a **confident** hope of possessing it (pp. 85-87, emp. added, parenthetical comment in orig.).

None of those discussed in these examples, nor, for that matter, any of the other people mentioned in Hebrews 11, acted without knowledge. They realized that faith is indeed the "confidence" [*hupostasis*—that which stands under, the foundation, hence that which produces confidence] of things hoped for, the "conviction" [*elengchos*—that which signifies proof, hence that which provides inner conviction] of things not seen. Viewed in this light, Hebrews 11:1 not only is **not** "unintelligible," but in fact captures the essence of biblical faith in a marvelous fashion.

Faith and Revelation

In addition to being produced by such things as sight, experiential knowledge, and credible testimony, biblical faith often is produced by revelation. Geisler and Feinberg have defined revelation as "a supernatural disclosure by God of truth which could not be discovered by the unaided powers of human reason" (1980, p. 255). David Elton Trueblood noted:

> While religion shares both faith and reason with other areas of experience, one religious concept, that of revelation, is unique. Revelation differs radically, both from reason and from epistemological faith, in that it claims to refer to an act or to acts of divine self-disclosure.... The main claim of revelation is not that the human recipient is made aware, by a special method, of a set of truths about God, but the far more exciting claim that he is made aware of **God Himself** (1957, pp. 27,29, emp. in orig.).

Again, skeptics have objected. English philosopher Herbert Spencer, an avowed agnostic, advocated the position that just as no bird ever has been able to fly out of the heavens, so no man ever has been able to penetrate with his finite mind the veil that hides the mind of the Infinite. This inability on the part of the finite (mankind), he concluded, prevented any knowledge of the Infinite (God) reaching the finite.

Such a premise is flawed internally because it wrongly assumes that the Infinite is equally incapable of penetrating the veil—a position that reduces the term "Infinite" to absurdity. An Infinite Being that is unable to express Itself is less finite than mortals who forever are expressing themselves. And an Infinite Being that is both capable of self-expression and aware of the perplexity and needs of mortal man, yet fails to break through the veil, is less moral than mortal man. As one writer expressed it:

> What **man** would stay in shrouded silence if he were the Infinite and knew that a word from him would resolve a thousand human complexes, integrate shattered personalities, mend broken lives, bring coveted light to baffled minds, and healing peace to disturbed hearts? (Samuel, 1950, p. 14, emp. added).

To be either correct or defensible, Spencer's proposition must work **both** ways. Finite man must be unable to penetrate the veil to the Infinite, but at the same time the Infinite likewise must be unable to penetrate the veil to the finite. By definition, however, the Infinite would possess the capability of breaking through any such veil. As Trueblood went on to note:

> There is nothing intrinsically unreasonable about the hypothesis that, if God really is, He is always reaching out to men in a vast variety of ways. Why should it be assumed that we are seeking Him, but that He is not seeking us? There is nothing implausible about the notion of a double search conducted simultaneously. The figure of speech involved in "Behold, I stand at the door and knock" (Revelation 3:20) may, indeed, be accurate... (1957, p. 28).

The theist contends that God has revealed Himself to mankind, via the sixty-six books of the Bible, in a most specific fashion. Speaking in general terms, there has been only one permanent revelation, i.e., the supernatural revelation found within the Scriptures. Actually, however, throughout human history God has disclosed Himself and His will in at least three different ways: theophanies, miracles, and direct communications.

Theophanies were appearances of God Himself. He is spoken of as dwelling between the cherubim (Psalm 80:1; 99:1). He appeared in fire and clouds and smoke (cf. Genesis 15:17; Exodus 3:2; 19:9,16ff.; 33:9; Psalm 78:14; 99:7; Matthew 17:5). He appeared in stormy winds (Job 38:1; 40:6; Psalm 18:10-16). Theophany reached its highest point in the incarnation, in which Jesus Christ became flesh and dwelt among men (John 3:16; 14:9; Colossians 1:19; 2:9).

God chose to reveal Himself through **miracles** that not only showcased His presence and power, but simultaneously emphasized great truths as well. The Maker of the Universe manifested His presence in the works of His creative genius (Psalm 19:1; Romans 1:20-21). Miracles confirmed the words of prophecy, and stood as evidence of God's omnipotence among the people that He had created.

God also disclosed Himself through **direct communications**. In doing so, He made His thoughts and will known to men. Sometimes it was through an audible voice (Genesis 2:16; 3:8-19; 3:9-16; 4:6-15; 9:1,8,12; 32:26; Exodus 19:9; Numbers 12:8; Deuteronomy 5:4-5; 1 Samuel 3:4; 1 Kings 19:12). He worked through visions and dreams (Genesis 20:3; Numbers 12:6; Deuteronomy 13:1-6; 1 Samuel 28:6; Isaiah 6; 21:6ff.; 29:10-11; Ezekiel 1-3; 8-11; Daniel 1:17; 2:19; 7-10; Amos 1:1; Joel 2:28). On unique occasions, He even made known His presence in such an unusual manner as to speak via the mouth of a donkey (Numbers 22:28). And lastly, God has communicated His thoughts and will to men via the Holy Spirit (Mark 13:11; Luke 12:12; John 14:17; 15:26; 16: 13; 20:22; Acts 6:10; 8:29; 2 Peter 1:20-21). Harold Lindsell, former editor of *Christianity Today*, wrote:

> Had God chosen not to reveal Himself, man could never have known Him. And man can never know more about God than God chooses to disclose.... Whatever knowledge of God is available exists solely because God has chosen to make it known. This is His self-revelation (1976, p. 28).

Lacking access to that "self-revelation" from God, we would have no accurate way of understanding what we needed to know regarding Him, His Son, our place in the creation, and many other topics of ultimate importance to humanity. We would have no objective standard upon which to base ethics and morals. We would know little of the ministry and message of Jesus of Nazareth. We would have no information regarding the theological purpose of His crucifixion and resurrection—namely, that they were essential ingredients in God's plan to offer ruined man a way of escape from the devastating consequences of his sin (Matthew 20:28; 26:28). We would know nothing of how to enter that sacred body of saved souls, the church (Ephesians 5:23; 1 Corinthians 12:13), or how, once we had entered, to worship God correctly. Without God's revelation, we would know nothing about these important spiritual matters that impact our eternal destiny. Perhaps it was with such things in mind that Arthur W. Pink wrote these beautiful words:

If it were announced upon reliable authority that on a certain date in the near future an angel from heaven would visit New York and would deliver a sermon upon the invisible world, the future destiny of man, or the secret deliverance from the power of sin, what an audience he would command! There is no building in that city large enough to accommodate the crowd which would throng to hear him. If upon the next day, the newspapers were to give a verbatim report of his discourse, how eagerly it would be read! And yet, we have between the covers of the Bible not merely an angelic communication, but a Divine revelation. How great then is our wickedness if we undervalue and despise it! And yet we do (1976, p. 103).

Truly, we should be grateful to God for providing us with a revelation that could be retained in a permanent form, studied faithfully, and used profitably by all of mankind. It is via that revelation that faith frequently is built and sustained. McGarvey wrote:

That great doctrine or fact on which the Church of Jesus Christ is built, the solid rock underlying it, is this: "Thou art the Christ, the Son of the living God." ...How is this faith begotten within a man? And then, after it is once begotten, how is it strengthened and deepened and enjoyed?...

First, our faith that the worlds were created by the word of God: whence did we obtain it? Not by reasoning about it; not by dreaming; not in answer to prayer: but we read, when we were little boys and girls, in chapter 1, verse 1, of God's holy word, "In the beginning God created the heavens and the earth." **We obtained it from God's word**.

Whence did Abraham obtain his conviction and confidence that led him to offer that lamb at the altar? We have very little information about that, but we know from the very nature of the case that he did not get it from any human source. It did not spring up from his own reasoning. No mortal man could have conceived from the results of his own ratiocination, that to slay a little innocent lamb and burn its flesh and sprinkle its blood, would procure a blessing upon him from the God of heaven. He must have obtained it from revelation. ...**He obtained it from the word of God**, communicated to him in some way.

...[H]ow did Noah obtain his conviction that a flood was coming upon the world, and his hope of escape from it for himself and his family?... **From the word of God** he obtained the conviction and the confidence.

How did Abraham obtain his conviction about the land when he did not know where it was? God said to him, "Come into a land which I will show thee, and I will make of thee a great nation, I will give it to thee for an inheritance." **From the word of God**....

But then you say, can it be possible that our faith in the Lord Jesus Christ is begotten in the same way? Well, just look into the workings of your own mind, and ask yourself how did it originate in your mind—the conviction that Jesus is the Christ, the Son of the living God? And every one of you must answer, I obtained it from God's word. But for that word, I would not have it.... Why, my friends, if God's word will not do it, what power is there in heaven or earth that you can conceive of, that could? (1958, pp. 88,89,90,91, emp. added).

Using capacities for proper reasoning, the Christian builds faith based upon numerous avenues of obtaining evidence. Sometimes (we might even say often) such evidence is based upon the testimony provided by revelation, which is why Paul wrote: "Faith cometh by hearing, and hearing by the Word of God" (Romans 10:17). Geisler and Feinberg observed that "the basic relation of reason and revelation is that the thinking Christian attempts to render the credible intelligible" (1980, p. 265). Is it credible to believe in God? Considering the amount and type of evidence available to establish His existence beyond any reasonable doubt (see Thompson, 2000, pp. 123-181), indeed it is! Is it credible to accept the Bible as His inspired Word? Considering the amount and type of evidence available to establish that fact beyond any reasonable doubt (see Thompson, 2000, pp. 183-242), indeed it is! Is it reasonable to accept Jesus Christ as the virgin-born, resurrected Son of God? Considering the amount and type of evidence available to establish such claims beyond any reasonable doubt (see Thompson, 2000, pp. 243-257), indeed it is!

Reason does indeed play an important role in building faith via revelation. As Trueblood remarked:

> The necessary conclusion is that reason and revelation, far from being incompatible, **need** to go together at all times. If reason is required to leave out all reference to revelation, it has no religious material that is worth discussing.... If, on the other hand, revelation is espoused without the critical examination which reason provides, we have no guarantee against superstition and ecclesiastical pretension.
>
> Revelation must be tested by reason for the simple reason that there are false claims of revelation. We know, in advance, that many alleged revelations are false, because there are absolutely contradictory claims. It cannot be true that there is only **one** way by which men may be saved and that there are **many** ways by which mean may be saved (1957, pp. 32, emp. in orig.).

By reasoning correctly, and by employing the Law of Rationality, Christians not only can refute erroneous claims made via false revelations, but simultaneously can establish the validity of the revelation that is God's Word. As Dave Miller put it:

> [T]he Bible **demands** that the thinker be rational in gathering information, examining the evidence, and reasoning properly about the evidence—drawing only warranted conclusions. The essentiality of the law of rationality was articulated by Paul: "Prove all things; hold fast to that which is good" (1 Ths. 5:21). John echoed the same thought: "Try the spirits" (1 John 4:1). These passages show that the New Testament Christian is one who stands ready to examine the issues. God expects him to put doctrines and beliefs to the test and draw only such conclusions as are warranted by the evidence (1988, 8[9]:10, emp. in orig.).

Christians continually must be reminded of the importance that revelation from God plays in building and sustaining their faith, and in protecting that faith from every possible threat. No doubt this is why McGarvey was moved to ask: "If God's word will not do it, what power is there in heaven or earth that you can conceive of, that could?"

Faith and Doubt

But does biblical faith in any way imply doubt? No, it does not. Biblical faith often is used of a subject (e.g, an individual person). And when it is, it is used in at least seven different ways. First, the Scriptures speak of faith as "belief" (John 12:42; Hebrews 11:6; et al.). Second, faith sometimes means "trust" (John 14:1; Romans 4:17-20). Third, faith often refers primarily to "obedience" (Numbers 20:12; John 3:36, ASV; Hebrews 10:23,38; Revelation 2:10; et al.). Fourth, faith is used to refer to what we might call "steadfastness," "loyalty," or "faithfulness" (Habakkuk 2:4; Galatians 3:9; Hebrews 10:23,38; Revelation 2:10, et al.). Fifth, faith is used objectively to refer to the **content** of faith, and generally is referred to in this context as "the faith" (Romans 10:9; Jude 3; Galatians 1:11,23; et al.). Sixth, faith sometimes is used to speak of strong personal conviction (Romans 14:2,23). And seventh, faith may be used to refer to a spiritual gift (Matthew 17:20; 1 Corinthians 12:8-9; 13:2; et al.).

But faith **never** implies doubt. In fact, that faith is the very antithesis of doubt can be seen by examining Romans 14:22-23 and James 1:6-7. In the passage in Romans, Paul wrote: "The faith which thou hast, have thou to thyself before God. Happy is he that judgeth not himself in that which he approveth. But **he that doubteth is condemned** if he eat, because he eateth not of faith; and whatsoever is not of faith is sin" (emp. added). In this connection, Paul observed in regard to Abraham's faith: "He staggered not at the promise of God through unbelief; but was strong in faith, giving glory to God; And being fully persuaded that, what he had promised, he was able also to perform" (Romans 4:20-21). The word "staggered" (*diakrithe*) is from the same root words translated as "doubt" in Romans 14:23 ("Abraham doubted not"), James 1:6-7, and elsewhere.

Further, in connection with the fact that Abraham as a man of faith did not doubt, the word *plerophoretheis* is used to describe the reason for his trust. That is, Abraham was fully persuaded ("fully convinced, assured, certain"—Schaeffer, 1968, p. 142) that God would do what he had promised. What motivated Abraham was neither a blind "leap into the dark," nor a slight "leap into the light." His was a faith without doubt; a simple trust in what he was fully persuaded that God would do.... The position that faith must entail even the slightest element of doubt means simply that one cannot be sure that the propositions in which ones trusts are true (Leatherwood, 1977, 8[3]:43,42, parenthetical item in orig.).

In James 1:6-7, James urged the faithful Christian to "ask in faith, nothing doubting: for he that doubteth is like the surge of the sea driven by the wind and tossed. For let not that man think that he shall receive anything of the Lord; a doubleminded man, unstable in all his ways."

As Peter began his walk on the water toward Jesus (Matthew 14:28-33), it is obvious that he did so with determination. And yet, when he glanced away from his Lord and saw the treacherous winds and waves licking at his feet, he lost his faith in the divine power that had borne him across the water to that point. When he returned to the boat, having been saved by the hand of the Master, Christ admonished him with these words: "O thou of little faith, wherefore didst thou doubt?" (14:31).

Throughout the New Testament, "doubt" is couched in negative terms. It is something we must avoid in our prayer life, for example (1 Timothy 2:8). Jesus explained to His disciples that they would be able to move mountains—if only they would believe, and not doubt (Matthew 21:21-22; Mark 11:23-24). Paul warned the Roman Christians that they would stand condemned if they doubted the propriety of eating food sacrificed to idols (14:23). And the classic example, of course, is that of "doubting Thomas," to whom Christ said, "Be not faithless, but believing" (John 20:27).

Doubt, then, is an impediment to faith. But doubt does not have to be viewed necessarily as the opposite of belief; it does not necessarily represent a blatant denial of faith. This would be **dis**belief —that is, believing a claim to be false. Rather, doubt is a matter of

unbelief—that is, an occasional inability to accept the truthfulness of a particular claim. It is a human failing that, on occasion, we simply cannot decide whether something is true. The different words translated as "doubt" in the New Testament carry with them the sense of being unstable, wavering, or contending with oneself. In relation to faith, doubt is a "lack of certainty concerning the teachings of Christianity or one's personal relationship to them" (Habermas, 1990, p. 10). In addressing the issue of doubt in the Christian's life, Trevor Major commented:

> Doubt, left unresolved, can become a serious problem. God holds us responsible for addressing the cause of our doubt, and for seeking the remedy so that doubt does not prevent us from doing what faith demands. If we do not know whether God answers prayers, then how can we honestly go to God in prayer? If we eat meat sacrificed to idols (or the modern equivalent), and yet we are not sure that this is something we should do, then how can we have a good conscience before God?
>
> These are the negative consequences of unresolved doubts, but doubt may also be resolved in favor of greater faith, or even faith itself. After all, converts will never be made of people who never doubt their rejection of Christ's saving blood.
>
> Doubt is a human weakness, but it is a serious matter when it affects one's faith. That Thomas and the other disciples could doubt serves as a warning to us. From our vantage point, they had every reason to be faithful, and yet still they struggled with unbelief. Christians must be able to recognize doubt in themselves so that they can, unreservedly, make the same good confession as the apostle Thomas (1995b, 15:94).

Being a Christian does not mean that our faith never will be challenged or strained, or that we never will experience doubt. But it is one thing to state that faith does not **imply** doubt, and entirely another to suggest that faith never will **encounter** doubt. In his book, *The Gift of Doubt*, Gary E. Parker addressed this fact when he wrote:

> If faith never encounters doubt, if truth never struggles with error, if good never battles with evil, how can faith know its own power? In my own pilgrimage, if I have to choose between a faith that has stared doubt in the eye and made it blink, or a naïve faith that has never known the firing line of doubt, I will choose the former every time (1990, p. 69).

In John 7:15, the inspired text indicates that when Jesus addressed the Jews in their own temple, they marveled at His teaching. But Jesus demurred, and said: "My teaching is not mine, but his that sent me. If any man **willeth** to do his will, he shall know of the teaching, whether it is of God, or whether I speak from myself" (John 7:16-17). Jesus' point to the devout temple Jews was simply that God has imbued mankind with the ability to **choose**. If a person **wills**, he can accept God and His teaching, but God never will force Himself on that person. As the apostle John brought the book of Revelation to a close, he wrote: "He that will, let him take the water of life freely" (Revelation 22:17). The operative phrase here, of course, is "he that will." Unbelief must be replaced by a strong determination and a renewed zeal—both of which are capable of sustaining our faith, even (or especially!) in the face of doubt.

Faith—A Blind Leap in the Dark, or a Secure Walk in the Light?

Biblical faith, as I have discussed above, is a conviction based upon credible evidence, regardless of whether that evidence derives from experiential knowledge, metaphysical intuition, reliable testimony, or divine revelation. But one thing must be stressed: the Bible nowhere discusses or recognizes the legitimacy of any concept such as a "leap of faith." Sztanyo explained the "leap of faith" hypothesis as follows:

> This is a popular view that suggests one go "as far as possible" on evidence, and "the rest of the way" on faith. In this case, "faith" gets all the way to its object. But since "faith" is divorced from knowledge, the person actually operates

with a non-biblical definition of the term "faith." Given this view, faith is little more than a volitional commitment (i.e., an act of the will). One may speak of the Christian's "leap of faith" as being "shorter" than the leap of faith required by an atheist, but since knowledge plays no role in such a "leap," neither the Christian nor the atheist can really establish his position as true (1996, pp. 28-29).

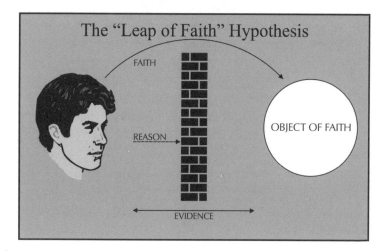

The "Leap of Faith" Hypothesis

FAITH

REASON

OBJECT OF FAITH

EVIDENCE

In an article on "Blind Faith," Dave Miller observed:

[T]he notion of "blind faith" is foreign to the Bible. People are called upon to have faith only after they receive adequate knowledge.... The God of the Bible is a God of truth. Throughout biblical history he has stressed the need for the acceptance of truth in contrast with error and falsehood. Those who, in fact, fail to **seek** truth are considered by God to be wicked (Jer. 5:1). The wise man urged, "Buy the truth, and sell it not" (Prov. 23:23). Paul, himself an accomplished logician, exhorted people to **love** the truth (2 Ths. 2:10-12). He stated the necessity of giving **diligence** to the task of dealing with the truth properly (2 Tim. 2:15). Jesus declared that only by **knowing** the truth is one made free (John 8:32). Luke ascribed nobility to those who were willing to search for and examine the evidence rather than being content to simply take someone's word for the truth (Acts 17:11). Peter admonished Christians to be prepared to give a defense (1 Pet. 3:15), which stands in stark contrast to those who, when questioned about proof of God or the credibility and comprehensibility of the Bible, triumphantly reply, "I don't know—I accept it by faith" (1988, 8[9]:10-11).

The late Guy N. Woods noted:

> Genuine faith derives from facts presented to the mind and from which proper and correct deductions are then drawn (John 20:30,31).... There is no such thing as "blind" faith. Faith itself is possible only when reason recognizes the trustworthiness of the testimony which produces it (1994, 125 [11]:2)

J.D. Thomas wrote:

> Faith cannot be totally blind or completely credulous. It must have a cognitive, "concept" content as its basic grounding. It is not really faith but mere credulity unless it really comes to grips with the intellectual, propositional concept and makes a response, which will be both intellectual assent and volitional commitment.... It would be impossible for one to come to God unless he accepts the intellectual statement that God exists. A man would not consent to place his money in a bank for safekeeping if he felt that the bank itself did not exist, or if it did not have a legal license to operate as a bank.... A person would not be willing to sit in a chair unless he were intellectually convinced that a chair was there.... So faith in God or any other kind of faith is impossible without a propositional, doctrinal statement accepted as true... (1965, pp. 258-259).

Faith always is evidence-based/knowledge-based. In a discussion titled, "Does Faith Contain an Element of Doubt?," Robert Camp remarked: "Thus, faith is not a leap in the dark, but rather a **walk in the light**" [1973, 4[2]:5, emp. in orig.]. He is absolutely right (cf. 1 John 1:5-7).

Types of Faith—and Man's Response

While we are examining the subject of faith, it might be good to note that, on occasion, various writers have presented discussions of different "types" of faith. For example, in his book, *Reasonable*

Faith, Winfried Corduan wrote: "We use the term faith in three ways in the context of Christian theology: saving faith, growing faith, and knowing faith" (1993, p. 17). In their *Handbook of Christian Apologetics*, Kreeft and Tacelli suggested: "We can distinguish at least four aspects or dimensions of religious faith...(a) emotional faith, (b) intellectual faith, (c) volitional faith and (d) heart faith" (1994, p. 30). How do these various types of faith tie together? What is the relationship among them, if any?

In Corduan's three groups, "knowing faith" (Kreeft and Tacelli's "intellectual faith") has to do with accepting statements and/or propositions as true. Or, as he put it:

> This faith refers to the way in which we may come to accept certain intellectual truths without which a trusting faith would be impossible. It is not possible to respond to the gospel without knowing the gospel; it is not possible to trust in Christ without knowing what Christ is all about. Thus even though we can only be redeemed through "saving faith," such saving faith presupposes some essential items of knowledge (p. 19).

But possessing the knowledge is not enough. **Acting** on that knowledge is required as well. Mark recorded the account of an unclean spirit's statement to Jesus: "I **know** thee who thou art" (1:24). And James reported that "the demons also **believe**, and shudder" (2:19). But neither their knowledge, nor their belief based on that knowledge, spurred them to an appropriate action. Richard England thus noted: "The Bible occasionally uses the term 'belief' with reference to simple mental acceptance without corresponding action (John 12:42-43). Such empty, tacit acquiescence to facts is characteristic of the devils" (2000, 142[12]:36). When Jesus said, "Ye shall **know** the truth, and the truth shall make you free" (John 8:32), the obvious implication of His statement was that the knowledge could make men free only if they acted upon it in a correct fashion.

"Growing faith" (roughly equivalent to Kreeft and Tacelli's "emotional faith") is the faith that increases as our knowledge base expands. This is the type of faith the apostle Peter had in mind when he said that he desired some of his readers to, "as newborn babes, long for the spiritual milk which is without guile, that ye may **grow thereby unto salvation**" (2 Peter 2:2). It is the same type of faith he had in mind when he urged those to whom he wrote to "**grow** in the grace and **knowledge** of our Lord and Saviour Jesus Christ" (2 Peter 3:17). Faith never was intended to be static or stagnant. Rather, it always was intended to be thriving and dynamic. As Paul wrote his second epistle to the young preacher, Timothy, he said that he was "reminded of the unfeigned faith that is in thee; which dwelt first in thy grandmother Lois, and thy mother Eunice; and, I am persuaded, in thee also" (2 Timothy 1:6). That "unfeigned faith" had grown first in his grandmother Lois, then in his mother Eunice, and finally in the budding evangelist Timothy. This always has been God's plan—that faith grow and be passed along from one generation to the next. Paul therefore told Timothy: "The things which thou hast heard from me among many witnesses, the same commit thou to faithful men, who shall be able to teach others also" (2 Timothy 2:2). This is how faith grows—and is spread.

Saving faith, as its name implies, is the type of faith that brings a person to salvation through belief in and obedience to Christ. This is the faith that causes people to realize that they cannot possibly redeem themselves, but instead are dependent solely on God and Christ for salvation. It is what might be called an "availing faith" (cf. Galatians 5:6) or a "reliant faith," since it relies (or trusts) on God and Christ for redemption. This would correspond roughly to what Kreeft and Tacelli refer to as "volitional/heart faith" In other words, it is "an act of the will, a commitment to obey God's will" (p. 30). Bierle commented on this point as follows:

> In spite of the knowledge concerning Jesus that we have gained, if we do not exercise our wills, we have all the faith we are every going to have—none. Unless we make a choice

concerning who Jesus is, there will be no faith. A consenting will is [an] essential component of the Bible's definition of faith (1992, p. 68).

In speaking to this point, Wayne Jackson wrote:

> But just what is this "faith" which is requisite to communion with God? Is it some blind leap into the dark? Is it an experience which is purely subjective? Is it an emotional phenomenon which is divorced from reason, evidence, and knowledge? Indeed not. The term "faith" as used in the Scriptures is of a comprehensive nature. It involves a **conviction** regarding certain facts (as based upon reasonable evidence), a disposition to **trust** the God of our existence, and a willingness to **submit** to his will (1974, p. 12, emp. and parenthetical item in orig.).

Or, as Bierle noted: "In other words, according to the teaching of the Bible, to qualify as legitimate, faith must consist of three components: knowledge, will, and response" (1992, p 69).

This is a good place to point out several important facts about "saving faith." First, we must remember that faith has not always—for all men, in all circumstances—required the same things. It always has required obedience, but obedience itself has not always demanded the same response.

For example, in God's earliest dealings with men, obedient faith required that those men offer animal sacrifices at the family altar (Genesis 4:4). Later, God dealt with the nation of Israel, giving the Israelites the law at Mount Sinai (Exodus 20). Under that law, animal sacrifices continued, along with the observance of certain feast days and festivals. Acceptable faith, under whatever law that was then in force, demanded obedience to the will of God. The Scriptures are clear that "obedience of faith" (Romans 1:5; 16:26) is based on the Word of God (Romans 10:13) and that both the faith and the obedience are demonstrated by **action**. Hebrews 11, in fact, devotes itself to an examination of that very concept. "By faith" Abel **offered**. "By faith" Noah **prepared**. "By faith" Abraham **obeyed**. "By faith," Moses **refused**. And so on. Even the casual reader cannot help but be impressed with the many heroes of faith listed in

Hebrews 11:32-40 and the **action** they took **because of their faith**. [When the four men lowered their palsied friend through a rooftop to Christ in order to be healed, Mark recorded that the Lord saw "their faith" (Mark 2:5). But what exactly did He "see"? It was their action.] Writing by inspiration, James observed that faith, divorced from works, is dead (2:26).

Is this to say, then, that man's faith and salvation are "works based"? The Bible clearly teaches that we are **not** saved by works (Titus 3:4-7; Ephesians 2:9). Yet the Bible clearly teaches we **are** saved by works (James 2:14-24). Since inspiration guarantees that the Scriptures never will contradict themselves, it is obvious that **two different kinds of works** are under consideration in these passages. And indeed, this is exactly the case.

The New Testament mentions at least four kinds of works: (1) works of the Law (Galatians 2:16; Romans 3:20); (2) works of the flesh (Galatians 5:19-21); (3) works of merit (Titus 3:4-7); and (4) works resulting from obedience of faith (James 2:14-24). This last category often is referred to as "works of God." This phrase does not mean works **performed by God**; rather, the intent is "works **required and approved by God**" (Thayer, 1958, p. 248, emp. added; cf. Jackson, 1997, 32:47). Consider the following example from Jesus' statements in John 6:27-29:

> Work not for the food which perisheth, but for the food which abideth unto eternal life.... They said therefore unto him, "What must we do, that we may work the **works of God**"? Jesus answered and said unto them, "This is the **work of God**, that ye believe on him whom he hath sent" (emp. added)

Within this context, Christ made it clear that there are certain works that humans must perform in order to receive eternal life. Moreover, the passage affirms that believing itself is a work ("This is the **work of God**, that ye **believe** on him whom he hath sent"). It follows, therefore, that if one is saved **without any type of works**, then he is saved **without faith**, because **faith is a work**. Such a conclusion would throw the Bible into hopeless confusion!

Jesus Himself stated in John 3:16: "For God so loved the world, that he gave his only begotten Son, that whosoever believeth on him should not perish, but have eternal life." The apostle Paul stated in Romans 5:1: "Being therefore justified **by faith**, we have peace with God through our Lord Jesus Christ." He stressed in Ephesians 2:8-9: "By grace have ye been saved **through faith**." To the Galatians, he wrote: "A man is not justified by the works of the law but **through faith** in Jesus Christ" (2:16). In Acts 16:31, his instructions to the Philippian jailor were: "Believe on the Lord Jesus, and thou shalt be saved."

In each of these instances, the words "believeth," "faith," and "believe" are synecdoches—i.e., a part representing the whole. That each of these means a great deal more than mere "mental assent" or "faith only" is evident from other passages of Scripture similarly associated with salvation. The only way to find the "road home" to heaven is to follow God's directions **exactly**. There are numerous things God has commanded that a person **must do** in order to enjoin the "obedience of faith" and thereby receive the free gift of salvation.

First, the New Testament quite plainly teaches that man cannot be saved by **faith only**. James, in his epistle, remarked that indeed, a man may be justified (i.e., saved), but "not only by faith" (2:24). This makes perfectly good sense, as James had observed only a few verses earlier: "Thou believest that God is one; thou doest well; the demons also believe, and shudder" (James 2:19). It is not enough merely to believe. Even the demons who inhabit the immortal regions of hell believe. But they hardly are saved (see 2 Peter 2:4). It is obvious, therefore, that "faith only" is insufficient to save mankind.

Second, hearing the gospel message is necessary to receive salvation (Romans 10:17). But "hearing only" is not sufficient. We know this to be the case because confession of the fact that Christ is the Son of God also is necessary for salvation (Matthew 10:32). But "confession only" is not sufficient. We know this is the case because God also commanded repentance (Luke 13:3; Acts 17:30;

cf. Acts 11:18 where the text speaks of the fact that to the Gentiles, "God granted repentance unto life"). Yet "repentance only" is not sufficient. We know this is the case because baptism similarly is necessary for salvation (Mark 16:16; Acts 2:38; 22:16; Romans 6:3-4; cf. 1 Peter 3:21 where the apostle stated that "even baptism doth also now save us"). But baptism only is not sufficient. We know this because God's Word teaches that it is necessary for a person who desires to be saved to do **all five** of these things—hear the gospel message, believe that Christ is the Son of God, confess Him as the Son of God, repent of past sins, and be baptized for remission of those sins—not just one of them!

Furthermore, faith and disobedience are set in vivid contrast in the Scriptures. Consider Jesus' statement in John 3:36: "He that **believeth** on the Son hath eternal life; but he that **obeyeth not** the Son shall not see life, but the wrath of God abideth on him." In Acts 14:1-2, Luke recorded: "A great multitude both of Jews and of Greeks **believed**. But the Jews that were **disobedient** stirred up the souls of the Gentiles." Examine also Hebrews 3:18-19, wherein those Israelites "that were **disobedient**" were condemned "because of **unbelief**" (cf. Hebrews 4:3,6). While John 3:16 does indeed promise eternal life to him that "**believeth**," Hebrews 5:9 attributes eternal salvation to those who "**obey**," thereby demonstrating that saving faith demands obedience to God's commands. To not obey is not to believe! As Blaine Hescht commented:

> We must understand that faith or belief does include an element of mental agreement. But we must also understand that faith or belief involves the aspect of obedience; a lack of faith or belief is a flagrant disregard for Jesus' authority and therefore for his commands (cf. John 14:15 and 1 John 5:1-3). In John 3:16-21 Jesus is comparing and contrasting faith or belief and faithlessness or disbelief. He concludes that not believing or having faith is essentially synonymous with not obeying (1984, 126[22]:692).

In the Sermon on the Mount, Jesus said: "Not every one that saith unto me, 'Lord, Lord, shall enter into the kingdom of heaven'; but he that **doeth** the will of my Father who is in heaven" (Matthew

7:21). This, no doubt, is why Paul repeatedly stressed the "obedience of faith" (Romans 1:5; 16:26). Faith without obedience is the same as faith without works—it is dead.

Conclusion

In discussing the importance of teaching correctly on the relationship between faith and knowledge, and the impact that such teaching would have, theologian Francis Schaeffer observed:

> Knowledge precedes faith. This is crucial in understanding the Bible. **To say, as a Christian should, that only the faith which believes God on the basis of knowledge is truth faith, is to say something which causes an explosion in the Twentieth Century world** (1968, p. 142, emp. in orig.).

Indeed it does. And well it should!

CHAPTER 3

"IN THE IMAGE AND LIKENESS OF GOD" [PART I]

The Hebrew slave who dwelt in Egypt 3500 years ago was considered to be the property of Pharaoh. All Egyptians detested that slave because of his association with shepherding (cf. Genesis 46:34). He labored rigorously from sunrise to sunset, building the impressive store-cities of Pithom and Raamases. The only one he knew who was considered to be like a god was Pharaoh, the supposed incarnation of the Sun god, Ra. Pharaoh also was considered the sole person who bore "the image of God." The Egyptian canal digger and the merchant, the taskmaster and the Hebrew slave, all were innately inferior because they were not divine image bearers (or so they had been told, and thus so they thought). Such a designation **never** was applied to the common man in Egypt, nor anywhere else for that matter. The rulers of empires were the sole beings referred to as "images" of their gods.*

---

* I am indebted to Eric Lyons, Director of Research at Apologetics Press, for his invaluable assistance in researching and writing this material.

What a joy, then, it must have been for a former slave in Egypt to find out that **he** was created in God's image. How delighted the Gentile convert must have been when he learned that he was as much an image bearer as any king. Outside the Bible, archaeologists and historians never have found where mankind in general was said to have been created in the "image" of a god. Three Akkadian texts from the Sargonic period of Assyria's history use the Akkadian cognate of *tselem* ("image"), but it is used only in a context where kings are being discussed (Miller, 1972, 91:294-295). Genesis 1:26-27 describes **all** mankind with language that previously had been applied only to the supreme rulers of nations.

> And God said, "Let us make man in our image, after our likeness: and let them have dominion over the fish of the sea, and over the birds of the heavens, and over the cattle, and over all the earth, and over every creeping thing that creepeth upon the earth." And God created man in his own image, in the image of God created he him; male and female created he them.

After generations of bondage in Egypt, the Israelite was humbled—and yet thrilled—to learn that he was as special in the eyes of Jehovah as Pharaoh thought he was in the eyes of Ra. The converted Gentile learned that high-ranking officials were not the only ones who bore God's image. Rather, mankind as a whole was created God's vice-regent.

The Creator of the Universe has honored mankind by endowing him with certain qualities that are intrinsic to His nature. Through the centuries, many have contemplated the meaning of the phrase "in the image and likeness of God." Much has been written on the subject, and no doubt much more is yet to be written. Here, however, I would like to take a logical approach in searching for this meaning. First, I intend to narrow the possibilities by eliminating inaccurate definitions. Second, I want to discuss whether the image of God in man has been "lost," as some have claimed. And third, I plan to deal with the actual meaning of the Bible's statement that man exists "in the image and likeness of God," and investigate the ramifications of that statement for people today who want to build and sustain a rock-solid faith.

"In the Image and Likeness of God"— What It Does *Not* Mean

Before I elaborate on what being created "in the image and likeness of God" means, it is appropriate to inquire as to what it does **not** mean. First, it does not mean that we are divine. Satan strives daily, of course, to persuade us to believe that we are God (cf. Genesis 3:5). In fact, deification of self is the central message of the New Age Movement (see Bromling, 1989, p. 39). Consider, for example, the following quotation from Ramtha, a so-called "channeled" spirit who allegedly speaks from a higher realm through New Ager J.Z. Knight:

> I am Ramtha, the Enlightened One, indeed. And who be you, my most illustrious brotheren [sic], who have gathered yourselves into this wondrous audience? **You be that which is termed Man**, you be that which is termed Christus, **you be that which is termed God**. Fallacy? Reality! You be of your importance and your value and your word far greater than that which you have first concluded yourself to be. **You be the totality of all that The Father is: God Supreme**. What else be there? What grander state is there? (see Ramtha, 1985, p. 22, emp. added).

This is the same message that leaps from the pages of the writings of Oscar-winning actress, Shirley MacLaine. In her book, *Out on a Limb*, she told of her discussions with a friend by the name of Kevin Ryerson who allegedly was able to "channel" John—a disembodied spirit from the days of Jesus' earthly sojourn. Once, when Ms. MacLaine was speaking with "John," he allegedly said to her: "[Y]our soul is a metaphor for God.... **You** are God. **You** know you are divine" (1983, pp. 188,209, emp. in orig.). In addressing what she refers to as her "higher self" in her book, *Dancing in the Light*, MacLaine said: "**I am God**, because all energy is plugged in to the same source. We are each aspects of that source. We are all part of God. We are individualized reflections of the God source. God is us and we are God" (1991, p. 339, emp. added). In her 1989 book, *Going Within*, she wrote: "I, for example, do a silent mantra with each of my hatha yoga poses. I hold each yoga position for twenty seconds and internally chant, 'I am God in Light'" (1989, p. 57).

In the book he authored refuting MacLaine's views, *Out on a Broken Limb*, lawyer F. LaGard Smith stated:

> The heart and soul of the New Age movement, which Ms. MacLaine embraces along with her reincarnation ideas, is nothing less than **self-deification**.... But it really should-n't be all that surprising. All we had to do was put the equation together: We are One; God is One; therefore, we are God. The cosmic conjugation is: I am God, you are God, we are God.... Surely if someone tells herself repeatedly that she is God, it won't be long before she actually believes it! (1986, pp. 178,179-180,181, emp. in orig.).

When Shirley MacLaine stands on the sands of the beach and yells out loud, "I am God," she literally means just what she says! But such a concept is not inherent in the biblical statement that mankind has been created "in the image and likeness of God." God's Word does not indicate that He created men and women in His **essence**, but in His **image** (Genesis 1:26). Only God is omnipotent, omnipresent, and omniscient. God revealed this truth when He told the king of Tyre through Ezekiel: "You say, 'I am a god, and sit in the seat of gods, in the midst of the seas,' yet, **you are a man and not a god**" (Ezekiel 28:2, emp. added). In the Bible, only the wicked elevate themselves to the status of deity. King Herod flirted with self-deification—and died in a horrific manner as a result. Luke reported the event as follows:

> So on a set day Herod, arrayed in royal apparel, sat on his throne and gave an oration to them. And the people kept shouting, "The voice of a god and not the voice of a man!" Then immediately an angel of the Lord struck him, because he did not give glory to God. And he was eaten of worms and died (Acts 12:21-23).

This stands in stark contradistinction to the reaction of Paul and Barnabas when the heathens at Lystra attempted to worship them (Acts 14:8-18). Had they held the same views as Shirley MacLaine and her New-Age kin, these two preachers would have encouraged the crowds in Lystra to recognize not only the preachers' deity but their own deity as well! Yet, consider the response they offered instead:

> They rent their garments, and sprang forth among the multitude, crying out and saying, "Sirs, why do ye these things? We also are men of like passions with you, and bring you good tidings, that ye should turn from these vain things unto a living God, who made the heaven and the earth and the sea, and all that in them is" (Acts 14:14-15).

The testimony of the Creation itself is not that man is God, but rather that God transcends both this world and its inhabitants. In Romans 1, the apostle Paul spoke directly to this point.

> For the wrath of God is revealed from heaven against all ungodliness and unrighteousness of men, who hinder the truth in unrighteousness; because that which is known of God is manifest in them; for God manifested it unto them. For the invisible things of him since the creation of the world are clearly seen, being perceived through the things that are made, even his everlasting power and divinity; that they may be without excuse: because that, knowing God, they glorified him not as God, neither gave thanks; but became vain in their reasonings, and their senseless heart was darkened. Professing themselves to be wise, they became fools, and changed the glory of the incorruptible God for the likeness of an image of corruptible man, and of birds, and four-footed beasts, and creeping things. Wherefore God gave them up in the lusts of their hearts unto uncleanness, that their bodies should be dishonored among themselves: for that they exchanged the truth of God for a lie, and worshipped and served the creature rather than the Creator, who is blessed for ever (Romans 1:18-25).

The idea of self-deification effectively eliminates the entire scheme of redemption and negates 4,000 years of Heaven's interaction in men's lives. It denies the role of Jesus in creation (John 1:1-3), the amazing prophetic accuracy of the Old and New Testaments (1 Peter 1:10-12), the providential preservation of the messianic seed (Galatians 3:16), the miraculous birth of Christ (Isaiah 7:14; Matthew 1:21-23), the significance of His resurrection (1 Corinthians 15), and the hope of His second coming (1 Thessalonians 4:13-18). When man decides to declare his own deity, he foments rebellion against the legitimate Inhabitant of heaven's throne. And he will bear the consequences of that rebellion, just as angels of old did (Jude 6). Certainly, then, the phrase recorded in Genesis 1:27 which states that "God created man in his own image" does not mean that man is, in fact, God.

Second, this description of man obviously does not refer to his physical appearance. It is true, of course, that some writers have suggested exactly the opposite, and have defended the view that when the Bible speaks of man being created "in the image of God," it means a **physical** image. Theodore Nöldeke argued as early as 1897 that the concept of the "image of God" basically had to do with man's physical appearance (see Miller, 1972, 91:292-293). Hermann Gunkel also took this position in his commentary on Genesis (1964, p. 112). In 1940, after respected theologian Paul Humbert published his now-famous word studies of *tselem* ("image") and *demuth* ("likeness"), the view that the "image of God" actually was something physical became more widely accepted by some critical scholars (Miller, 91:293).

Others, although careful to place more emphasis on the fact that man was indeed created in the **spiritual** image of God, nevertheless have suggested that "in some sense, therefore, even man's body is in God's image in a way not true of animals" (Morris, 1976, p. 74). In his book, *The Genesis Record*, Henry M. Morris wrote:

> There is something about the human body, therefore, which is uniquely appropriate to God's manifestation of Himself, and (since God knows all His works from the beginning of the world—Acts 15:18), He must have designed man's body with this in mind. Accordingly, He designed it, not like the an-

imals, but with an erect posture, with an upward gazing coun-
tenance, capable of facial expressions corresponding to emotional feelings, and with a brain and tongue capable of articu-
late, symbolic speech (1976, p. 4, parenthetical comment in
orig.).

While it might be tempting to believe such an interpretation of
Genesis 1:26-27, the phrase "image of God" does **not** refer to the
fact that man's physical being has a form or shape like God. It does
not mean that God has two eyes, two ears, two arms, and two legs.
As T. Pierce Brown noted:

The fact that God is spoken about as one who has eyes, hands,
ears, and so on, has no bearing on the subject for two reasons. First, if God is trying to let us know that He can observe
us, hear us, and minister to us, He has to do it in words that
mean something to us. These expressions are called "anthro-
pomorphisms" or "forms of man" figures of speech. Second,
a bird or a fish may have eyes without being in the form of a
man. So it is not without reason to speak of God's eyes, ears,
or hands, although He is Spirit (1993, 135[8]:50).

Nor does man's creation in God's image have anything to do
with man's posture, as Morris suggested in the last sentence of his
assessment. Some have attempted to make a connection between
Genesis 1:26-27 and Ecclesiastes 7:29 where it is stated: "God hath
made man upright." But as L.S. Chafer correctly noted, "God, being
incorporeal, is neither perpendicular nor horizontal in His posture"
(1943, 100:481). Gordon H. Clark addressed this topic when he
wrote:

This image cannot be man's body for two reasons. First, God
is spirit or mind and has no body. Hence a body would not
be an image of him. Second, animals have bodies, yet they
are not created in God's image. If anyone should suggest that
man walks upright, so that his bodily position could be the
image, the reply is not merely that birds also walk on two legs,
but that Genesis distinguishes man from animals by the image and not by any physiological structure (1969, 12:216).

In their commentary on the Pentateuch, Keil and Delitzsch remarked:
"There is more difficulty in deciding in what the likeness to God consisted. Certainly not in the bodily form, the upright position, or the

commanding aspect of man, since God has no bodily form, and the man's body was formed from the dust of the ground" (1996, 1:39). Being made in the image of God, then, does not refer to the physical body, the posture, or the authoritative aspect of man.

Although it is true that the word "image" (Hebrew *tselem*) is a term used in certain contexts within the Old Testament to refer to a model or to idols (and thus can refer to a similarity in physical appearance), it cannot, and does not, denote such meaning in Genesis 1:26-27, nor in any of the other passages referring to the *imago Dei* ("image of God"). God is not "like unto gold, or silver, or stone" (i.e., He is not physical; Acts 17:29). As Ashby Camp observed: "God, of course, is a spirit (Jn. 4:24), and the O.T. stresses his incorporeality and invisibility (see Ex. 20:1-4; Deut. 4:15-16), so the resemblance no doubt relates to some nonphysical aspect(s) of humanity" (1999, p. 44). Since it is the case that a spirit "hath not flesh and bones" (Luke 24:39; cf. Matthew 16:17), clearly, then, man does not bear the image of God in his physical nature.

Third, the "image" (*tselem*) of God does not refer to something different than the "likeness" (*demuth*) of God. The so-called Greek and Latin "church fathers" frequently suggested a distinction between the two words. They taught that *tselem* referred to the physical, and *demuth* to the ethical, part of the divine image (Feinberg, 1972, 129:237). Other theologians, like Irenaeus (A.D. 130-c.200), taught that "image" denoted man's unchangeable essence (i.e., his freedom and rationality), whereas "likeness" referred to the changing part of man (i.e., his relationship with God). The first thus related to the very nature of man, while the second was that which could be lost (Crawford, 1966, p. 233). As of 1972, this still was the official view of the Roman Catholic Church (Feinberg, 129:237). It is not a correct view, however, as Hoekema has pointed out:

> The word translated as **image** is *tselem*; the word rendered as **likeness** is *demuth*. In the Hebrew there is no conjunction between the two expressions; the text says simply "let us make man in our image, after our likeness." Both the Septuagint and the Vulgate insert an **and** between the two expressions, giving the impression that "image" and "likeness"

refer to different things. The Hebrew text, however, makes it clear that there is no essential difference between the two: "after our likeness" is only a different way of saying "in our image." This is borne out by examining the usage of these words in this passage and in the two other passages in Genesis. In Genesis 1:26, both **image** and **likeness** are used; in Genesis 1:27 only **image** is used, while in 5:1 only the word **likeness** is used. In 5:3 the two words are used again but this time in a different order: **in his likeness, after his image**. And again in 9:6 only the word **image** is used. If these words were intended to describe different aspects of the human being, they would not be used as we have seen them used, that is, almost interchangeably.... The two words together tell us that man is a representation of God who is like God in certain respects (1986, p. 13, emp. in orig.).

Despite the influence of those who claim that these words carry very different ideas about the image of God, a careful study of such passages as Genesis 1:26-27, 5:1-3, and 9:6 reveals that, in fact, these two Hebrew words do **not** speak of two different entities. "Likeness" simply emphasizes the "image." As William Dyrness noted in regard to *tselem* and *demuth*: "[T]he two words should be seen as having complimentary rather than competing meanings. The first stresses its being shaped and the second its being like the original in significant ways" (1972, 15[3]:162). Charles Feinberg, writing on "The Image of God" in the respected religious journal *Bibliotheca Sacra*, agreed when he remarked:

A careful study of Genesis 1:26-27; 5:1,3; and 9:6 will show beyond question that it is impossible to avoid the conclusion that the two Hebrew terms are not referring to two different entities. In short, use reveals the words are used interchangeably (129:237).

There actually is no good evidence for making any distinction between the two and, in fact, the words are essentially synonymous in this context. Keil and Delitzsch remarked in their commentary on Genesis that the two words are "merely combined to add intensity to the thought" (1996, 1:39). As Clark put it: "Man is not two images. To distinguish between image and likeness is fanciful exegesis" (1969, 12:216).

Fourth, the "image" has nothing to do with the sexual distinction between man and woman. Karl Barth, one of the most popular theologians of the twentieth century, suggested, however, that it did (see Clark, 1969, 12:221). Yet how could this be the image of God in man if a sexual distinction also is present in animals? Furthermore, since there are no sexual distinctions in the Godhead (spirits do not have a gender), one wonders how this could be the image at all. Realistically, sexuality could not be the image of God that man possesses.

Fifth, the "image" is not man's domination of the lower creation around him. In a "letter to the editor" that Norman Snaith wrote to the *Expository Times* in 1974, he boldly claimed:

> The meaning is that God created man to be his agent, his representative in ruling all living creatures, and he was given sufficient (to quote the psalm) "honour and glory" to do this. ...Biblically speaking, the phrase "image of God" has nothing to do with morals or any sort of ideals; **it refers only to man's domination of the world and everything that is in it**. It says nothing about the nature of God, but everything concerning the **function** of man (1974, p. 24, emp. added, parenthetical comment in orig.).

In regard to this kind of thinking, we would be wise to remember that

> man must exist before dominion can be invested in him, and that man has authority because of the truth that he is made in the image or likeness of God. The authority is not the **cause** of the image or likeness, but the image and likeness is the **ground** of the authority (Chafer, 1943, 100:481, emp. added).

In commenting on this subject James Hastings wrote:

> The view that the Divine image consists in dominion over the creatures cannot be held without an almost inconceivable weakening of the figure, and is inconsistent with the sequel, where the rule over the creatures is, by a separate benediction, conferred on man, already made in the image of God. The truth is that the image marks the distinction between man and the animals, and so qualifies him for dominion: **the latter is the consequence, not the essence, of the Divine image** (1976,1:48, emp. added).

"Dominion," Keil and Delitzsch noted, "is unquestionably ascribed to man simply as the consequence or effluence of his likeness to God" (1996, 1:39). As William H. Baker commented: "[I]t is the presence of the image of God in people that makes them able to exercise dominion over the earth. **Dominion itself is not what constitutes the image**" (1991, p. 39, emp. in orig.). Although somewhat closely related to the image of God, exercising dominion over the world is not itself that image.

Was the "Image of God" Destroyed by Sin?

Through the years, numerous scholars have suggested that the image of God spoken of in Genesis 1:26-27 refers to some sort of "spiritual perfection" that was lost at the time of man's fall, and thus is incomprehensible to us today. Martin Luther claimed that the image was an original righteousness that was lost completely. He proclaimed: "I am afraid that **since the loss of this image through sin** we cannot understand it to any extent" (as quoted in Dyrness, 1972, p. 163, emp. added). John Calvin similarly spoke of the image of God as having been destroyed by sin, obliterated by the Fall, and utterly defaced by man's unrighteousness (see Hoekema, 1986, p. 43). At other times, he took a less "hard-core" approach and vacillated between a complete loss and a partial loss of the image. In his commentary on Genesis, he wrote: "But now, although **some** obscure lineaments of that image are found remaining in us, yet are they so vitiated and maimed, that **they may truly be said to be destroyed**" (as quoted in Hoekema, p. 45, emp. added). Keil and Delitzsch remarked that the "concrete essence of the divine likeness was shattered by sin; and it is only through Christ, the brightness of the glory of God and the expression of His essence (Heb. 1:3), that our nature is transformed into the image of God again (Col. 3:10; Eph. 4:24)" [1:39]. Famed Canadian anthropologist Arthur C. Custance, in his book, *Man in Adam and in Christ*, observed:

> Genesis tells us that man was created in a special way, bearing the stamp of God upon him which the animals did not bear. **Genesis also tells us that he lost it**.... Now while Adam himself was created with this image, his disobedience so robbed him of it that all his children thereafter bore not the image of God but his—and even his **likeness** (1975, pp. 103, 109, first emp. added, last emp. in orig.).

When we are told in Genesis 1:26-27 that man was created "in the image and likeness of God," does the language refer **only to Adam and Eve** as these writers would have us to believe? Or does it refer to **all mankind** in general?

It is my position that the "image of God" spoken of in Genesis 1:26-27 does not refer to some kind of "spiritual perfection," especially considering the fact that the members of the Godhead (Who created man) are omniscient and therefore knew that man would sin. Why would Deity create man with an image that demanded spiritual perfection, knowing ahead of time that man was going to sin and thereby "lose" that image? Granted, **if** this phrase referred **just** to a sinless condition, **then** it would have been lost in the Fall and man no longer could be called God's image bearer. Yet the Bible clearly reveals that man still retained the image of God **after** the Fall. In addressing this fact, Gordon H. Clark remarked:

> Since Adam remained Adam after the fall, it looks as if some "part" of the image survived; but since also Adam lost his original innocence and Cain committed murder, was not some "part" of the image lost?... Can man still be in the image of God? Yes, the image is still there. Paradoxical though it may seem, man could not be the sinner he is, if he were not still God's image. Sinning presupposes rationality and voluntary decision. Animals cannot sin. Sin therefore requires God's image because man is responsible for his sins. If there were no responsibility, there could be nothing properly called sin. Sin is an offense against God, and God calls us to account. If we were not answerable to God, repentance would be useless and even nonsense. Reprobation and hell would also be impossible.... [T]he fall and its effects, which have so puzzled some theologians as they studied the doctrine of the image,

are most easily understood by identifying the image with man's mind.... "Out of the heart proceed evil thoughts." Note that in the Bible the term **heart** usually designates the intellect, and only once in ten times the emotions; it is the heart that thinks. Sin thus interferes with our thinking. It does not, however, prevent us from thinking. Sin does not eradicate or annihilate the image. It causes a malfunction, but man still remains man (1969, 12:216,217-218, emp. in orig.).

L.S. Chafer similarly concluded:

Though much is said throughout the Bible of man's sinfulness and of the depths to which he has descended, it is not said that he has lost the image of God. In fact, as has been declared, the Bible directly teaches that fallen man retains that image and that it is this reality which determines the extent of his degradation (1943, 100:490).

Robert Morey noted:

This is not to say that man is no longer God's image-bearer. In James 3:9, man is still viewed as being made in the image of God. But this image has been marred and defaced by man's sin. While man is still **man**, he is now a **sinful** man.... In terms of our self-image, we should view ourselves as rebel sinners as well as image bearers. In fact, it is man's capacity as God's image bearer that makes sin so awful. Man's creation purpose magnifies his sin and rebellion (1984, pp. 38, 39, emp. in orig.).

Various writers have suggested that the image of God in man has been **damaged** by sin, **but not destroyed**. Feinberg, in speaking of the image of God as what he called an "inalienable part of man's constitution," spoke of that image as presently being in a "marred, corrupted, and impaired state" (1972, 129:245). Harold Hazelip commented in a similar vein when he observed: "We have marred the image of God in ourselves by sin. But the image is not destroyed" (1980, 2[2]:30). Hoekema elaborated on the same point when he wrote:

In other words, there is also a sense in which human beings no longer properly bear the image of God, and therefore need to be renewed in that image. We could say that in this latter

sense the image of God in man has been marred and corrupted by sin. We must still see fallen man as an image-bearer
of God, but as one who by nature...images God in a distorted
way (1986, p. 31).

The well-known British writer of Oxford University, C.S. Lewis, expressed this very fact in a most unforgettable manner via a personal
letter to one of his friends.

[I]ndeed the only way in which I can make real to myself what
theology teaches about the heinousness of sin is to remember that every sin is the distortion of an energy breathed into
us.... We poison the wine as He decants it into us; murder a
melody He would play with us as the instrument. We caricature the self-portrait He would paint. Hence all sin, whatever else it is, is sacrilege (1966, pp. 71-72).

While the fall of man was tragic, and the consequences far-reach-
ing, man's sin did not so completely shatter the image of God within him that it no longer existed. Man still possessed the ability to discern right from wrong. He still had the desire, and the capability, to
worship his Creator. The late Reuel Lemmons, while editor of the
Firm Foundation, devoted one of his editorials to this concept.

The fall did not impair man's ability to reason nor destroy
his desire to worship. If so, then where did Abel's sacrifice
come from? If Calvin's view were right, then the world would
have been left completely without a witness to the very existence of God from Adam at least until Jesus. If the link were
completely shattered, and man was a wandering star, consigned to the blackness of unrelatedness with God, then where
did the Old Testament come from?

The fact is that man was then and is now in the image of God.
He never lost the capacity to respond to God, even though
separated from God because of his rebellion. His sacrifices
throughout the Patriarchal age, and his submission to ten commandment law in the Mosaic age, demonstrates the fact that
his "image" was never totally shattered. He retained his capacity to recognize the law of the Lord, and even to correct
his wayward ways through repentance. Although dimmed
and obscured by rebellion, the image was still visible (1980,
97:546).

G. Campbell Morgan, in his book, *The Crises of the Christ*, lamented: "By the act of sin, the image and likeness of God in man was not destroyed but defaced, and in all the history contained in the Old Testament Scripture, is seen a degraded ideal" (1903, p. 26). In his book, *Feet Firmly Planted*, Ashby Camp rightly observed: "Since the image of God is an inherent aspect of human nature, it was not lost through the introduction of sin into the human world. This is almost certainly the point of Gen. 5:1-3" (1999, p. 45). In the passage in Genesis 5:1-3 to which Camp referred, Moses recorded:

> In the day that God created man, in the likeness of God made he him; male and female created he them, and blessed them, and called their name Adam, in the day when they were created. And Adam lived a hundred and thirty years, and begat a son in his own likeness, after his image; and called his name Seth.

There would be no point in once again proclaiming Adam and Eve as image bearers if, by this time, the divine likeness already had vanished. Thus, in spite of Custance's insistence that Adam's "children thereafter bore not the image of God but his," the real truth is that "the likeness of God that stamped Adam (and Eve) was perpetuated in his offspring, despite the corruption caused by sin" (Camp, p. 45, parenthetical item in orig.). That is to say, Seth, being made in the likeness of Adam, must have retained the same "image of God" that Adam possessed. In addressing the fact that man's sin did not result in the loss of his humanity, Feinberg wrote:

> Nowhere does the Old Testament indicate that the divine image and likeness are lost.... When one contemplates Genesis 9:6; James 3:9; and 1 Corinthians 11:7, it can be seen that it is incorrect to say unqualifiedly that the image of God was lost through sin. There are references where man's nature after the fall is still the "work and creature of God" (see Deut. 32:6; Isa. 45:11; 54:5; 64:8; Acts 17:25; Rev. 4:11; Job 10:8-12; Ps. 139:14-16). The insurmountable obstacle to the position that the image of God is entirely lost through the fall is the fact that even fallen man is man and is not short

> of his humanity.... [T]hat which relates to rationality, con-
> science, and self-consciousness cannot be less, for then man
> would cease to be man. In spite of the fall, man did not become
> a beast or a demon, but retained his humanity (1972, 129:
> 245).

Perhaps an even stronger argument is found in the passage in Genesis 9:6, to which Feinberg referred. It states: "Whoso shed-deth man's blood, by man shall his blood be shed: For **in the image of God** made he man" (emp. added). According to this passage, fallen man still bears the image of God. The account of Adam and Eve's fall had been recorded earlier in the book; that man had become a rank sinner is stated unequivocally in the immediate context of the passage. "Never again will I curse the ground because of man, even though every inclination of his heart is evil from childhood" (8:21). Although God's assessment was correct in regard to mankind, "in Genesis 9:6 murder is forbidden because man was made in the image of God—that is, he still bears that image" (Hoekema, 1986, p. 17). Chafer rightly commented:

> To sin against man either by murder or by slander is reprov-
> able on the ground of the divine image being resident in man.
> A definite sacredness appertains to human life. Man must
> respect his fellowman, not on the ground of kinship, but on
> the ground of the exalted truth that human life belongs to
> God. To injure man is to injure one who bears the image of
> God (1969, 100:489-490).

Anderson and Reichenbach added: "To kill a human is to forfeit one's own life, for the denial of another's image is a denial of one's own. This value emphasis is reiterated in Jas 3:9, where to curse persons is to fail to properly recognize the image of God in them" (1990, 33:198).

If one argues that Genesis 9:6 is referring only to the past and says nothing about the future, then he does violence to the meaning and intent of the passage. Moses, writing approximately 2,500 years after the Fall, said that the reason murder is wrong is because the victim **is** someone created in the image of God. If man no longer bore the image of God after the Fall (and apart from redemption), these words would have been completely meaningless to the Israelites (and, subsequently, are valueless for man today). Without doubt, this passage teaches that man still bears the image of God. Notice what King David wrote about man approximately 3,000 years after his initial sin in the Garden of Eden.

> What is man, that thou art mindful of him? And the son of man, that thou visitest him? For thou hast made him but little lower than God, And crownest him with glory and honor. Thou makest him to have dominion over the works of thy hands; Thou hast put all things under his feet (Psalm 8:4-6).

Although this statement does not contain the phrase, "image of God," it nevertheless reminds one of the proclamation contained in Genesis 1:26-27. David used powerful, poetic language to describe contemporary mankind as having "all things under his feet." As Keil and Delitzsch affirmed: "...[I]t is the **existing generation** of man that is spoken of. Man, as we see him in ourselves and others...**is** a being in the image of God" (1996, 5:94-95, emp. added). The *imago Dei*

> does not necessarily include moral and spiritual perfection; **it must include the possibility of achieving it;** it reveals the Divine purpose that man should achieve it; but **man, even after he has sinned, still retains the "image of God"** in the sense in which it is attributed to him in the Hebrew Scriptures. **It belongs to his nature, not to his character** (Hastings, 1976, 1:51, emp. added).

Nowhere does the Old Testament indicate that the divine image was lost. Thus, it is incorrect to say (at least unqualifiedly) that the image of God vanished when sin entered the world.

In the New Testament, one can read where the apostle Paul, in addressing the then-current subject of head coverings, said: "Man indeed ought not to have his head veiled, forasmuch as **he is the image and glory of God**" (1 Corinthians 11:7, emp. added). Paul used a present active participle in describing man's nature to note that man "is" the image, not that he "was" or "used to be" the image of God. Elsewhere in the New Testament, James wrote: "But the tongue can no man tame; it is a restless evil, it is full of deadly poison. Therewith bless we the Lord and Father; and therewith curse we men, **who are made after the likeness of God**" (3:8-9, emp. added). The English verb "are made" (ASV) derives from the Greek *gegonotas*, which is the perfect participle of the verb *ginomai*. The perfect tense in Greek is used to describe an action brought to completion in the past, but whose effects are felt in the present (Mounce, 1993, p. 219). For example, when the Bible says "it is written," this usually is stated in the perfect tense. That is to say, scripture was written in the past, but is applicable in the present. The thrust of the Greek expression, *kath' homoisosin theou gegonotas* ("who are made after the likeness of God"), is that humans in the past have been made according to the likeness of God and **they still are bearers of that likeness**. For this reason, as Hoekema noted, "It is inconsistent to praise God and curse men with the same tongue, since the human creatures whom we curse [whether Christians or non-Christians—BT] still bear the likeness of God" (1986, p. 20).

A final text that speaks to the fact that man still bears God's image can be found in Acts 17:28-29 where Paul, preaching to the pagan Gentiles in Athens, quoted from their own poets and proclaimed that the whole human race is of the offspring of God. He did not say that man was a divine image bearer and then lost that image. He said, "we **are** (*esmen*) also his offspring" (17:28). The Greek *esmen* is the first person plural of *eimi* (to be). This recognition—of being God's offspring—served as a basis for the apostle's argument, as the next verse clearly indicates: "**Being** then the **offspring of God**..." (Acts 17:29, emp. added).

None of the above verses can be viewed as teaching that the image of God has been **lost**. But this fact does not minimize the devastating impact of sin, which always has been repulsive and always will be. According to biblical instruction, sin did not **destroy** the divine image stamped upon man by Jehovah. While it is true that after the Flood, God referred to the imagination of man's heart as being evil "from his youth" (Genesis 8:21), it also is true that just a few lines later, Moses recorded God as telling Noah that murder is wrong **because man is a divine image bearer** (9:6). Thus, Hoekema correctly commented:

> We may indeed think of the image of God as having been tarnished through man's fall into sin, but to affirm that man had by this time completely lost the image of God is to affirm something that the sacred text does not say (1986, p. 15).

If, then, it is the case that the image of God does not refer to spiritual perfection, how does one correlate the "image" that Christ possessed and "the renewed image" that Christians possess with such passages as Genesis 1:26-27, Genesis 9:6, and James 3:9—each of which teaches that man innately bears God's image? The answer lies in the fact that the "image of God" applied to Jesus and His followers in the New Testament is a "fuller" term than is intended in the usage found in Genesis 1:26-27. The image Jesus possessed (2 Corinthians 4:3-4; Colossians 1:15; Hebrews 1:3) is one that included spiritual flawlessness and the glory that emanated from the Lord's divine nature (two traits, incidentally, that humans do not, and cannot, possess). It is obvious that Jesus represented the "image of God" in a very unique sense. As Morey remarked:

> This is why the Apostle Paul could refer to Jesus as the messianic image-bearer of God (Col. 1:15). As the second Adam, Christ was the full and complete image-bearer. This is why Christ could say that to see Him was to see the Father (John 14:9). Christ reflected on a finite level as the second Adam what the Father was like on an infinite level (1984, p. 37).

While it is true—as both Old and New Testament testimony makes clear—that God created man in His image, the Bible also teaches that Christ bore the image of God. He was the **perfect** image— an unsurpassed example of what God wants each of us to be like. When Paul wrote in 2 Corinthians 4:3-4 about how "the god of this world hath blinded the minds of the unbelieving, that the light of the gospel of the glory of **Christ, who is the image of God**, should not dawn upon them," he used the word *eikon* for "image"—the Greek equivalent of *tselem*. Verse 6 of that same chapter elaborates on what, exactly, he meant by his use of that term: "Seeing it is God that said, 'Light shall shine out of darkness,' who shined in our hearts, **to give the light of the knowledge of the glory of God in the face of Jesus Christ**." Paul reiterated this same fact when he wrote in Colossians 1:15 of Jesus, "who is the **image of the invisible God**." This is precisely the point Christ Himself was making when He said to Philip: "He that hath seen me hath seen the Father" (John 14:9). Boiled down to their essence, the two passages amount to this: If you look carefully at Christ, you will see God, since Jesus is His **perfect image**. There is a remarkable corollary in Hebrews 1:1-4:

> God, who at various times and in various ways spoke in time past to the fathers by the prophets, has in these last days spoken to us by His Son, whom He has appointed heir of all things, through whom also He made the worlds; who **being the brightness of His glory and the express image of His person**, and upholding all things by the word of His power, when He had by Himself purged our sins, sat down at the right hand of the Majesty on high, having become so much better than the angels, as He has by inheritance obtained a more excellent name than they (NKJV, emp. added).

According to W.E. Vine, the word translated in this passage as "image" (*charakter*), denotes "a stamp or impress, as on a coin or a seal, in which case the seal or die which makes an impression bears the image produced by it, and, vice versa, **all the features of the image correspond respectively with those of the instrument producing it**" (1966, p. 247, emp. added). Just as one can look at a coin and know exactly what the die was like that produced it, so we can look at Christ and know exactly what the Father is like. In remarking on the Greek word *charakter* that Paul used, Hoekema commented: "It is hard to imagine a stronger figure to convey the thought that Christ is a perfect reproduction of the Father. Every trait, every characteristic, every quality found in the Father is also found in the Son, who is the Father's **exact representation**" (1986, p. 21, emp. in orig.). In their book, *Science and Faith*, Harry Poe and Jimmy Davis commented regarding the message concerning Christ that is found within the book of Hebrews:

> The writer of Hebrews explores the passage as the ultimate intersection of God and humanity. The destiny of humanity is tried to the manifestation of God in the created order. Human destiny is tied to relationship with the Creator. In Christ, God became one of his creatures.... **This passage from Hebrews explains that the incarnation makes knowledge of God possible** (2000, p. 133, emp. added).

Indeed it does! As S.G. Wilson put it:

> As the image of God, Christ has a threefold function: creator, **revealer**, and redeemer.... Christ does not merely resemble God but is an exact representation of his essence. Image and revelation are again connected: the invisible **God is revealed in Christ**, his image. And as an image Christ is not a poor substitute for the real thing, for he is uniquely related to God (1974, 85[12]:357, emp. added).

Ashby Camp elaborated on the fact that Christ is indeed "uniquely related" to God.

> Jesus is the image of God in a unique sense. He is the Uncreated One who took the form of a human being (Phil 2:7). As a man, Jesus certainly shares mankind's resemblance to God, but he transcends that resemblance. He is the perfect image of God (2 Cor. 4:4; Col. 1:15; Heb. 1:3), and in his face is the glory of God (2 Cor. 4:6). **"Image of God" is designed to emphasize his oneness with God, not his oneness with us.** It is a fuller term than intended in Gen. 1:26-27, one that includes moral perfection and the glory of the Lord's divine being (1999, p. 46, emp. added).

When we reflect on the fact that Christ is the perfect image of God and is one with Him, it helps us understand just how much we are able to see God through Christ. Since Christ was without sin (Hebrews 4:15), we can witness the image of God in all of its perfection. As Hoekema explained:

> As a skillful teacher uses visual aids to help his or her pupils understand what is being taught, so God the Father has given us in Jesus Christ a visual example of what the image of God is. There is no better way of seeing the image of God than to look at Jesus Christ. What we see and hear in Christ is what God intended for man.... [W]e must learn to know what the image of God is by looking at Jesus Christ (1986, p. 24).

Christ bore the image of God in a way that man cannot. For example, when Paul referenced Psalm 8:6 in his letter to the Corinthians ("He has put all things under His feet"—1 Corinthians 15:27), he took a passage of Scripture that applies to all men and applied it in a distinctive fashion to Christ. Although God has put all things under the feet of mankind, He has given His Son dominion over "all things" in a deeper, more permanently abiding sense. For example, while men can control and dominate the animal kingdom, they cannot cause donkeys to speak (Numbers 22:21-30) or shut the mouths of hungry lions (Daniel 6:11-24; 1 Kings 13:28). One can see clearly that the language applied to man likewise applied to Christ, yet when applied to Christ, it was used in an exclusive manner.

Using the same type of logic, it also is reasonable to conclude that the image of God possessed by Christians (Colossians 3:10; Ephesians 4:22-24) simply is one that is more "refined" than what non-Christians possess. In commenting on Colossians 3:10, Camp stated:

> Paul here implies that sin makes man less like God than he **should** be, but I believe he is using "image of his Creator" in a fuller sense than intended in Gen. 1:26-27. Man is like God in some aspects of his nature and therefore has the **potential** (and duty) of being like God in action. The sinner is less like God in action, even if the divine aspects of his nature are unchanged, and therefore can be said to be less like his Creator (1999, p. 47, emp. added, parenthetical item in orig.).

Realistically then, "the things that make mankind in the image of God are still present in the worst sinner as well as in the best saint" (Brown, 1993, 135[8]:50). All kings and servants, all sinners and saints, possess God's image; it is the **use** of this image that makes the difference in man's relationship with God.

CHAPTER 4

"IN THE IMAGE AND LIKENESS OF GOD" [PART II]

What, Then, *Is* The "Image of God?"

What is it that actually makes man a divine image-bearer? Or, is it even possible for one to know what it means at all? The great reformer Martin Luther believed that man cannot comprehend the meaning of *imago Dei*. He wrote:

> [W]hen we speak about that image, we are speaking about something unknown. Not only have we had no experience of it, but we continually experience the opposite; and so we hear nothing but bare words.... **Through sin this image was so obscured and corrupted that we cannot grasp it even with our intellect** (as quoted in Chaney, 1970, p. 18, emp. added).

Admittedly, it is much easier to speak of what the "image of God" is **not** than what it **is**. The simple fact is, in most cases, wrong answers are easier to eliminate than right ones are to defend. In commenting on Genesis 1:26-27, Henry Morris wrote: "This is a profound and mysterious truth, **impossible to fully comprehend**"

(1976, p. 73, emp. added). Camp agreed: "Several elements of our nature seem to distinguish us from animals, but without scriptural guidance **it is impossible to be certain which are intended**" (1999, p. 44, emp. added). Wilson suggested: "The only way in which Genesis explains the image of God is to define its purpose —man's dominion over creation—rather than its nature or location" (1974, p. 356).

Part of the difficulty in ascertaining the meaning of the "image of God" is the fact that the Bible does not define what being created in the image of God means; it simply states the fact that to be human is to bear God's image. Hence "whatever meaning is to be ascribed to the concept in its Biblical locus must be derived from its usage" (Anderson and Reichenbach, 1990, 33:201). How, then, is it used in Genesis 1:26-27? Speaking in a broad sense, as Morey has explained,

> [d]espite all the elaborate attempts to read highly technical, theological, and philosophical concepts into the biblical words "image of God," we should take them in their simplest meaning as they would have been understood by the people to whom Moses wrote. In this sense, "image of God" simply meant that man was created to be and do on a finite level what God was and did on an infinite level. Man was created to reflect God in the created order. Thus, we do not need to divide up the image of God into such categories as "inner and outer," "higher and lower," etc. Neither should we reduce the image-bearing capacity of man to one of his functions such as reason, language, or emotion. The "image of God" simply means that man reflects his creator in those capacities and capabilities which separate him from the rest of the creation. The nobility, uniqueness, meaning, worth and significance of man all rest on his being made in the image of God and being placed over the world as God's prophet, priest, and king (Gen. 1:26,27) [1984, p. 37].

When Moses wrote of man's creation in the "image of God," he did indeed "separate him from the rest of the creation." In fact, Moses' entire discussion appears in the context of man being different from animals. As Morris correctly observed:

> [M]an was to be more than simply a very complex and highly organized animal. There was to be something in man which was not only quantitatively greater, but qualitatively distinctive, something not possessed in any degree by the animals. ...[T]here can be little doubt that the "image of God" in which man was created must entail those aspects of human nature which are not shared by animals—attributes such as a moral consciousness, the ability to think abstractly, an understanding of beauty and emotion, and, above all, the capacity for worshiping and loving God (1976, p. 74).

It is apparent from the text of Genesis 1 and 2 that the creation of man differed markedly from that of all other life on Earth in at least the following ways.

(1) The account of man's creation as recorded in Genesis 1 indicates that a "divine conference" of sorts preceded the forming of man. "Then God said, 'Let **us** make man in **our** image, after **our** likeness'" (Genesis 1: 26, emp. added). Such a statement never is recorded in the text in speaking of the creation of animals. Feinberg noted:

> ...[M]an is the apex of all creation. Man's creation by God comes as the last and highest phase of God's creative activity.... Now there is counsel or deliberation in the Godhead. No others can be included here, such as angels, for none has been even intimated thus far in the narrative. Thus the creation of man took place not by a word alone, but as the result of a divine decree (1972, 129:238).

Hoekema remarked:

> It should also be noted that a divine counsel or deliberation preceded the creation of man: "Let us make man...." This again brings out the uniqueness of man's creation. In connection with no other creature is such a divine counsel mentioned (1986, p. 12).

(2) Man's creation was unique in that God "breathed life" into him (Genesis 2:7). As James Orr wrote in his classic text, *God's Image in Man*:

> The true uniqueness in man's formation, however, is expressed by the act of the divine inbreathing.... This is an act peculiar to the creation of man; no similar statement is made about the animals. The breath of Jehovah imparts to man the life which is his own, and awakens him to conscious possession of it (1906, pp. 41,46).

(3) The sexes of mankind were not created simultaneously, as in the case of the animals. Rather, the first female was "built" from a section of the first male's flesh and bone.

(4) Unlike animals, mankind is not broken down into species (i.e., "according to their kind" or "all kinds of"), but instead is designated by sexuality. God created them **male** and **female** (see Hamilton, 1990, p. 138).

(5) The Psalmist (8:5) spoke of man as being created a little lower than the angels (*elohiym*; ASV "God"). As Keil and Delitzsch put it in their commentary on Psalms:

> According to Genesis 1:27 man is created in the image of God; he is a being in the image of God, and, therefore,...since he is only a little less than divine, he is also only a little less than angelic (1996, p. 154).

Leupold, in his *Exposition of Genesis*, commented: "Man is not only made after the deliberate plan and purpose of God but is also very definitely patterned after Him" (1942, p. 88). The psalmist's point was that man, because he bears the image of God, is indeed "patterned after Him."

(6) Only man is endowed with an immortal soul; animals do not possess such a soul (see Thompson and Estabrook, 1999, 19:89-92). Unlike animals, man possesses a God-given spirit that returns to Him when man dies (Ecclesiastes 12:7). Such never is affirmed of animals. Scripture refers to Adam, the first man, as the son of God (Luke 3:38), and to mankind in general as "the offspring of God" (Acts 17:29). No animal ever was described by such language. **Man** is the only physical being upon this Earth that possesses an immortal soul given to him by God—the Father of Spirits (Hebrews

12:9). This immortal spirit that is given by God (and that one day will return to Him) most assuredly makes us divine image-bearers. It likens us to God, separates us from the lower creation, and gives us a reason to live—and to live in accordance to God's will!

(7) Finally, the text of Genesis 1 explicitly states that **mankind alone** was created in the image of God. Nowhere is such a statement made concerning the rest of Earth's life forms.

Unlike the other creatures that God created, man alone bears a special resemblance to Him. Of all the living beings that dwell on planet Earth, one solitary creature was made "in the image of God." What is it that composes the critical essence of man that distinguishes him from all of creation, and what are the ramifications of this distinction?

I believe it is unwise to restrict the meaning of the "image of God" to one particular "feature" as some have tried to do. The apostle Paul declared that man is "the offspring of God" (Acts 17:29). Such a concept certainly would consist of more than one bond of similarity (cf. Chafer, 1943, 100:481). As Victor Hamilton observed: "Any approach that focuses on one aspect of man...to the neglect of the rest of man's constituent features seems doomed to failure" (1990, p. 137). Or, as Poe and Davis wrote: "The idea of the image of God represents a far more complex matter, however, than one essential thing" (2000, p. 136). I agree wholeheartedly. It is evident from the context in Genesis 1 that the "image of God" denotes how man resembles God, and yet at the same time is distinct from animals, in a number of ways. The features that make up this image link humankind to what is above, and separate him from what is below (see Marais, 1939, 1:146). What, then, are the characteristics peculiar to man that liken him to God, differentiate him from the lower creation, and allow him to subdue the Earth? As Feinberg observed:

> The image of God constitutes all that differentiates man from the lower creation.... It has in mind the will, freedom of choice, self-consciousness, self-transcendence, self-determination, rationality, morality, and spirituality of man. The ability

to know and love God must stand forth prominently in any attempt to ascertain precisely what the image of God is (1972, 129:246).

In his *Exposition of Genesis*, Leupold stated concerning Genesis 1:26 and mankind's creation "in the image of God":

> Taking the verse as a whole, we cannot but notice that it sets forth the picture of a being that stands on a very high level, a creature of singular nobility and endowed with phenomenal powers and attributes, not a type of being that by its brute imperfections is seen to be on the same level with the animal world, but a being that towers high above all other creatures, their king and their crown (1942, pp. 92-93).

But in what way do humans "tower high above all other creatures"? What do the Scriptures mean when they speak of men and women having been created in the image of God? There are numerous different aspects that deserve to be explored in responding to such a question. Those that follow certainly would be included, but are not discussed in any specific order of importance or priority.

First, man is **capable of speaking**. Although some may consider this to be a trivial feature in man's likeness to God, the Scriptures teach otherwise. God, in His dealings with men, has revealed Himself as a speaking God. "And God said" appears ten times in Genesis one alone. God Almighty **spoke to create** the "heaven and earth, the sea, and all that in them is" (Exodus 20:11; Psalm 33:6-9), and He **spoke to communicate** to man (Genesis 1:28). Then, very soon after God created Adam, He expected him to name the creatures brought before him (Genesis 2:19). Adam named the animals of the Earth; he spoke of the helper God created for him as "woman"; and later, when attempting to justify his sinful actions, he "creatively" offered excuses and placed blame on others (Genesis 3:9-13). This indicates that man was created with the ability to speak. As Werner Gitt observed in his fascinating book, *The Wonder of Man*:

> Only man has the gift of speech, a characteristic otherwise only possessed by God. This separates us clearly from the animal kingdom. We are able to use words creatively, but we are unable to create anything by speaking, as God can do. ...We are able to express all our feelings in words, and we can enter into trusting relationships like no other beings on Earth. In addition to the necessary "software" for speech, we have also been provided with the required "hardware" (1999, p. 101).

The famous language researcher from MIT, Noam Chomsky, has championed the idea that humans are born with a "built-in universal grammar"—a series of biological switches for complex language that is set in place in the early years of childhood. This, he believes, is why children can grasp elaborate language rules even at an early age. Powerful support for Chomsky's theory emerged from a decade-long study of 500 deaf children in Managua, Nicaragua, which was reported in the December 1995 issue of *Scientific American* (Horgan, 1995, 273[6]:18-19). These children started attending special schools in 1979, but none used or was taught a formal sign language. Within a few years, and under no direction from teachers or other adults, they began to develop a basic "pidgin" sign language. This quickly was modified by younger children entering school, with the current version taking on a complex and consistent grammar. If Chomsky is correct, where, then, did humans get their innate ability for language? Chomsky himself will not even hazard a guess. In his opinion, "very few people are concerned with the origin of language because most consider it a hopeless question" (1991, 264[4]:46). The development of language, he admits, is a "mystery." The fundamental failing of naturalistic theories is that they are inadequate to explain the origins of something so complex and information-rich as human language, which itself is a gift of God and part of man's having been created "in His image."

The fact is, no animal is capable of speaking in the manner in which people can speak. Speech is a peculiarly **human** trait. In an article titled "Chimp-Speak" that dealt with this very point, Trevor Major wrote:

First, chimps do not possess the anatomical ability to speak. Second, the sign language they learn is not natural, even for humans. Chimps have to be trained to communicate with this language; it is not something they do in the wild. And unlike humans, trained chimps do not seem to pass this skill on to their young. Third, chimps never know more than a few hundred words—considerably less than most young children.... [E]volutionists have no way to bridge the gap from innate ability to language relying on natural selection or any other purely natural cause. Why? Because language is complex and carries information—the trademarks of intelligent design (1994, 14[3]:1).

The Bible mentions only two (supernaturally caused) exceptions to this rule—the serpent in the Garden of Eden (Genesis 3:1-6) and Balaam's donkey (Numbers 22:28-30). However, unlike man, both of these animals were controlled externally; Satan controlled the serpent, and God controlled the donkey. It is clear that only man was given the gift of speech. It is a fundamental part of his nature that associates him with God and separates him from the rest of creation.

Second, man can **write, improve his education, accumulate knowledge, and build on past achievements**. The Bible mentions two occasions when God Himself wrote something. The first, of course, was on Mount Sinai when He gave Moses the Ten Commandments: "And he gave unto Moses, when he had made an end of communing with him upon mount Sinai, the two tables of the testimony, tables of stone, written with the finger of God" (Exodus 31:18). The second time was during Belshazzar's feast: "In the same hour came forth the fingers of a man's hand, and wrote over against the candlestick upon the plaster of the wall of the king's palace: and the king saw the part of the hand that wrote" (Daniel 5:5; cf. also 5:24-28). Werner Gitt thus observed:

Various writing systems have been devised by man, who is now able to record thoughts and ideas. The invention of writing is one of the greatest achievements of the human intellect. The human memory span is brief and the storage capacity of the brain, though vast, is limited. Both these problems are overcome by recording information in writing. Written information can communicate over vast distances; written records may last for many years, even centuries. Only nations possessing the skill of writing can develop literature, historiography, and high levels of technology. Nations and tribes without writing are thus restricted to a certain level of cultural development. Written language offers the possibility of storing information so that inventions and discoveries (like medical and technological advances) are not lost, but can be developed even further (1999, p. 103, parenthetical comment in orig.).

It is this ability to "develop even further" that allows mankind to improve his own educational levels, accumulate knowledge, and build on past achievements. The adage that we "learn from our mistakes" contains more than just a kernel of truth. It actually represents the basis of cumulative human knowledge. Human society today is in many ways a far better place than it was, say, two thousand years ago. We have eradicated smallpox, cracked the human genome, and landed a robotic rover on Mars. Today the citizens of most civilized countries are better fed, better clothed, and healthier than they have ever been. Transportation, educational, medical, industrial, and even recreational facilities are vastly improved compared to those of previous generations. Prospects for mankind's future hardly could be brighter.

But compare mankind's achievements to those of the animal kingdom. Animals possess no greater knowledge today than they did 200—or 2,000—years ago. Insofar as improvements to their habitats, knowledge base, or past achievements are concerned, animals of today fare little better than their ancestors from previous generations. We not only learn from our mistakes, but also build for the distant future. No animal does that. Man, as a part of his endowment in the "image of God," has the ability to improve and progress—a trait conspicuously lacking in any of the inhabitants of the animal kingdom.

Third, **man is creative**. In Genesis 1-2, the words "created" (*bara*) and "made" (*asah*) are used fifteen times to refer to God's work. His omnipotence is seen in His ability to create something out of nothing simply by speaking it into existence (cf. Hebrews 1: 3). The amazing and intricate design of His creation testifies to His creative prowess (see Ackerman, 1990, p. 48). Like God, man also is able to create and invent, although he does so on a distinctly different level. Consider the creativeness in Picasso's paintings, Mozart's music, or Goethe's writings. Man has built spaceships that travel 240,000 miles to the Moon; he has made artificial hearts for the sick; and he continues to construct computers that can process billions of pieces of information in a fraction of a second. Animals cannot do such things because they lack the inherent creative ability with which God has endowed man. Beavers may build huts, birds may build nests, and spiders may weave webs, but they are guided by instinct.

Exhaustive attempts have been made to teach animals to express themselves in art, music, writing, etc., but none has produced the hoped-for success. Beyond the simple and clumsy drawing of a circle, no attempt at creative expression has ever been observed. There is an enormous, unbridgeable gap between humans and animals in the realm of creativity and aesthetics. In his *Great Texts of the Bible* series, James Hastings commented in the volume on Genesis:

> As regards his intellectual powers, consider that man is, like God, a creator. Works of art, whether useful or ornamental, are, and are often called, creations. How manifold are the new discoveries, the new inventions, which man draws forth, years after year, from his creative genius—the timepiece, the microscope, the steamship, the steam-carriage, the sun-picture, the electric telegraph! All these things originally lay wrapped up in the human brain, and are its offspring. Look at the whole fabric of civilization, which is built up by the several arts. What a creation it is—how curious, how varied, how wonderful in all its districts!... It may possibly suggest itself here that some of the lower animals are producers no less than man. And so they are, in virtue of the instinct with which the Almighty has endowed them. The bird is the artisan of her nest, the bee of his cell, and beaver of his hut. But they are

artisans only, working by a rule furnished to them, not architects, designing out of their own mental resources. They are producers only, not creators; they never make a variation, in the way of improvement, on forgone productions; and we argue conclusively that because they **do** not make it, they **can** never make it. Instinct dictates to them, as they work, "line upon line, precept upon precept"; but there is no single instance of their rising above this level—of their speculating upon an original design, and contriving the means whereby it may carried into effect (1976, 1:53-54, emp. in orig.).

When one considers the genius of man's creativeness in areas such as literature, art, science, medicine, technology, etc., it is clear that a huge, gap separates man from all members of the animal kingdom—and that this gap is indeed unbridgeable. Certainly, in his creativity, man is made "in the image of God."

Fourth, closely related to man's creative ability is his gift of **reasoning**. Admittedly, animals possess a measure of understanding. They can learn to respond to commands and signs, and in some cases even can be trained to use minimal portions of sign language, as in the case of a chimpanzee named Washoe who was taught certain portions of American Sign Language. But, as biologist John N. Moore has pointed out:

Although the chimpanzee Washoe has been taught the American Sign Language, such an accomplishment is **primarily** an increase in an ability of the anthropoid to respond to direct presentation of **signs**. And, further, the learned capability of the chimpanzee Lana to utilize push buttons connected with a computer to "converse" with a human trainer depends fundamentally upon increased conditional reflex response to **signs** (1983, p. 341, emp. in orig.).

Even though apes, dogs, and birds can be "trained" to do certain things, they cannot reason and communicate ideas with others so as to have true mental communion. The intelligence of animals is unlike that of humankind. As Moore went on to discuss,

[t]he purest and most complex manifestation of man's symbolic nature is his capacity for conceptual thought, that is, for thought involving sustained and high order abstraction and

generalization. Conceptual thought enables man to make himself independent of stimulus boundness that characterizes animal thinking. Animals, especially primates, give undeniable evidence of something **analogous** to human thought—analogous yet medically different in that their thought is bound to the immediate stimulus situation and to the felt impulse of the organism. Animal thinking, too, is riveted to the realm of survival (broadly taken) and therefore encompasses a variety of needs pertinent to the species as well as to the individual. These differences account for the distinction between **conceptual** thought, which is the exclusive prerogative of man, and **perceptual** thought, a cognitive function based directly upon sense perception, which man shares with other animals (1983, p. 344, emp. in orig.).

Thus, the issue is not "can animals think?," but rather "can they think the way humans do?" The answer, obviously, is a resounding "No!" In summarizing his thoughts on this subject, Trevor Major offered the following conclusion concerning the intelligence of chimpanzees.

Are chimps intelligent? The answer is yes. Do chimps possess the **same kind** of intelligence as humans? The answer would have to be no. Humans are more intelligent, **and** they possess additional forms of intelligence. What we must remember, also, is that the greatest capabilities of the apes belong to a handful of superstars like Kanzi and Sheba. Even these animals lack the empathy, foresight, and language capabilities of all but the youngest or most intellectually challenged of our own species (1995a, 15:88, emp. in orig.).

Moore commented further:

Animals can think in several ways...though only on the perceptual, not on the conceptual level. The key difference here is one between conceptual and perceptual thinking. The latter, which is typical of animal thinking, requires the actual or nearly immediate presence of the pertinent objects. Man's thinking, on the other hand, is independent of the presence of pertinent objects. It is, in fact, independent of objects altogether, as is the case with logical or mathematical exercises. Secondly, the difference between human and animal thinking resides in the fact that, whether or not the object of the mental operation is present, animals cannot make judgments or engage in reasoning. For example, animals are unable to conclude that such and such **is** or **is not** the case in a given situation or that **if** such and such is the case, **then** so and so is not (1983, p. 344, emp. and ellipses in orig.).

In any examination of the intellectual capacity of God's creation, one of the most obvious differences between humans and animals is that animals do not posses the ability to know and love God. As Hazelip remarked:

Animals go in herds and have some traces of "civilization," but they do not know real fellowship, nor can they develop cultures. The animal may fear punishment, but he does not have a conscience. He may realize man's superiority, but he certainly knows nothing of the supreme God. Obviously man is something other than an animal, just as an animal is something other than a plant (1980, 2[2]:26).

Animals cannot look at the heavens and understand them as God's handiwork (cf. Psalm 19:1); they cannot perceive that there is a God based upon what is made (cf. Romans 1:20; Hebrews 3:4); neither can they understand God's written revelation. For this reason, animals are neither righteous nor sinful. Feinberg was absolutely correct when he wrote that this feature "must stand forth prominently in any attempt to ascertain precisely what the image of God is" (1972, 129:246). Some writers, such as Gordon Clark, have argued that "**The image must be reason** because God is truth, and fellowship with him—a most important purpose in creation—requires thinking and understanding" (1969, 12:218, emp. added). While I never would go so far as Clark and limit the "image" to reason alone, it most assuredly plays a critical role in man's rule over God's creation and in his unique relationship to God—a relationship that animals cannot have, partly because they lack the intelligence for such.

A fifth characteristic included in the "image of God" is man's **free-will capacity** to make rational choices. God Himself is a Being of free will, as the Scriptures repeatedly document. The psalmist recorded: "Whatever the Lord pleases, he does" (135:6). God's free will is apparent in Romans 9:15: "I will have mercy on whom I have mercy, and I will have compassion on whom I have compassion." He is a God Who "would have all men to be saved, and come to the knowledge of the truth" (1 Timothy 2:4). God has free will, and has employed it on behalf of humanity.

As a **volitional** creature endowed with what we often refer to as "free moral agency," man likewise possesses free will. And as such, he is capable of choosing his own destiny. In his book, *The Crises of the Christ*, G. Campbell Morgan remarked:

> In God intelligence is unlimited, emotion is unlimited, will is unlimited. In man, all three facts are found, but in each case within limitations. He does not know all things, his intelligence being limited, his emotional nature also can only act within comparatively narrow limitations, and the exercise of his will is limited by the demand for a cause, which is never perfectly found within himself (1903, p. 28).

Thomas Aquinas often is quoted as one who thought the image most assuredly implied an intelligent being endowed with free choice and self-movement (*Summa Theologica II*, p. 609), which is yet another distinguishing characteristic that separates him from the animals.

Whenever animals react to their environment, they are guided by instinct. The Arctic tern travels from the Arctic to the Antarctic and home again every year—a round trip of 22,000 miles—without concern for changes in climate or in the environment (see Devoe, 1964, p. 311). Salmon are able to find their way back home through thousands of miles of trackless ocean to the same river and gravel bed where they once were hatched (Thompson and Jackson, 1982, p. 24). These animals, along with thousands of other creatures, are guided by the amazing trait we refer to as "instinct."

But unlike animals, man does not rely primarily upon instinct for his survival. Rather, God gave him the ability to plot the course of his own life and then to carry out his plans in a rational manner. Adam and Eve freely chose to eat of the tree of knowledge of good and evil, even after being instructed otherwise (Genesis 2:16-17). Joshua challenged Israel to serve either Jehovah or some false god (Joshua 24:15). Jesus condemned the Pharisees of His day because they were "not willing" to accept Him as the Son of God (John 5: 39-40). **But Adam, Eve, the Israelites, and the Pharisees did have a choice!**

Today, in a similar fashion, each person has a choice regarding whether or not he or she accepts the invitation of Jesus (Revelation 22:17; Matthew 11:28-30). Unlike all of God's other creatures that act primarily on instinct, human beings are able to think rationally and act willfully in regard to the choices they make. As Gitt commented:

> God did not create puppets which can only do what the puppeteer wants. He did not create robots which function according to pre-determined programs. He did not create trained creatures, mindlessly carrying out their practiced routines— we are not performing circus animals (1999, p. 104).

And, as numerous scholars have noted, it is this ability to choose that helps explain why there frequently is so much evil, pain, and suffering in the world. The simple fact is, we do not always choose correctly.

Sixth, of all the creatures upon the Earth only man has the ability to choose between **right and wrong**. As Clifford Newell Jr. noted:

> Involved in man's rationality is his capability of being a moral being. In fact, man has the capacity to be properly concerned about what is right and what is wrong—to be concerned about God's will. God wants men to come to Him, to love Him. But He wants them to come and to love on their own free will. God respects man's free moral agency—He does not violate man's free will (2001, p. 16).

Animals do not possess any innate sense of moral "oughtness." A dog might be taught by his master not to do certain things, and even may fear punishment, but he does not possess a conscience. A Doberman Pincher does not feel sorry about biting the paperboy; nor does he feel guilty after eating his master's birthday cake. A lion has no pangs of conscience because it kills a young gazelle for an afternoon meal. There is simply no evidence that shows beasts have any sense of morality or ethics.

True morality is based on the fact of the unchanging nature of Almighty God. He is eternal (Psalm 90:2; 1 Timothy 1:17), holy (Isaiah 6:3; Revelation 4:8), just and righteous (Psalm 89:14), and forever consistent (Malachi 3:6). In the ultimate sense, only He is good (Mark 10:18). Furthermore, since He is perfect (Matthew 5:48), the morality that issues from such a God is good, unchanging, just, and consistent—i.e., exactly the opposite of the relativistic, deterministic, or situational ethics of the world.

There is within each man, woman, and child a sense of moral responsibility which derives from the fact that God is our Creator (Psalm 100:3) and that we have been fashioned in His spiritual image (Genesis 1:26-27). As the potter has sovereign right over the clay with which he works (Romans 9:21), so our Maker has the sovereign right over His creation since in His hand "is the soul of every living thing" (Job 12:10). As the patriarch Job learned much too late, God is not a man with whom one can argue (Job 9:32; 38:1-3; 42:1-6).

Whatever God does, commands, and approves is good (Psalm 119:39,68; cf. Genesis 18:25). What He has commanded results from the essence of His being—Who He is—and therefore also is good. In the Old Testament, the prophet Micah declared of God: "He showed thee, O man, what is good; and what doth Jehovah require of thee, but to do justly, and to love kindness, and walk humbly with thy God" (Micah 6:8). In the New Testament, the apostle Peter admonished: "As he who called you is holy, be ye yourselves also holy in all manner of living; because it is written, 'Ye shall be holy: for I am holy'" (1 Peter 1:15-16).

The basic thrust of God-based ethics concerns the relationship of man to the One Who created and sustains him. God Himself is the unchanging standard of moral law. His perfectly holy nature is the ground or basis upon which "right" and "wrong," "good" and "evil" are determined. The Divine will—expressive of the very nature of God—constitutes the ultimate ground of moral obligation. Why are we to pursue holiness? Because God is holy (Leviticus 19:2; 1 Peter 1:16). Why are we not to lie, cheat, or steal (Colossians 3:9)? Because God's nature is such that He cannot lie (Titus 1:2; Hebrews 6:18). Since God's nature is unchanging, it follows that moral law, which reflects the divine nature, is equally immutable.

While there have been times in human history when each man "did that which was right in his own eyes" (Judges 17:6), that never was God's plan. Hastings spoke to this point when he wrote:

> That the wickedness of mankind has made fearful confusion between right and wrong, and that men very often by their conduct appear to approve of that which they ought not to approve, is very true; and that man may fall, by a course of vice, into such a condition that their moral sense is fearfully blunted, is also true; but this does not prove the absence of a sense of right and wrong from a healthy mind, any more than the case of ever so many blind men would prove that there is no such thing as sight (1976, 1:55-56).

God has not left us to our own devices to determine what is right and wrong because He knew that through sin man's heart would become "exceedingly corrupt" (Jeremiah 17:9). Therefore, God has "spoken" (Hebrews 1:1), and in so doing He has made known to man His laws and precepts through the revelation He has provided in written form within the Bible (1 Corinthians 2:11ff.; 2 Timothy 3:16-17; 2 Peter 1:20-21). Thus, mankind is expected to act in a morally responsible manner (Matthew 19:9; Acts 14:15-16; 17:30; Hebrews 10:28ff.) in accordance with biblical laws and precepts. This is a part of our having been fashioned "in the image of God."

Seventh, man possesses a **conscience**. While writing to the Christians in Rome, Paul argued that even the ancient Gentiles, who had no written law from God, had a type of law "written in their hearts" (Romans 2:14-15). Hence, their consciences either accused them or excused them. John Henry Newman assessed the situation like this:

> Inanimate things cannot stir our affections; these are corre-
> lative with persons. If, as is the case, we feel responsibility,
> are ashamed, are frightened, at transgressing the voice of
> conscience, this implies that there is One to whom we are
> responsible, before whom we are ashamed, whose claims up-
> on us we fear.... [W]e are not affectionate towards a stone,
> nor do we feel shame before a horse or a dog; we have no re-
> morse or compunction on breaking mere human law...and
> thus the phenomena of conscience, as a dictate, avails to
> impress the imagination with the picture of a Supreme Gov-
> ernor, a Judge, holy, just, powerful, all-seeing, retributive
> (1887, pp. 105,106).

When man violates his conscience, he feels guilt. Although one's
environment plays a major role in his **concept** of morality, the
need for morality is acknowledged universally by humans around
the globe.

Furthermore, the conscience must work in close concert with
our judgment in order to prompt us to review that judgment (i.e.,
our concept of right and wrong) to determine if we are acting in accordance with it. One of the best and most comprehensive discussions I have seen on this subject can be found in Guy N. Woods'
book, *Questions and Answers.*

> [C]onscience is thus a safe guide in ascertaining whether our
> conduct is in harmony with our judgement; and, so long as
> it is not allowed to become hardened, seared over and callous,
> it serves effectively in the area which God designed for it.
> But, it was not intended to serve as a standard of right and
> wrong; and, it is not a "creature of education" so as to be
> equipped for such action. If we think what we are doing is
> right, we have a **good** conscience (Acts 23:1; I Tim. 1:5,19;
> Heb. 13:18; I Pet. 3:16,21), a pure conscience (I Tim. 3:9;
> II Tim. 1:3); and a conscience **void of offence** (Acts 24:
> 16). If we think we are doing wrong, our conscience is **evil**
> (I Tim. 4:2). What we **think**, however, does not determine
> what is right and wrong and, like Paul when he persecuted the
> saints, we may have "a good conscience" though we are griev-
> ously in error. In such instances, it is the judgement which is
> at fault, and which must be "educated." When this is done,
> the conscience will swing around and approve that which it

> formerly condemned, and oppose that which it before approved.... It is wrong to disregard the promptings of our conscience, because it is designed to lead us to review our judgement; but, it is our judgement (our concept of right and wrong) which determines whether the conscience approves or condemns us (1976, pp. 213-214, emp. in orig.).

How does one explain all of this? The only way to explain it is to acknowledge that man was given a conscience "in the beginning" as a part of having been created in the image of God.

Eighth, like God, man can **experience heart-felt emotions**. Camp addressed this fact when he wrote:

> Several elements of our nature seem to distinguish us from animals.... Perhaps the most fundamental difference is self-transcendence, the capacity to make oneself and the world the object of reflection. Other aspects of our uniqueness, some of which flow from self-transcendence, include moral and spiritual awareness, creativity, and abstract reasoning. We also have a unique capacity for worship, love, fellowship, and emotional experience (1999, p. 44).

As an example of this point, consider 1 John 4:8,16, wherein the apostle recorded that "God is love." If we were created by God in His image, then we, too, should be capable of, and radiate, love. This is why Christ told His disciples: "By this shall all men know that ye are my disciples, if ye have love one to another" (John 13: 35). And this is why Paul admonished first-century Christians: "Let all that ye do be done in love" (1 Corinthians 16:14).

God can experience anger or righteous indignation [as He did when the Israelites built and worshiped a golden calf (Exodus 32), and as Christ did when He ran the moneychangers out of the Temple (Matthew 21:12)]. Thus, we, too, can experience righteous indignation ("Be ye angry, and sin not," Ephesians 4:26).

God can be merciful, as Paul wrote in 2 Corinthians 1:3-5:

> Blessed be the God and Father of our Lord Jesus Christ, the Father of mercies and God of all comfort; who comforteth us in all our affliction, that we may be able to comfort them that are in any affliction, through the comfort wherewith we ourselves are comforted of God.

Consequently, we, too, should strive to be merciful, just as Christ urged us to do when He said: "Be ye merciful, even as your Father is merciful" (Luke 6:36).

God is compassionate, as is evident from the fact that He said: "As I live...I have no pleasure in the death of the wicked; but that the wicked turn from his way and live: turn ye, turn ye from your evil ways; for why will ye die" (Ezekiel 33:11). Furthermore, he is "longsuffering to you-ward, not wishing that any should perish" (2 Peter 3:9). This is exactly why Christ commanded us: "But love your enemies, and do them good" (Luke 6:35). And so on.

Ninth, man alone possesses a unique, inherent **religious inclination**; he has both the desire and the ability to worship. Regardless of how "primitive" or "advanced" he may be, and despite living isolated from all other humans, man always has sought to worship a higher being. And even when man departs from the true God, he still worships something. It might be a tree, a rock, or even himself. As one writer observed, evidence reveals that "no race or tribe of men, however degraded and apparently atheistic, lacks that spark of religious capacity which may be fanned and fed into a mighty flame" (Dummelow, 1944, p. ci). The steadily accumulating historical and scientific evidence forced unbelievers to accept this fact decades ago. In their book titled *Infidels and Heretics: An Agnostic's Anthology,* Clarence Darrow and Wallace Rice quote the famous skeptic, John Tyndall:

> Religion lives not by the force and aid of dogma, but because **it is ingrained in the nature of man**. To draw a metaphor from metallurgy, the moulds have been broken and reconstructed over and over again, but the molten ore abides in the ladle of humanity. An influence so **deep and permanent** is not likely soon to disappear... (1929, p. 146, emp. added).

More than twenty years ago, evolutionist Edward O. Wilson of Harvard University admitted: "The predisposition to religious belief is the most complex and powerful force in the human mind and in all probability an ineradicable part of human nature" (1978, p. 167). Thus, both believers and nonbelievers readily admit that **religion is "ingrained" in man**. Yet no chimpanzee or dog ever stopped to build an altar, sing a hymn of praise, or give a prayer of thanks. Man's unique **inclination to worship** someone or something, and the fact that he alone is amenable to God (Acts 17:30; Hebrews 14:13) is an important part of the image of God that he bears.

Finally, and very likely most important, is the fact that man bears the spiritual imprint of God due to the fact that he possesses an **immortal soul**. As Poe and Davis noted:

> In whatever sense people are made in the image of God, this image or likeness refers to the sense in which people are like God. People are like all other animals in many respects related to the physical world, but people are like God in many respects related to the **spiritual** world (2000, p. 134, emp. added).

Or, as Anderson and Reichenbach stated it: "Since the *imago Dei* designates the unique feature of human persons it must relate to the essence of man.... Since God is spirit, that which images him must likewise be **spiritual**" (1990, 33:200, emp. added). Morgan wrote:

> In what sense was man created in the image of God? The answer to the enquiry may be found by suggesting another question. What is man essentially, for it is in his essential nature that he is in the image of God. Man essentially is spirit, his present body being his probational dwelling place, that through which he receives impressions, and that through which he expresses the fact of his own being.... The essential fact in man therefore is his **spirit**, and it is in **spiritual essence** that man is made in the image of God.... God is a Spirit, having intelligence, having emotion, having will. Man is in the shadow of God. He also is a spirit, having intelligence, having emotion, having will (1903, pp. 26,27).

Leupold perhaps summarized the matter best when he stated that "...the spiritual and inner side of the image of God is, without a doubt, the most important one" (1942, p. 90). Henry Morris agreed when he wrote that the image of God "involves many things, but **surely the essential fact is that man has an eternal spirit**, capable of fellowship with his Creator" (1965, p. 65, emp. added). This is why, to use Hastings' words, man is "fitted to hold communion with God" (1976, 1:57).

Hastings allowed that "in man God objectified Himself, made Himself visible. God intended man to be the incarnation of Himself, for He 'made man in His own image.' What a stupendous truth!" (p. 63). But equally as stupendous is the fact that, as God uniquely "formed" man's body from the dust of the ground (Genesis 2:7), He "formeth the **spirit** of man within him" (Zechariah 12:1, emp. added). The Hebrew word *yatsar* (form) is used in both Genesis 2:7 and Zechariah 12:1, and is defined as to form, fashion, or shape (as in a potter working with clay; Harris, et al., 1980, 1:396). Thus, God molded and fashioned both man's physical body and his spiritual nature.

Man and animals **do not share kinship**—all the claims of evolutionists (and those sympathetic to them) notwithstanding. The apostle Paul stressed this fact in 1 Corinthians 15 when he wrote: "**All flesh is not the same flesh**: but there is one flesh of men, and another flesh of beasts, and another flesh of birds, and another of fishes" (v. 15, emp. added). As Stuart Walker correctly commented: "Genesis 1:26-30 and 2:7,21-25 clearly state that man was a special creation with no phylogenetic relationship to any other creature. Thus, there is a phylogenetic **discontinuity** between man and animals—**we are not physically interrelated**" (1991, 5[2]:21, emp. added). As Adam previewed the animals in the Garden of Eden for a mate and went about naming them (Genesis 2:18-20), this "discontinuity" became clear. Among all the animals that God had created, there was none that corresponded to him. Not one sufficed to remove him from his personal isolation of being "alone" (Genesis 2:18). As Walker went on to note:

> Thus, we share in the life principle, but it is not the life principle itself that is precious.... Ontological continuity cannot be established upon the experiences of life, the intrinsic value

of life itself, or physical parallels between animals and humans; rather, **we are separated from the animal world by an impassable gulf**—a chasm of essential difference in who we are (5[2]:22, emp. added).

Further, man was commanded to "subdue and have dominion over the fish of the sea, and over the birds of the heavens, and over every living thing that moveth upon the earth" (Genesis 1:28). The Hebrew word for "subdue" (*kabash*) is described in *Strong's Exhaustive Concordance* as meaning "to tread down," "to bring under subjection," etc. The same word is used in Numbers 32:22, 29 and Joshua 18:1 where it is used to describe the subduing and pacifying of Israel's enemies. To *kabash*, therefore, is to

> face that which opposes us and is inimical in its present state to our goals and well-being, and bring it into conformity with our needs—completely pacifying it....Thus it can be inferred that when God gave Adam dominion over the creative order, He was describing a pre-emptive authority which man would wield over the creation as he interpreted the cosmos and manipulated its functions to man's benefit... (Walker, 5[2]:25).

Man's "pre-emptive authority" over the creation, including the animal kingdom, was demonstrated quite forcefully in a single stroke when God granted mankind permission to kill and eat animals for food (Genesis 9:3-4). Interestingly, however, within the same context God specifically forbade manslaughter "for in the image of God made he man" (Genesis 9:5-6). If man "shares kinship" with animals or if animals possess immortal souls, why would God permit him to kill his own kin—relatives whose souls are no different than his own? As Neale Pryor commented: "Animals also have a *ruach* [a Hebrew word for "breath" or "life"—BT] (Genesis 6:17). Killing one who has a *ruach* or *nephesh* would not necessarily constitute murder; otherwise animals could not be sacrificed or slaughtered" (1974, 5[3]:34). God's prohibition against murder carried over even into New Testament times (Matthew 19:18). At the same time, however, God broadened the list of animals that men could kill and eat (Acts 10:9-14). Why was it that men **could not** kill other men, but **could** kill animals? The answer lies, of course, in the fact that animals were not created "in the image of God."

Additionally, although it is true that at times the Bible uses the same terms to refer to the life principle/force in both humans and animals (e.g. Genesis 7:22), and although it is true that those terms may be used to refer to the immortal souls of humans (Ecclesiastes 12:7; Matthew 10:28), they **never** are employed by Bible writers to refer to an immortal soul in animals. In their *Commentary on the Old Testament*, Keil and Delitzsch observed:

> The beasts arose at the creative word of God, and **no communication of the spirit is mentioned** even in ch. ii:19; the origin of their soul was coincident with that of their corporeality, and their life was merely the individualization of the universal life, with which all matter was filled in the beginning by the Spirit of God. On the other hand, the human spirit is not a mere individualization of the divine breath which breathed upon the material of the world, or of the universal spirit of nature; nor is his body merely a production of the earth when stimulated by the creative word of God. The earth does not bring forth his body, but God Himself puts His hand to the work and forms him; nor does the life already imparted to the world by the Spirit of God individualize itself in him, but God breathes it directly into the nostrils of the one man, in the whole fulness of His personality, the breath of life, that **in a manner corresponding to the personality of God he may become a living soul** (1996, 1:79-80, emp. added).

Man alone was created "in the image and likeness of God" (Genesis 1:26-27)—something that may not be said of animals. Walker therefore asked:

> If the putative parallels either do not exist or are insignificant before God, what then is the critical essence of man that distinguishes him from all of creation, and what are the ramifications of this distinction? The key is found in Genesis 1:26-28, 2:18-25, and 9:5-7; it is that **only man is created in the image of God** (1991, 5[2]:22, emp. added).

Gary Anderson addressed this same point when he wrote:

Man's concepts of spiritual values, his recognition of morals and his universal acknowledgement that he is responsible for his own behavior set him far apart from the animal world. That is to say, they have no immortal soul, as the following point documents. The spirit of man returns to God who gave it when one dies (Eccl. 12:7). Such is not said of the animal! Adam is called the son of God in Luke 3:38, obviously by creation. **What animal is called the son of God or offspring of God**? (1989, p. 76, emp. added).

Nowhere does God's Word indicate that animals were created in God's image. As Philip Hughes commented:

Only of man is it said that God created him in his image. It is in this charter of his constitution that man's uniqueness is specifically affirmed as a creature radically distinguished from all other creatures. In this respect a line is defined which links man directly and responsibly to God in a way that is unknown to any other creature. Nothing is more basic than the recognition that being constituted in the image of God is of the very essence of and absolutely central to the humanness of man. It is the key that unlocks the meaning of his authentic humanity (1989, p. 30, emp. added).

Conclusion

The Bible paints a picture of man as a being that stands on a different level from all other creatures upon the Earth. He towers high above all earthly creation because of the phenomenal powers and attributes that God Almighty has freely given him. No other living being was given the capacities and capabilities, the potential and the dignity, that God instilled in each man and woman. Indeed, humankind is the peak, the pinnacle, the crown, the apex of God's creation. And what a difference that should make in our lives. As Poe and Davis put it:

Whether people are an aspect of God or creatures of God has profound implications for human existence on earth. If people are the result of the creative activity of God based on God's intentional, self-conscious decision to make people, then creation results from the purpose of God. People have a purpose, and this purpose emerges from the Creator-creature relationship. If, on the other hand, people are aspects of a...unity of which all things are a part, but which lacks self-consciousness, then life has no purpose. It merely exists (2000, p. 128).

There are, no doubt, additional ways in which man bears God's image. For example, only human beings yearn to know a cause for things. Only humans are concerned with their origin, their present purpose, and their destiny. No animal—regardless of how "close" to mankind certain evolutionists think that animal may be—ever pondered such things. Also, only human beings contemplate death, practice funeral rituals, and bury their dead. God has indeed "placed eternity" in our hearts (Ecclesiastes 3:11). Human civilizations from time immemorial have believed in life after death and attempted to make some plans for it. One look at the Egyptian pyramids is enough to establish this fact. Additionally, only humans are historical beings. We record past events, recount them, discuss them, and even are able to learn from them.

Although in some aspects man is very different from the infinite God (i.e. man is not omnipotent, omniscient, etc.), the passages of Scripture that speak of the *imago Dei* reveal his likeness to Him. Thus, we are justified in concluding that man was created "**to be and do on a finite level what God was and did on an infinite level**" (Morey, 1984, p. 37, emp. added). Man did not evolve from an "imageless" lower creation. Rather, God created him with the unique abilities I have discussed here. How thrilling, and yet how humbling, it is to know that we alone bear God's image! And oh, how such knowledge should help us build, and sustain, a rock-solid faith.

CHAPTER 5

KNOWING AND
DEFEATING THE ENEMY

As we make our way through this pilgrimage called "life," surely we would count among the strongest aspirations of the human heart the desire to be content and happy—not in the mediocre sense of those words, but instead to be genuinely fulfilled and at peace both with ourselves and with the world in general. Oh, how we would like to be able to say with the writer of old (and actually mean it): "This is the day which Jehovah hath made; we will rejoice and be glad in it" (Psalm 118:24).

But, as each of us knows all too well from personal experience, not every day causes us to "rejoice and be glad." The simple truth is that things do not always go our way. Plans go awry. Fortunes are forfeited. Friendships are broken. Lives are lost. To echo the words of that ancient patriarch so famous for his perseverance in the face of adversity, "Man that is born of a woman is of few days, and full of trouble" (Job 14:1).

Facing the routine vicissitudes of life would be difficult enough on its own, without any outside force "stacking the deck." Unfortunately, however, there **is** an outside force marshaled against us.

Within the pages of Holy Writ, that "outside force" is identified by a variety of designations, but likely the best known and most widely used is the name—**Satan**.

In the Old Testament (where we first are introduced to the word, and where it is used approximately nineteen times), etymologically the Hebrew term *satan* is related to an Aramaic verb that means "to lie in wait," "to oppose," or "to set oneself in opposition to." On occasion, the name was employed to describe in non-specific terms any adversary, but whenever it was accompanied by the definite article (i.e., **the** adversary), it always indicated a proper name associated with mankind's greatest adversary, Satan (Hiebert, 1975, 5:282).

In the New Testament (where the term Satan is used thirty-six times), the Greek word for Satan (*satanas*) indicates an adversary, opponent, or enemy, and "is always used of 'Satan,' the adversary" (Vine, et al., 1985, p. 547). Another designation for our Great Adversary—"devil"—is used thirty-three times in the New Testament, and "...came into English through the German language from the Greek word *diabolos*. *Diabolos* means a slanderer, treacherous informer and, traitor" (Overton, 1976, 5[4]:3).

Exactly who is this devil, Satan, who has established himself as God's archfiend and mankind's ardent foe? Is he real? If he is, what is his origin? Why has he arrayed himself against both God and man? What is his mission? What are his powers? And what is his ultimate destiny? These are questions that cry out from the human heart for answers. Fortunately, God's Word provides those answers.

Is Satan Real?

Throughout history, both those who do not accept the Bible as the Word of God (unbelievers), and those who accept it but only marginally so (religious liberals), have disavowed the existence of Satan as a real, personal, spiritual being. Rather, they speak of him as a "myth," and of his dealings with mankind as "legends" invented as vehicles of "moral teaching" intended to impart great spiritual truths. But neither he nor his activities is accepted as historical reality. For example, atheistic writer Isaac Asimov, who was serving as president of the American Humanist Association at the time of his death in 1992, wrote:

> By New Testament times, the Jews had developed, in full detail, the **legend** that Satan had been the leader of the "fallen angels." These were angels who rebelled against God by refusing to bow down before Adam when that first man was created, using as their argument that they were made of light and man only of clay. Satan, the leader of the rebels, thought, in his pride, to supplant God. The rebelling angels were, however, hurled out of heaven and into Hell. By the time this legend was developed the Jews had come under Greek influence and they may have perhaps been swayed by Greek myths concerning the attempts of the Titans, and later the Giants, to defeat Zeus and assume mastery of the universe. Both Titans and Giants were defeated and imprisoned underground. But whether Greek-inspired or not, the **legend** came to be firmly fixed in Jewish consciousness (1968, p. 540, emp. added; see also pp. 408-410).

The assessment of liberal-leaning religious writers does not sound much different. Andrew Zenos of Presbyterian Theological Seminary in Chicago suggested:

> The apparent incongruity of a person (i.e., Satan) with such a frame of mind consorting with the other "sons of God" in the courts of heaven, giving an account of himself to, and speaking on familiar terms with, God, disappears when the narrative is seen to be constructed, not as a picture of realities, but as a vehicle of moral teaching... (1936, p. 811).

Forty-five years later, Neal D. Buffaloe and N. Patrick Murray co-authored a text in which they wrote: "By contrast [to the literal, historical view of Genesis—BT], the mainstream of Biblical scholarship rejects the literal historicity of the Genesis stories prior to Chapter 12, and finds the literature of parable and symbol in the early chapters of Genesis." Later, in referring to the events of these chapters, including Satan's temptation of Eve in the Garden of Eden, the authors stated that "these things never were..." (1981, pp. 5,8).

Because unbelievers reject belief in the spirit entity known as God (and, not coincidentally, the Bible as His Word), it hardly is shocking that they simultaneously repudiate belief in the spirit being known as Satan (whose actual existence can be documented only within God's Word). Skepticism of, and opposition to, spiritual matters on the part of unbelievers should be expected. Skepticism of, and opposition to, such matters on the part of those professing to be believers should not.

The same Bible that informs the religious liberal about the existence of the God in Whom he proclaims **to believe**, also informs him of the existence of Satan—in whom he does **not believe**. Where is the consistency? Furthermore, consider the emphasis on Satan within the whole of the Sacred Text, the importance placed on the fact of his existence by both the biblical writers and the Son of God Himself, and the critical role he has played in the necessity of God's great plan of salvation for mankind.

The Reality of Satan in the Old Testament

From the first book of the Bible (Genesis) to the last (Revelation), the existence of the devil as a real, literal adversary is affirmed. Our first introduction to Satan occurs in Genesis 3 as he arrives on the scene in the form of a serpent to tempt Eve. Speaking of the historical nature of this account, Melancthon W. Jacobus observed:

> That there was a real serpent in this transaction cannot be doubted any more than we can doubt the real history throughout. Here, where the facts speak, further explanations are not necessary, nor fitted to the time of the beginning. (1) The real serpent is contrasted with the other animals, (vs. 1). (2) In the New Testament allusion is made to a real serpent in referring to the history (2 Cor. 11:3,14; 1 Jn. 3:8; Rev. 20:2). Yet (3) that there was in the transaction a superior agent, Satan himself, who made use of the serpent, is plain from his being referred to as "the old Serpent, called the Devil and Satan," (Rev. 12:9)—"a murderer from the beginning" (Jn. 8:44) [1864, 1:112].

Additional Old Testament testimony addresses the historical existence of Satan. In 1 Chronicles 21:1, the text states: "And Satan stood up against Israel, and moved David to number Israel." Six verses later, this simple statement is found: "And God was displeased with this thing; therefore he smote Israel" (1 Chronicles 21:7). Israel suffered as a direct result of Satan's workings in the life of her monarch.

In the book of Job, Satan retains a place of great prominence —more, perhaps, than in any other Bible book. In the first two chapters alone, he is mentioned at least fourteen times. In fact, Job 2: 1-2 records a conversation between this mendacious despot and God:

> Again it came to pass on the day when the sons of God came to present themselves before Jehovah, that Satan came also among them to present himself before Jehovah. And Jehovah said unto Satan, "From whence comest thou?" And Satan answered Jehovah, and said, "From going to and fro in the earth, and from walking up and down in it."

The entire theological thrust of the book of Job is utterly dependent upon the actual existence of Satan, his adversarial nature toward God and mankind, and Heaven's ultimate superiority over him. Further, the New Testament book of James boldly refers to Job's dealings with Satan: "Behold, we call them blessed that endured: ye have heard of the patience of Job, and have seen the end of the Lord, how that the Lord is full of pity, and merciful" (5:11). What possible meaning could this have had to first-century saints who were enduring extreme persecution and intense suffering as a result of their faith? An imaginary fight between a non-existent devil and a mythical patriarch could not, and would not, provide much comfort to those whose lives were in eminent danger. A promise that "the Lord is full of pity, and merciful"—based on real, historical events—could, would, and did provide such comfort in times of peril.

In Zechariah 3:1-10, the prophet recorded a vision "intended to show that Jehovah's people, conditioned upon a moral and spiritual reformation, could again enjoy prosperity" (Jackson, 1980, p. 75). In Zechariah's vision, Satan appeared as an adversary of Joshua the high priest, who was clothed with dirty garments that symbolized "the sins of the whole nation, of which he was the representative" (Hengstenberg, n.d., p. 972).

> And he showed me Joshua the high priest standing before the angel of Jehovah, and Satan standing at his right hand to be his adversary. And Jehovah said unto Satan, "Jehovah rebuke thee, O Satan; yea, Jehovah that hath chosen Jerusalem rebuke thee: is not this a brand plucked out of the fire?" (3:1-2).

In describing the spiritual importance of this scene, one writer commented: "Satan was ready to challenge the Lord's own institution for the forgiveness of sin, to deny the right of God to pardon the sinner. He seeks to overthrow the Throne of Grace, so hateful to him, and to turn it into a seat of judgment and condemnation" (Laetsch, 1956, p. 422; cf. also Psalm 109:3-8). The part that Satan played in this scenario cannot be overstated. Without his act of overt condemnation, and God's response to it, Zechariah's message would be lost. The activity and historical reality of Satan in the Old Covenant sets the stage for the urgency of God's plan of salvation in the New.

The Reality of Satan in the New Testament

Within the pages of the New Testament, the existence of Satan is reaffirmed, and more of his cunning, deceit, and hypocrisy is revealed. Of paramount importance is the record of his temptation of the Son of God (Matthew 4:1-11; cf. Luke 4:1-13). Erich Sauer has noted:

> The whole story of the temptation of Jesus proves beyond all doubt that we are here concerned with a factual and personal conflict between two protagonists. The accounts of the evan-

gelists and the behaviour and words of Jesus show clearly that we are not here concerned with a mere "principle" of evil, but with a real, factually present, speaking and active person, not "the evil" but "the evil one" (1962, p. 64).

A few chapters later, Jesus referred to Satan as "Beelzebub" (Matthew 12:27), a term that originally meant "lord of refuse," "lord of the flies," or "lord of dung" (Easton, 1996). As such, it was an expression of contempt signifying all that was the opposite of holiness and purity—hardly a name the Lord would apply to some harmless, legendary, mythical character of antiquity. Wayne Jackson suggested:

> As the serpent seduced Eve (Gen. 3:6) through the manifold channels of the lust of the flesh, lust of the eye, and the vainglory of life (I John 2:16), so he sought to solicit Christ to sin similarly (Matt. 4:1-11). Interestingly, he is denominated "the tempter" in that narrative. The Greek term is *peirazon*, a present tense participle—literally expanded, "the always tempting one"—which suggests his characteristic activity. Had the devil succeeded in causing Christ to sin, the Lord could not have served as the blemishless sin-offering (I Peter 1:19; II Cor. 5:21), and the entire human race would have been forever lost! (1980, p. 76).

Christ's apostles also addressed the fact of Satan's existence. And certainly they knew of which they spoke, since Satan is depicted within the pages of the New Testament as their ardent enemy. For example, the Lord informed Peter: "Simon, Simon, behold, Satan asked to have you that he might sift you as wheat" (Luke 22:31). A fact often overlooked within this text is that the pronoun "you" in the Greek is plural, indicating that Satan wanted **all** of the apostles (see Jackson, 1980, p. 76). The apostle Paul spoke of "the prince of the power of the air" (Ephesians 2:2) who has "devices" (2 Corinthians 2:11) and "ministers" who disguise themselves as righteous (2 Corinthians 11:15). The apostle John noted that "the devil sinneth from the beginning" (1 John 3:8), and lamented the fact that "the whole world lieth in the evil one" (1 John 5:19). Further, Paul's thorn in the flesh was said to have been "a messenger of Satan" (2 Corinthians 12:7). But perhaps most sinister is the fact that it was Satan who "put into the heart of Judas Iscariot" the idea to betray his Lord (John 13:2).

In addition, various New Testament writers referred to Satan as the author of sin (1 John 3:8), sickness (Acts 10:38), and death (Hebrews 2:14), as well as the one who leads men astray (2 Thessalonians 2:9-10). The authors of *Vine's Expository Dictionary* made an important observation when they stated:

> "Satan" is not simply the personification of evil influences in the heart, for he tempted Christ, in whose heart no evil thought could ever have arisen (John 14:30; 2 Cor. 5:21; Heb. 4:15); moreover his personality is asserted in both the OT and NT, and especially in the latter, whereas if the OT language was intended to be figurative, the NT would have made this evident (1985, p. 547).

What the New Testament makes evident, however, is exactly the opposite—i.e., that Satan is **not** figurative, but very real.

Satan's Origin

The Bible does not address specifically the origin of Satan, yet there is adequate information to draw a logical, well-reasoned conclusion as to how he came into existence. Consider the following.

Is Satan Deity?

Although quite powerful, Satan does not enjoy the status of deity. Clues to this fact are scattered throughout the pages of Holy Writ. Deity is **eternal**. Scripture speaks of "the eternal God" (Deuteronomy 33:27) Whose "years shall have no end" (Psalm 102:27), and Who is "the Alpha and the Omega..., who is and who was and who is to come" (Revelation 1:8). Deity is **omnipotent**. He is referred to as "God Almighty" (Genesis 17:1) Who cannot "be restrained" (Job 42:2). By "the thunder of his power" (Job 26:13-14) He has the might to create (Genesis 1:1; Isaiah 45:12) or destroy (2 Peter 3:10). He alone retains the power to instill life (Genesis 2:7) and to raise the dead (Ephesians 1:20). Deity is **omnipresent**. "[T]here is no creature that is not manifest in his sight: but all things are naked and laid open before the eyes of him with whom we have to do" (Hebrews 4:13). He is "at hand" and "afar off" (Jeremiah 23:23-24). He is able to "bring every work into judgment ...every hidden thing, whether it be good, or whether it be evil" (Ecclesiastes 12:14). Deity is **omniscient**. The psalmist wrote:

> O Jehovah, thou hast searched me, and known me. Thou knowest my downsitting and mine uprising; Thou understandest my thought afar off. Thou searchest out my path and my lying down, and art acquainted with all my ways. For there is not a word in my tongue, but, lo, O Jehovah, thou knowest it altogether.... Such knowledge is too wonderful for me; it is high, I cannot attain unto it (139:1-6).

God not only knows the past and the present, but the future as well (Acts 15:18). Indeed, "how unsearchable are his judgments, and his ways past tracing out" (Romans 11:33).

Satan, by comparison, does not possess these qualities. For example, he is not omnipotent. Scripture affirms: "Greater is he [God] that is in you than he [Satan] that is in the world" (1 John 4:4). When he sought to "sift" the apostles as wheat, he first had to "ask" for them (Luke 22:31). Satan is not omnipresent. His position as "god of this world" (2 Corinthians 4:4) was "delivered" unto him (Luke 4:6). When he eventually is cast permanently into his place of eternal torment, the devil will be powerless to resist (Revelation 20:10). In discussing the apocalyptic literature of the book of Revelation, which speaks of Satan's being "bound" (20:2), Hardeman Nichols observed: "The binding of Satan, we conclude, equally means that his work will be restrained in a certain realm..." (1978, p. 262). Omnipresence, by definition, is not restrained. Further, Satan is not omniscient. If we are sufficiently knowledgeable of the Word of God, and carefully wield that knowledge to resist him, the devil does not possess a superior knowledge sufficient to overcome us, but will "flee" (James 4:17; cf. Matthew 4:4). He is not intelligent enough to outwit us in order to "snatch" us from the Lord's hand (John 10:28).

The only possible conclusion regarding Satan is that he is not deity. But such a conclusion has serious implications. If Satan does not partake of the nature of deity, then he cannot be eternal. Thus, he must be a **created being**. That, as Wayne Jackson has explained, is exactly what he is.

> ...[S]ince the devil is not of the nature of deity, it is obvious that he is a created being, for **all** things and beings (outside the class of deity) are the result of creation—"for in him were all things created, in the heavens and upon the earth, things visible and things invisible, whether thrones or dominions or principalities or powers" (Col. 1:16); this would include Satan as he originally was (1980, p. 78; emp. in orig.).

Was Satan Created "Evil"?

But what was Satan originally? When was he created? And was he created "evil"? The biblical evidence may be summarized as follows. The Scriptures categorically state that all things, as they had been created originally, were good. Genesis 1:31 records: "And God saw **everything** that he had made, and, behold, it was **very good**" (emp. added). In their Old Testament commentary on the Pentateuch, Keil and Delitzsch observed:

> By the application of the term "good" to everything that God made, and the repetition of the word with the emphasis "very" at the close of the whole creation, the existence of anything evil in the creation of God is absolutely denied, and the hypothesis entirely refuted, that the six days' work merely subdued and fettered an ungodly, evil principle, which had already forced its way into it (1968, 1:67).

Thus, whatever else Satan may have been originally, he was **good**. God did not **create** Satan as an evil adversary; rather, Satan **became** evil. Some, however, have suggested that God's statement in Isaiah 45:7—"I form the light, and create darkness; I make peace, and **create evil**. I am Jehovah, that doeth all these things"—indicates that God does, in fact, create things that are evil. This view results from a misunderstanding of the use of the word "evil" within the context of that passage. The statement obviously can have no reference to moral evil, since such is contrary to God's holy nature (see Isaiah 6:3). Deuteronomy 32:4 describes Jehovah as the "God of faithfulness and without iniquity." An in-depth examination of the passage in Isaiah reveals that God, through the prophet, was announcing to the (as yet unborn) Cyrus, King of Persia, his intention to use the monarch as an instrument for punishment. Notice in Isaiah 45:7 how the word "evil" is employed in direct contrast to "peace." God's point was this: "I form light and create darkness [viz., I control nature]; I make peace and create evil [viz., I also control nations]; I am Jehovah that doeth all these things."

Later in chapter 47, there is a commentary that further explains how the word "evil" is used in chapter 45, verse 7. In verse 11, as he described the coming judgment upon Babylon, Isaiah said:

> Therefore shall **evil** come upon thee; thou shalt not know the dawning thereof: and mischief shall fall upon thee; thou shalt not be able to put it away: and desolation shall come upon thee suddenly, which thou knowest not (emp. added).

The "evil" that God "created" was **desolation** due to the wickedness of the Babylonian empire. In Isaiah 31:1-2, God similarly warned Israel that if the Hebrew nation forged an untoward alliance with Egypt, He would bring "evil" (i.e., punishment) upon them. "Thus, scholars have observed that 'evil' can be used with a purely secular meaning to denote physical injury (Jeremiah 39:12) or times of distress (Amos 6:3), and that is its significance in Isaiah 45:7" (Jackson, 1984, 1:84). When Job's wife proposed that he curse God and die, his rejoinder was: "Thou speakest as one of the foolish women speaketh. What? Shall we receive good at the hand of God, and shall we not receive **evil**?" (Job 2:10; emp. added). Job's meaning is clear: Shall we not receive **punishment and correction** from the hand of Jehovah, as well as innumerable blessings? The late Rex A. Turner Sr. noted:

Solomon wrote: "A prudent man seeth the evil, and hideth himself; But the simple pass on, and suffer for it" (Prov. 22:3). The meaning of this statement from Solomon is that the prudent man sees public calamity approaching, and he uses all lawful means to secure himself. Evil here is put for dangers and calamities that befall men. Thus, God creates evil only in the sense that he brings punishment or calamity upon those who do evil. In no sense, therefore, has God created criminal or moral evil. In no sense has God provoked or brought about evil in any angel or man (1989, p. 79).

Is Satan a Fallen Angel?

There is compelling textual evidence within the Bible which indicates that originally Satan was one of the angels who inhabited the heavenly realm, and that he (along with others) departed from a righteous state and rebelled against God. There is a hint of this in the Old Testament book of Job. Eliphaz said of God: "Behold, he putteth no trust in his servants; and his angels he chargeth with folly" (Job 4:18). In discussing this wording, renowned commentator Albert Barnes wrote:

> Language like this would hardly be employed unless there was a belief that even the holiness of the angels was not incorruptible, and that there had been some revolt there among a part, which rendered it **possible** that others might revolt also (1949, 1:lxiii; emp. in orig.).

Indeed, the New Testament seems to confirm that such a revolt **did** take place. In two separate passages, reference is made to just such an event. The apostle Peter said that "God spared not angels when they sinned, but cast them down to hell, and committed them to pits of darkness, to be reserved unto judgment" (2 Peter 2:4). Another inspired New Testament writer wrote: "And angels that kept not their own principality, but left their proper habitation, he hath kept in everlasting bonds under darkness unto the judgment of the great day" (Jude 6). Since the Bible also refers to Satan as "the prince of demons" (Matthew 12:24), and speaks of "the devil and **his** angels" (Matthew 25:41, emp. added), "...the only possible conclusion is that the devil is the leader of a group of angels who rebelled against God and were therefore expelled from heaven to eventually spend eternity in hell" (Workman, 1981a, 1[5]:4).

From references such as these, it is clear that God created angels (just as He has men) with the powers of reason and free will, which made it possible for them both to think and to choose. Turner commented:

> This is to say that angels had the freedom of choice—the freedom to fear and serve God, and the freedom to refuse to fear and serve God. Without intellect and freedom of absolute choice, angels could not be holy as God is holy. In the absence of free will, coupled with responsibility, there can be no true holiness (1989, p. 82).

But, as Lloyd Ecrement has noted:

> They, therefore, have the ability to choose good or evil. It is possible, but certainly not necessary, for them to sin. If they choose evil rather than good, that is no reflection upon their Creator, but simply a rebellion against Him—they abuse the powers of reason and a free will given to them by God (1961, p. 33).

Apparently, certain of the angels chose wrongly, which is why Peter referred to the "angels when they **sinned**." But John wrote that sin is "lawlessness" (i.e., transgression of God's law; 1 John 3:4). In some fashion, then, the angels' sin consisted of breaking God's law by not keeping their "proper habitation," but instead departing from whatever appropriate position it was that God had established for them.

Since Scripture speaks of "the devil and his angels," it becomes reasonable to suggest that Satan was either the instigator, or leader (or both), of this heavenly revolt. What brought about this Satanic rebellion? Nichols, in addressing the topic of sedition against legitimately established authority, suggested that "...rebellion is generally attempted only by the headstrong and obstinate" (1978, p. 262). Henry Morris similarly observed:

The root of all sin, in both man and angels, is the twin sin of unbelief and pride—the refusal to submit to God's will as revealed by His own Word and the accompanying assertion of self-sufficiency which enthrones the creature and his own will in the place of God. This was the original sin of Satan, rejecting God's Word and trying to become God Himself (1971, pp. 214-215).

Victor Knowles added:

Perhaps Satan became proud of his position as an angel and reached out, wanting more power and authority. What else could there be in heaven to battle for? It is possible that he may have harbored bitter envy and selfish ambition in his heart, for James says that such "wisdom" is "of the devil" (Jas. 3: 14,15) [1994, p. 70].

Is Satan Lucifer?

It is sad, but nevertheless true, that on occasion Bible students attribute to God's Word facts and concepts that it neither teaches nor advocates. These ill-advised beliefs run the entire gamut—from harmless misinterpretations to potentially soul-threatening false doctrines.

Although there are numerous examples from both categories that could be listed, perhaps one of the most popular misconceptions among Bible believers is that Satan also is designated as "Lucifer" within the pages of the Bible. What is the origin of the name Lucifer, what is its meaning, and is it a synonym for "Satan"? Here are the facts.

The word "Lucifer" is used in the King James Version only once, in Isaiah 14:12: "How art thou fallen from heaven, O Lucifer, son of the morning! how art thou cut down to the ground, which didst weaken the nations!" The Hebrew word translated "Lucifer" is *hēlēl* (or *heylel*), from the root, *hâlâl*, meaning "to shine" or "to bear light." Keil and Delitzsch noted that "[i]t derives its name in other ancient languages also from its striking brilliancy, and is here called *ben-shachar* (son of the dawn)..." (1982, 7:311). However, the KJV translators did not translate *hēlēl* as Lucifer because of something inherent in the Hebrew term itself. Instead, they borrowed the name from Jerome's Bible translation (A.D. 383-405) known as the *Latin Vulgate*. Jerome, likely believing that the term described the planet Venus, employed the Latin word "Lucifer" ("light-bearing") to designate "the morning star" (Venus). Only later did the suggestion originate that Isaiah 14:12ff. was speaking of the devil. Eventually, the name Lucifer came to be synonymous with Satan. But is Satan "Lucifer"?

No, he is not. The context into which verse 12 fits begins in verse 4 where God told Isaiah to "take up this parable against the **king of Babylon**, and say, 'How hath the oppressor ceased! the golden city ceased!'" In his commentary on Isaiah, Albert Barnes explained that God's wrath was kindled against the king because the ruler "intended not to acknowledge any superior either in heaven or earth, but designed that himself and his laws should be regarded as supreme" (1950, 1:272). The chest-pounding boast of the impudent potentate was:

> I will ascend into heaven, I will exalt my throne above the stars of God; and I will sit upon the mount of congregation, in the uttermost parts of the north; I will ascend above the heights of the clouds; I will make myself like the Most High (vss. 13-14).

As a result of his egotistical self-deification, the pagan monarch eventually would experience both the collapse of his kingdom and the loss of his life—an ignominious end that is described in vivid and powerful terms. "Sheol from beneath is moved for thee to meet thee at thy coming," the prophet proclaimed to the once-powerful king. And when the ruler finally descends into his eternal grave, captives of that hidden realm will taunt him by saying, "Is this the man that made the earth to tremble, that did shake kingdoms?" (vs. 16). He is denominated as a "man" (vs. 16) who would die in disrepute and whose body would be buried, not in a king's sarcophagus, but in pits reserved for the downtrodden masses (vss. 19-20). Worms would eat his body, and hedgehogs would trample his grave (vss. 11,23).

It was in this context that Isaiah referred to the king of Babylon as "the morning star" ("son of the morning"; "son of the dawn") to depict the once-shining-but-now-dimmed, once-lofty-but-now-diminished, status of the (soon to be former) ruler. In his *Bible Commentary*, E.M. Zerr observed that such phrases were "…used figuratively in this verse to symbolize the dignity and splendor of the Babylonian monarch. His complete overthrow was likened to the falling of the morning star" (1954, 3:265). This kind of phraseology should not be surprising since "[i]n the O.T., the demise of corrupt national powers is frequently depicted under the imagery of falling heavenly luminaries (cf. Isa. 13:10; Ezek. 32:7), hence, quite appropriately in this context the Babylonian monarch is described as a fallen star [cf. ASV]" (Jackson, 1987b, 23:15).

Nowhere within the context of Isaiah 14, however, is Satan depicted as Lucifer. In fact, quite the opposite is true. In his commentary on Isaiah, Burton Coffman wrote: "We are glad that our version (ASV) leaves the word *Lucifer* out of this rendition, because…Satan does not enter into this passage as a subject at all" (1990, p. 141). The Babylonian ruler was to die and be buried—fates neither of which Satan is destined to endure. The king was called "a man" whose body was to be eaten by worms, but Satan, as a spirit, has no physical body. The monarch lived in and abided over a "golden city" (vs. 4), but Satan is the monarch of a kingdom of spiritual darkness (cf. Ephesians 6:12). And so on.

The context presented in Isaiah 4:4-16 not only does not portray Satan as Lucifer, but actually militates against it. Keil and Delitzsch firmly proclaimed that "Lucifer," as a synonym, "…is a perfectly appropriate one for the king of Babel, on account of the early date of the Babylonian culture, which reached back as far as the grey twilight of primeval times, and also because of its predominate astrological character" (1982, p. 312). They then correctly concluded that "Lucifer, as a name given to the devil, was derived from this passage…without any warrant whatever, as relating to the apostasy and punishment of the angelic leaders" (pp. 312-313).

When Did Satan Become Evil?

But when, exactly, did all of this take place? Through the ages, numerous trustworthy and intelligent people have seen angels (cf. Luke 1:11,26ff.; Acts 12:7ff., etc.). Thus, at some point the Lord created them. But when? Truthfully, we have no way of knowing the exact time of their creation since the Holy Spirit has not seen fit to reveal that information to us in God's Word. In his book, *All the Angels in the Bible*, respected Bible scholar Herbert W. Lockyer observed regarding these heavenly messengers: "But just when, in the mysterious revolutions of eternity, they were called into existence is not a subject of divine revelation" (1995, p. 14). Wayne Jackson noted that there is an "absence of explicit testimony" regarding the creation of angels (1993, p. 208). Both writers are correct. Yet there are some "hints" in Scripture.

For example, we know that angels must have been created **on** or **before** the first day of Creation, because Job 38:1-7 makes it clear that "the sons of God [i.e., angels] shouted for joy" when God laid the foundations of the Earth (vss. 6-7). This certainly indicates that the angels were present as eyewitnesses to the creation of the Universe. Thus, the question then becomes, did the creation of angels occur on day one of the Creation week, or at some point before day one?

Through the years, numerous conservative scholars have suggested that likely the creation of the angels occurred during the first day of the Creation week, but prior to the creation of the Earth itself (see Jackson, 1980, p. 78; Kelly, 1997, p. 93; Knowles, 1994, p. 69; Turner, 1989, p. 80; Whitcomb, 1972, p. 43). It is important to remember that angels are messengers, thus necessitating someone to whom they could deliver a message. Jackson therefore has suggested that "...a plausible opinion would be that they were brought into existence at the commencement of the creation week" (1993, p. 208). Why might this be so? Lockyer explained as follows:

> The heavens include all that are in them created by God, and among these must be the angels (Genesis 2:1). Among the hosts of heaven the angels are the principal part. They are expressly called "**the heavenly host**" and "**the armies of heaven**" (Luke 2:13) [p. 14, emp. in orig.].

Nehemiah 9:6 also speaks to the very point Dr. Lockyer was making.

> Thou art Jehovah, even thou alone; **thou hast made... the heaven of heavens, with all their host,** the earth and all things that are thereon, the seas and all that is in them, and thou preservest them all; and **the host of heaven worshippeth thee** (emp. added).

In commenting on this passage, Hebrew language expert Weston W. Fields wrote:

> While the passages in Genesis...mention only the making of the firmament, sun, moon, stars, and animals, it must be carefully marked by the reader that in Nehemiah 9:6 the objects of God's making include the **heavens**, the **heaven of heavens**, and the **earth**, and **everything contained in and on it**, and the **seas and everything they contain**, as well as the **hosts of heaven** (probably angels) [1976, p. 61, emp. and parenthetical comment in orig.].

If you combine the passages and concepts discussed by Lockyer, Jackson, and Fields, it seems to allow for a "plausible opinion" that the angels "were brought into existence at the commencement of the creation week." In speaking of God and His original creation, Knowles commented: "Before creation of the world He created the angels, for they observed the process and rejoiced over it (Psa. 148: 2,5)" [1994, p. 69]. John C. Whitcomb concurred when he wrote that the angels "must have been created at the very beginning of the first day of creation, for Job 38:6,7 tells of their singing and their shout for joy at the creation of the earth" (1972, p. 43). Douglas Kelly also advocated such a position, but stressed caution, when he wrote:

Neither Genesis, nor any other text in Scripture, states when the angelic beings were actually created. What is definite is that angels are creatures, and thus do have a beginning. They are immortal, but only the Triune God is eternal, without beginning or endings. Reserve is necessary on such a speculative subject that has not been revealed to us by God in his Word....

Perhaps the angels were brought into being on the very first day of creation. In Job 38:4-7 we are told that the angels were present when the foundations of the earth were laid, and were rejoicing over it all. Psalm 104:2-5 speaks of the shining of God's light during the original creative process, and mentions the angels just before reference to "laying the foundations of the earth." Thus they appear after the creation of all things and before the earth is made a solid body.... These passages from Job and Psalms are certainly poetic, and are presumably not meant to be interpreted in the same precise, chronological sense required by Genesis 1 and 2. Poetic though its literary form is, it must mean something, and bear reference to a true state of affairs. Such passages may take us as far as we can go safely in consideration of the question: when were the angels first created? (1997, pp. 93,94).

It is significant to remember, of course, that angels are finite, created spirits who were (and are) amenable to God's law. Regardless of the exact time of their creation, the fact remains that certain of the angels, Satan among them, disobeyed that law, and as a result were cast from their spiritual abode. It is accurate to state, therefore, that Satan, and those dismissed from the heavenly realm with him, are fallen angels, and that their creation and transgression occurred sometime prior to God's bringing the Earth into existence.

Why Has Satan Arrayed Himself Against Both God and Man?

In any study of Satan, the question is bound to arise: **Why** has Satan established himself as God's archfiend and man's ardent foe? No doubt a portion of the answer can be found in the fact that he, too, once inhabited the heavenly realm but, as a result of his defiant rebellion against the great "I Am," was cast "down to hell"

(2 Peter 2:4). Satan's insurrection failed miserably, and that failure had dire, eternal consequences. His obstinate attempt to usurp God's authority cost him his position among the heavenly host and doomed him to "everlasting bonds under darkness" (Jude 6). In the end, his sedition gained him nothing and cost him everything. Regardless of the battle plan he adopted to challenge the Creator of the Universe, regardless of the battlefield he chose as his theater of war, and regardless of the strength or numbers of his army, the simple fact of the matter is that—in the most important contest of his existence—**He lost**!

The conditions of his ultimate surrender were harsh. Although his armies had been thoroughly routed, although he had been completely vanquished, and although the Victor had imposed the worst kind of permanent exile, Satan was determined not to go gently into the night. While he had lost the war, he nevertheless planned future skirmishes. Vindictive by nature (Revelation 12:12), in possession of cunning devices (2 Corinthians 2:11), and determined to be "the deceiver of the whole world" (Revelation 12:9), he set his face against all that is righteous and holy—and never once looked back. His anger at having been defeated fueled his determination to strike back in revenge.

But strike back at whom? It was futile to attempt a second mutiny. God's power was too great, and His omnipotence too all-consuming (Job 42:2; 1 John 4:4). Another target was needed; another repository of satanic revenge would have to be found. And who better to serve as the recipient of hell's **un**righteous indignation than mankind—the only creature in the Universe made "in the image and likeness of God" (Genesis 1:26-27)? As Turner suggested: "Satan cannot attack God directly, thus he employs various methods to attack man, God's master creation" (1989, p. 89). Sweet revenge—despoiling the "apple of God's eye" and the zenith of His creative genius! Thus, with the creation of man, the battle was on—and has been ever since. Basil Overton warned: "Satan is out to get us. He will take advantage of us if we let him. It is a fight to the finish!" (1976, 5[4]:3).

It was through mankind that Satan would exact his revenge—the emphasis being on the word "through." As the apostle Paul stated in Romans 5:12: "Therefore, as **through** one man sin entered into the world, and death through sin; and so death passed unto all men, for that all sinned" (emp. added). Man thus became the agent who caused sin to be in the world. Richard Batey wrote: "Paul's point is rather that since the power of sin is a universal human experience (Rom. 1:18-32; 3:9-23), this power must have come into the world through the representative man, Adam" (1969, 1: 72). As the "prince of this world" (John 12:31), Satan stalks about "as a roaring lion,...seeking whom he may devour" (1 Peter 5:8). He, and his ignominious band of outlaws ("sons of the evil one"; Matthew 13:38), have worked their ruthless quackery on mankind from the moment the serpent met Eve in the Garden of Eden. Their goal is the spiritual annihilation of mankind which, no doubt, is why Satan is identified within Scripture as the "king of the abyss," the "Destroyer" ("Apollyon," Revelation 9:11; see Easton, 1996), and the "wicked one" ("Belial," 2 Corinthians 6:15; see Vine, et al., 1985, p. 60).

In his war against Heaven, Satan will stop at nothing; it is a "no holds barred/winner take all" battle. Witness, for example, his cruel deception of Eve (Genesis 3:1-6) with its temporal and eternal consequences of physical/spiritual death (1 Corinthians 15:21; Ezekiel 18:20). Recall the trials, tribulations, and tragedies visited upon the Old Testament patriarch, Job (Job 1-2). Take notice of Israel's beloved monarch, King David, being tempted and convinced to sin (1 Chronicles 21:1,7). Remember the devil as Joshua's adversary (Zechariah 3:1ff.). Commit to memory Beelzebub's part in Paul's thorn in the flesh (2 Corinthians 12:7), or how he hindered the apostle's missionary efforts (1 Thessalonians 2:18). Cower in fear (as the early church did—Acts 5:11) at the results of his having persuaded Ananias to lie to the Godhead (Acts 5:3). Weep in sadness at the Great Adversary's so successfully convincing Judas to betray His Lord (John 13:2) that Christ referred to him as "the devil" (John 6:70).

Or, tremble in dismay at the potential ruin of humanity, had Satan succeeded in causing Christ to sin when he tempted Him in the wilderness those many years ago (Matthew 4:1-11). Had Jesus yielded, there would have remained "no more a sacrifice for sins" (Hebrews 10:26), and man would have been doomed—destined to inhabit forever the "blackness of darkness" (Jude 13) in the eternal **presence** of his most vituperative enemy, but, more important, in the eternal **absence** of His Creator-God.

Make no mistake about it. Satan **has** arrayed himself against both God and man. He **is** God's archfiend, and man's ardent foe. Nothing short of an absolute victory will assuage him; nothing short of a hell filled with every single member of the human race will dissuade him. He is, indeed, "the enemy" (Matthew 13:39).

Why Has God Allowed Satan to Continue to Exist?

As we study this enemy, another question comes to mind: **Why** has God allowed Satan to continue to exist? Since he is denominated within the pages of Scripture as "a murderer" (John 8:44), why not simply impose on him the same death penalty that civilized nations have imposed on murderers practically from time immemorial (cf. Numbers 35:16)? What possible justification could God have for allowing one so wicked to continue to live?

The answer, I am convinced, has to do with the nature of God and the nature of the spirit beings (angels) that He created. There is a clue regarding this point in the text of Luke 20:33-36. Within this passage, Jesus spoke of the righteous who one day would inhabit heaven, and stated that "neither can they die any more, for they are equal unto the angels." If righteous humans who will inhabit heaven cannot die, and if they are equal to the angels, then it follows logically that angels cannot die. While the Godhead is eternal, humans and angels are immortal. As Douglas Kelly correctly observed, angels (and this certainly would include Satan prior to his fall) "are immortal, but only the Triune God is eternal" (1997, p. 93).

In his thought-provoking work, *Systematic Theology,* Turner addressed the issue of Satan's continued existence when he wrote:

> Why did God not destroy Satan when he sinned? Why let Satan continue to exist and influence others to sin? The answer here lies in God's nature—his eternal nature which he has passed on to angels as well as to men—for there will never be a time when the spirits or angels, the evil as well as the good, will cease to exist. Punishments and prescribed limits have been passed upon evil spirits, and the more will be passed upon them, but they will always exist (1989, p. 83).

Scripture delineates angelic beings as immortal; thus, they—whether righteous or sinful—never will cease to exist. However, there may be more to Satan's continued existence than simply the angels' immortal nature. In addressing the question of exactly why Satan persists, Lloyd Ecrement has suggested:

> Perhaps the reason might well be expressed in the words the Lord asked Moses to say to wicked Pharaoh: "For by now I could have put forth my hand and struck you and your people with pestilence, and you would have been cut off from the earth; but for this purpose have I let you live, to show you my power, so that my name may be declared throughout all the Earth" (Exodus 9:15,16) [1961, p. 33].

Indeed, from a purely human vantage point, the continuation of evil—even for a brief period—generally is not viewed as either desirable or ideal. But, as T. Pierce Brown has proposed, God may have "allowed Satan to retain his power, temporarily, until he is through using him to test and purify a people for his ultimate glory and purposes" (1974, 91:245). Certainly, God's glory was exemplified by mankind's creation because Isaiah, speaking for Jehovah, said that man was "created for my glory" (Isaiah 43:7).

In John 9, the story is told of a man who had been born blind. When Jesus' disciples inquired as to the reason for his predicament, He responded that it was so that "the **works of God should be made manifest** in him" (John 9:3, emp. added). What all this entails, we certainly may not profess to know, realizing that the "secret things belong unto Jehovah our God" (Deuteronomy 29:29).

But the Scriptures do reveal enough information for us to conclude that Satan's continued existence follows logically from the immortal nature of angelic beings. They also reveal that the devil's existence is not at variance with Heaven's eternal plan, since at times it affords opportunities for mankind to witness God working amidst His creation.

What Is Satan's Mission?

Were Satan made of flesh and bone, we might employ the oft'-used phrase to describe him as a "man with a mission." But do not let the fact that he is spirit rather than flesh trick you into thinking he has no mission. He most certainly does—and has since the day he was cast from the heavenly portals. Simply stated, that mission is the complete destruction of all humanity in hell.

Within Scripture, Satan (i.e., our "adversary"; Zechariah 3:1) routinely is denominated by such unseemly designations as: (a) the devil (i.e., slanderer; Matthew 4:1); (b) "the god of this world" (2 Corinthians 4:4); (c) "the prince of the powers of the air" (Ephesians 2:2); (d) the father of lies (John 8:44); (e) the "Great Dragon" (Revelation 12:9); (f) "Beelzebub" (i.e., prince of demons; Matthew 12:24). (g) the "wicked one" (Matthew 13:38); (h) "the prince of this world" (John 12:31); (i) the ruler of darkness (Ephesians 6:12); (j) "the tempter" (1 Thessalonians 3:5); (k) "accuser of the brethren" (Revelation 12:10); (l) a "murderer" (John 8:44); (m) "the enemy" (Matthew 13:39); (n) "a roaring lion" (1 Peter 5:8); (o) a "serpent" (2 Corinthians 11:3); (p) "Belial" (i.e., "wicked one"; 2 Corinthians 6:15); and (q) "angel of the bottomless pit" (Revelation 9:11).

After even a cursory glance at these appellations, surely we could agree with L.O. Sanderson when he wrote: "These alone should make us fearfully concerned" (1978, 120:678). Satan's names describe his mission. His primary goal is to alienate men from God by causing them to sin. His main objective is to make men his slaves, thereby robbing them of the freedom that God's Word alone can impart (John 8:32). But how, exactly, does Satan do this?

How Does Satan Carry Out
His Mission Against Humanity?

The Bible makes it clear that the devil is the originator, the father, of sin. John wrote: "[H]e that doeth sin is of the devil; for the devil sinneth from the beginning" (1 John 3:8). In speaking to this point, Wayne Jackson has written: "Disease, infirmity and death are ultimately the responsibility of Satan, for by his introduction of sin into the world, he brought about such woes and hence he is really the murderer of the human family (John 8:44)" [1980, p. 76].

However, it is important to recognize that while Satan is the **originator** of sin, he is not the immediate **cause** of sin.

> Satan tempts, but he cannot compel men to do evil against their wills. A man must yield to Satan's temptation and desire before he becomes guilty of sin. To be tempted is not sin, but to yield to temptation is sin. We are answerable and responsible for our own sins, notwithstanding the temptation and influence of the devil. God endowed us with reason and a free will, therefore we have the ability to choose good or evil; in other words, we are free moral agents. So our sins are our own, and our own responsibility (Ecrement, 1961, p. 34).

Satan's constant coercion and tantalizing temptation do not, and cannot, override man's free will. James affirmed this in his epistle when he wrote:

> But each man is tempted, when he is drawn away by his own lust, and enticed. Then the lust, when it hath conceived, beareth sin: and the sin, when it is fullgrown, bringeth forth death (1:14-15).

As an example of this point, consider the apostle who betrayed the Son of God. Overcome by the grotesque nature of his dastardly deed, Judas eventually lamented: "**I** have sinned in that **I** betrayed innocent blood" (Matthew 27:4). Even in his final hours, he did not attempt to lay the blame for his sin at someone else's feet.

Similar lessons are taught in Acts 5 and 2 Samuel 12. In Acts 5, when Ananias and Sapphira lied about the amount they had received from the sale of a piece of land (and the amount they subsequently professed to have donated to the church), Peter inquired of Ananias: "How is it that **thou** hast conceived this thing in **thy** heart? **Thou** has not lied unto men, but unto God" (Acts 5:4, emp. added). The apostle wanted Ananias to know that he, personally, bore the guilt for his sin. He could not claim (with any legitimacy): "The devil made me do it." In 2 Samuel 12, the prophet Nathan was sent by God to convict King David of the sin of adultery with Bathsheba, wife of Urriah the Hittite. This he did. After hearing the evidence against him, "David said unto Nathan, **I** have sinned against Jehovah" (12:13). To his credit, David realized that not even powerful potentates are immune to the personal responsibility that accompanies transgression of God's law.

If we are responsible for our own actions, how, then, does Satan influence us to sin? In 2 Corinthians 2:11, Paul spoke of the fact that "no advantage may be gained over us by Satan: for we are not ignorant of his devices." The word "devices" in this text derives from the Greek *noemata*, which "refers to intelligent notions, purposes, designs, devices, etc." (Overton, 1976, 5[4]:3). In Ephesians 6:11, Paul admonished Christians to "put on the whole armor of God, that ye may be able to stand against the wiles of the devil." The word "wiles" derives from the Greek *methodeias*, from which we get our word "methods." *Methodeias* "is from the Greek verb that means to trace; to investigate; to handle methodically; to handle cunningly.... The devil is a skilled artisan. He will deceive you if you do not work at the job of fighting back at him" (Overton, 5[4]:3).

Indeed, deceit is perhaps Satan's most powerful tool. Through his "devices" and "wiles," Satan pressures us "with all deceit of unrighteousness" (2 Thessalonians 2:10). Sanderson has suggested that Satan's traits "clearly show the Devil to be a cunning, deceitful hypocrite. He is truthless, dishonest, and fraudulent in *every* possible way" (1978, 120:678). Adding to this assessment, L.M. Sweet wrote: "Satan's power consists principally in his ability to deceive. It is interesting and characteristic that according to the

Bible, Satan is fundamentally a liar and his kingdom is a kingdom founded upon lies and deceit" (1939, 4:2693). The New Testament provides ample evidence to substantiate such a conclusion. Wayne Jackson summarized a portion of that evidence when he acknowledged that the deceiver:

> (1) Delights in blinding the minds of the unbelieving that the light of the gospel should not dawn upon them (II Cor. 4:4). (2) To accomplish this he does not hesitate to transform himself into an angel of light along with his ministers who pretend to be ministers of righteousness (II Cor. 11:14,15). (3) When people are inclined not to believe the truth, the devil takes the gospel from their hearts (Luke 8:12). (4) He is full of trickery. He has his snares (I Tim. 3:7), and employs his "wiles"—a deliberate planning or system (Eph. 4:14; 6:11) [1980, p. 81].

But what power does Satan have that allows him to accomplish his task of deceiving humanity? How extensive is that power, and how is it wielded?

What Are Satan's Powers?

There can be no doubt that, as "god of this world" (2 Corinthians 4:4), Satan is powerful in his own right. When the devil tempted the Son of God in the wilderness, he offered Him all the power and glory of the kingdoms of this world, if only He would fall down and worship him (Matthew 4:9). His justification for this insidious offer was based on his claim that, as the lord of this planet, he could give its possessions to "whomsoever I will" (Luke 4:6). Interestingly, Jesus refuted neither Satan's position as "god of this world" nor his ability to impose his will upon it. Erich Sauer therefore concluded:

> This whole offer would have been unreal from the first for the Lord as a temptation, if some such legal basis for Satan's dominion in the world had not existed. Otherwise Jesus would only have had to point out that the necessary presuppositions for Satan's legal claim to and ability to dispose of the glory of the world simply did not exist. The Lord however left this claim of the devil's uncontradicted and merely declared that man should worship and serve God alone (Luke 4:8).

> With this He recognized in principle the tempter's right to dis-
> pose of the kingdoms of this world in this present age. This
> same thought lies behind the various sayings of Jesus in which
> He calls Satan "the Prince of this world" (John 12:31; 14:30;
> 16:11) [1962, p. 66].

We would do well to recognize the same thing the Son of God recognized: Satan is an important and powerful foe!

As powerful as he is, however, Satan is not omnipotent—a fact that even he recognized. During his temptation of Christ, he admitted that his earthly reign "hath been delivered unto me" (Luke 4:6). When the devil robbed Job of his family and earthly possessions, and even when he afflicted Job physically, he did so only with the express permission of God (Job 1:12; 2:6). When he sought to "sift" Christ's apostles as wheat, he first had to "ask" for them (Luke 22:31). The Scriptures make it clear, therefore, that his powers do have limits.

But exactly what powers are in his possession? When T. Pierce Brown observed that "apparently he is able to make some sort of suggestions to the heart" (1974, 91:245), he provided a picture window into which we may peer to observe the way Satan works among men. Among Satan's powers are these. He perverts the Word of God (Genesis 3:1-4). He instigates false doctrine (1 Timothy 4:1-3). He blinds men to the truth (2 Corinthians 4:4). He sows tares among God's wheat (Matthew 13:24-30,36-43). He steals the Word of God from human hearts (Matthew 13:19). He lays snares for men (2 Timothy 2:26; 1 Timothy 3:7). He tempts (Matthew 4:1; Ephesians 6:11). He afflicts (Job 2:7; Luke 13:16; Acts 10:38; 2 Corinthians 12:7). He deceives (Revelation 12:9; 20:8-10). He undermines the sanctity of the home (1 Corinthians 7:3-5). He prompts both saints and sinners to transgress the laws of God (1 Chronicles 21:1; Matthew 16:22-23; John 13:2; Acts 5:3). He hinders the work of God's servants (1 Thessalonians 2:18). And he even makes accusations against God's children before Heaven's throne (Job 1:6-11; 2:3-6; 21:1-5; Zechariah 3:1-4; Revelation 12:9-10).

Satan employs his power of "suggestions to the heart" to pervert the truth. In his book, *Get Thee Behind Me Satan*, Virgil Leach assessed our much-feared, other-worldly adversary in these words:

> He is the great pretender and the first liar and hypocrite with special skills in deception.... No one escapes his trickery; every man knows something of deception. He will influence men to conceal or distort truth for the purpose of misleading, cheating and fraud. If he cannot overthrow truth he will neutralize it, water it down to dilute it. Qualities of guile, craftiness, dissimulation and pretense are used in all his maneuvers. Satan is a master of deceit and is well aware that half lies mixed with half truths more often do the trick and will more easily be swallowed and digested, not that he will not use an out-and-out lie should it fit the occasion. Loving darkness, he would prefer a tree to hide behind than an open field and would prefer an ambush over an open warfare. Our adversary would desire to plant his "Judas kiss" on the cheek of every man (1977, pp. 14-15).

Like a carnivorous lion ready for the hunt (1 Peter 5:8), Satan waits to devour us via his "suggestions to the heart." Like a well-hidden, coiled snake (Revelation 20:2), he is able to strike in an instant, injecting the poison of his venom into the minds of men. Or, using what is perhaps the most insidious disguise at his disposal, he even may portray himself as an "angel of light" (2 Corinthians 11:14) who feigns humility, piety, and righteousness, yet whose intentions all the while are as insincere as they are sanctimonious.

What awesome powers the devil commands! What subtle meanness he exhibits! One moment he presents himself as an innocent-faced, sweet-talking "angel"; the next he is a ravenous mammal or slithering reptile. Little wonder Paul wrote to the Thessalonians:

> For this cause I also, when I could no longer forbear, sent that I might know your faith, lest by any means the tempter had tempted you, and our labor should be in vain (1 Thessalonians 3:5).

The apostle's inner stirrings on behalf of those he had worked so long, and so hard, to wrest from the devil's grasp were based on his knowledge that they faced daily a formidable foe who was more than capable of ravishing both their bodies and their souls.

What Is Satan's Ultimate Destiny?

Is all lost, then? Hardly! Although the Scriptures repeatedly affirm Satan's immense power, they likewise affirm that "he [God] that is in you is greater than he [Satan] that is in the world" (1 John 4:4). We know this to be the case because the Scriptures testify eloquently to the fact that Satan—far from having free reign—has been "bound."

The concluding book of the New Testament, Revelation, was written to offer encouragement to first-century Christians who, because of their professed faith in the Son of God, were threatened hourly with severe persecution "even unto death" (Revelation 2: 10). Within this book, which is written in apocalyptic literature that is highly figurative, the message is one not only of comfort, but of ultimate victory over the devil and his forces. The twentieth chapter, especially, presents a picture of God's archfiend and man's ardent enemy, Satan, as being "bound" (vs. 2) and "cast into the abyss" (vs. 3). As Hardeman Nichols has suggested:

> If in our study of Revelation 20 we fail to see the final overthrow of Satan and his collaborators, we have missed a major truth. If we do not appreciate the final triumph of every righteous person, we have not been sufficiently blessed by this study (1978, p. 260).

Concerning the devil, Nichols went on to write that "[w]hen, in the unspecified eternity before the world he initiated his rebellion, God put a restraint upon him" (p. 263).

That restraint never has been removed. And, in fact, it has been tightened. While it is true that in the first century the devil and his minions were able to affect people **physically** (cf. Luke 4:41; 8: 26-33), fortunately that no longer is the case. For example, when the prophet Zechariah foretold of the coming of the Messiah, and spoke of the blessings that would attend His reign, he stated that eventually the Lord would "cause the prophets and the **unclean spirit** to pass out of the land" (13:1-2). Concerning Zechariah's prophecy, the late Homer Hailey remarked:

> Likewise, unclean spirits, the antithesis of the prophets, would cease. In the conquest of Christ over Satan and his forces, unclean spirits have ceased to control men as they did in the time of the ministry of Christ and the apostles (1972, p. 392).

L.M. Sweet correctly observed that in our day and age there is no evidence that "Satan is able to any extent to introduce disorder into the physical universe or directly operate in the lives of men" (1939, p. 2694). [For a more in-depth discussion of these points than the limited space here allows, the reader is referred to Jackson, 1990b, 1998a.]

"Resist the Devil"

The warfare for the souls of men has continued ever since Eve first fell prey to Satan's deceit in the great long ago (Genesis 3:1-6; cf. 1 Timothy 2:14). At times, it seems that humanity has taken one step forward and two steps backward in this critical conflict between good and evil. One ancient, inspired writer lamented: "[F]or all have sinned, and fall short of the glory of God" (Romans 3:23), with the end result being that "the wages of sin is death" (Romans 6:23). One modern, non-inspired writer lamented: "Even now there are millions who consciously worship Satan and many more millions who are increasingly open in their hatred of God" (Morris, 1971, p. 215).

Not a very pretty picture, is it? Is our battle against God's arch-fiend and man's ardent enemy a losing one? Are Satan's powers too great for us to overcome? Shall we simply give in, give up, and raise the white flag in ultimate surrender, knowing that we are beaten down and destroyed by a foe whose powers know no limits? What shall be the end of this matter?

While we never should underestimate Satan's power and ability, neither should we underestimate the power and ability of our great God and His Word. Satan may have the power to ensnare us, but Jehovah has the power to remove us from that snare (2 Timothy 2:26). Truly, "the Lord knoweth how to deliver the godly out of temptation" (2 Peter 2:9).

But we have a part to play in that deliverance. Steadfast, unmovable faith is the key (1 Peter 5:9; 1 Corinthians 15:58). John wrote: "For whatsoever is begotten of God overcometh the world: and this is the victory that hath overcome the world, even our faith" (1 John 5:4). We must not, we cannot, be "ignorant of his devices" (2 Corinthians 2:11). Neither can we be double-minded (James 1:8), nor lukewarm (Revelation 3:15-16). Rather, we must be alert to the ever-present danger that our enemy represents. Like Abraham of old, we must stand firm. Abraham, "looking unto the promise of God, wavered not through unbelief, but waxed strong through faith, giving glory to God, and being fully assured that what he had promised, he was able also to perform" (Romans 4:20-21).

But how do we accomplish this? What weapons may be found in our arsenal? And how may they be employed successfully against this, the most pervasive and powerful of enemies? First, we need battle armor, which is why Paul wrote:

> Put on the whole armor of God, that ye may be able to stand against the wiles of the devil. For our wrestling is not against flesh and blood, but against the principalities, against the powers, against the world-rulers of this darkness, against the spiritual hosts of wickedness in the heavenly places. Wherefore take up the whole armor of God, that ye may be able to withstand in the evil day, and, having done all, to stand (Ephesians 6:10-13).

What, exactly, is the "whole armor of God"? The apostle went on to explain himself in the same context when he wrote:

> Stand therefore, having girded your loins with truth, and having put on the breastplate of righteousness, and having shod your feet with the preparation of the gospel of peace; withal taking up the shield of faith, wherewith ye shall be able to quench all the fiery darts of the evil one. And take the helmet of salvation, and the sword of the Spirit, which is the word of God: with all prayer and supplication praying at all seasons in the Spirit, and watching thereunto in all perseverance and supplication for all the saints (Ephesians 6:14-18).

Is not this the exact same weaponry employed by our Lord in His spiritual struggle with Satan in the wilderness? Each time the devil tempted Him, the Lord's resistance was couched in the repetitive refrain: "It is written..." (Matthew 4:4,7,10), after which the Scriptures state simply: "Then the devil leaveth him" (Matthew 4:11).

Seizing upon Christ's example, years later the inspired James would write: "**Resist the devil, and he will flee from you**" (James 4:7, emp. added). If we steep ourselves in a working knowledge of God's Word, if we take courage and press on, if we adamantly refuse to give in or give up, we, like Paul, can say:

> Who shall separate us from the love of Christ? Shall tribulation, or anguish, or persecution, or famine, or nakedness, or peril, or sword? Even as it is written, "For thy sake we are killed all the day long; We were accounted as sheep for the slaughter." Nay, in all these things we are more than conquerors through him that loved us. For I am persuaded, that neither death, nor life, nor angels, nor principalities, nor things present, nor things to come, nor powers, nor height, nor depth, nor any other creature, shall be able to separate us from the love of God, which is in Christ Jesus our Lord (Romans 8:35-39).

Second, we must realize that while God will not necessarily act to prevent our temptation by Satan, neither will He allow us to be tempted beyond what we are able to endure. Paul wrote: "There hath no temptation taken you but such as man can bear: but God is faithful, who will not suffer you to be tempted above that ye are able; but will with the temptation make also the way of escape, that ye may be able to endure it" (1 Corinthians 10:13).

Third, we should remember that while Satan indeed may be the "accuser of the brethren" (Revelation 12:10), we have an Advocate —Jesus the Christ—Who stands with us, pleads our case, protects us, and refuses to forsake us. The same apostle that wrote the beautiful book of Revelation to comfort first-century saints who were losing their lives daily to the "evil one" also wrote: "We have an

Advocate with the Father, Jesus Christ the righteous" (1 John 2: 1). The writer of Hebrews said that "he is able to save to the uttermost them that draw near unto God through him, seeing he ever liveth to make intercession for them" (7:25). What a great consolation—to know that the Son of God stands before the great white throne in the city set foursquare to plead our case before the "Judge of all the earth" Who will "do what is right" (Genesis 18:25).

Fourth, let us never forget that victory is within our grasp. The outcome of the battle for the souls of men already has been decided. As Paul said: "And the God of peace shall bruise Satan under your feet shortly" (Romans 16:20). We may defect from God's army if we so desire, and become "AWOL" as a result. Through the millennia, many have done exactly that. They grew weary of the battle, and gave up. They set aside the "whole armor of God." They stripped away the loincloth of truth. They discarded the breastplate of righteousness. They took off the shoes of the gospel of peace. They laid down the shield of faith. They removed the helmet of salvation. But they did so at their own peril.

Judas, for example, became so filled with the essence of Satan that Jesus referred to him as the "devil" (John 6:70). When Paul wrote the Ephesian Christians, he warned: "Leave no loop-hole for the devil" (4:27, NEB). But some did. Two early Christians, Hymenaeus and Alexander, were so overcome by the devil that Paul told Timothy he had "delivered [them] unto Satan" (1 Timothy 1: 20). When God spoke through John to the church at Thyatira, He indicated that some of those Christians had become so wicked as to know the "deep things of Satan" (Revelation 2:24). What a horrible indictment!

And what a needless waste! Obviously, these individuals had ignored the Lord's admonition: "Watch and pray, that ye enter not into temptation" (Matthew 26:41). As a result, they never would be able to say with the great apostle to the Gentiles, and with the faithful of all the ages: "But thanks be to God, who giveth us the victory through our Lord Jesus Christ" (1 Corinthians 15:57).

Conclusion

God not only "bound" Satan, but sealed his ultimate doom. Our Lord will be victorious over Heaven's Great Adversary, for "to this end was the Son of God manifested, that he might destroy the works of the devil" (1 John 3:8). It is via the power inherent in His own death and resurrection that He will "bring to nought him that had the power of death, that is, the devil" (Hebrews 2:14). The fate that awaits this traitorous tyrant is clear:

> And the devil that deceived them was cast into the lake of fire and brimstone, where are also the beast and the false prophet; and they shall be tormented day and night for ever and ever (Revelation 20:10).

Eternal punishment in hell has been "prepared for the devil and his angels" (Matthew 25:41).

God's covenant pledge, made with our forefathers in Genesis 3:15, then will be fulfilled once and for all: "He [Christ] shall bruise thy [Satan's] head." The paradise lost of Genesis will have become the paradise regained of Revelation. With the earthly reign of Satan brought to an end, and the eternal bliss of God's saints secure, then we shall be able to say with the psalmist of old: "This is the day that Jehovah hath made; we will rejoice and be glad in it" (118:24).

CHAPTER 6

THE ORIGIN, NATURE, AND DESTINY OF THE SOUL—[PART I]

Throughout the whole of human history, man has struggled to find answers to any number of important (yet often difficult) questions that have to do with his origin, existence, nature, and destiny. Such queries as "Whence have I come?," "Why am I here?," and "Where am I going?" routinely intrigue and enthrall each of us. Securing clues to the exact makeup of the creature known popularly as *Homo sapiens* always has been one of mankind's keenest intellectual pursuits. And along the way, perhaps no single topic has perplexed us, or piqued our interest, as much as that pertaining to the origin, nature, and destiny of the soul.

Contemplate, if you will, the concept of the soul and the issues that spring from it. What is the definition of a soul? If the soul actually exists, what is its origin? Do humans possess a soul? Do animals? If souls do, in fact, exist, are they purely temporal—thus living only as long as our corporeal nature exists? Or are they immortal—surviving the death of the physical body? What is the difference, if any, between the "soul" and the "spirit"? What is the ultimate destiny of the soul? And what part does the soul play in the biblical statement that men and women were created "in the image of God" (Genesis 1:27)? These are the kinds of issues that I would like to investigate in this chapter and in the four that follow.

The subject of the soul—including its origin, nature, and destiny —has long been controversial. Some people believe that there is no such thing as a soul. Certain individuals advocate the position that only humans possess a soul, but that it ceases to exist at the death of the body. Others seek to maintain that both humans and animals possess a soul, and that those souls likewise die when the physical body dies. Still others are convinced that both animals and humans possess an immortal soul. And finally, there are those who have concluded that humans possess an immortal soul, but that animals do not. What, then, is the truth of the matter?

Science certainly cannot provide the answers to such questions, for they lie far beyond the purview of the scientific method. In her best-selling book, *The Fire in the Equations*, award-winning science writer Kitty Ferguson addressed this very issue. While discussing the efforts of several renowned, modern-day scientists (like eminent physicists Stephen Hawking and Paul Davies, to mention just two) to uncover what they view as a grand, unified "Theory of Everything," she asked:

> Is there anything else? We needn't get spooky about it. Part of the "anything else" might be human minds and personalities. Can we entirely account for our self-awareness, our minds, personalities, intuitions, and emotions, by means of a physical explanation? This is a matter of enormous significance for many of the questions we are asking in this book, and we will return to it frequently. If we are super-complex computing machines—the sum of our physical parts and their mechanical workings, which in turn exist as a result of the process of evolution—then science may ultimately be able to tell us everything there is to know about us. Even if no computer can ever assimilate the human mind, science may find another complete physical explanation. But **we have at**

present no scientific reason to rule out the possibility that there is more to self-awareness, our minds, and our personalities than any such explanation can encompass. Is there such a thing as the soul? If there is, does its existence begin and end with our material existence? Despite some impressive advances in the field of artificial intelligence, and an increasing understanding of the way our minds work, certainly no-one would claim to be able to say at present, except on faith, whether science will eventually be able to assimilate the phenomena of self-awareness, mind, and personality into the materialistic picture. **If science can't, then there is truth beyond the range of scientific explanation**.

Another part of the "anything else" may be what we call the supernatural. Perhaps it is simply figments of imagination, psychological events, not so much to be explained by science as to be explained away. Or perhaps these are real events which are at present unexplainable because we lack complete understanding of the full potential of the physical world. If either is the case, then the supernatural ought eventually to fall into the realm of scientific explanation. However, **if the supernatural world exists**, and if it is inherently beyond testing by the scientific method, **then there is truth beyond the range of scientific explanation**. There may indeed be more in heaven and earth than is dreamed of in our science (if not our philosophy) [1994, pp. 82-83, emp. added].

I would like to seize upon Ferguson's "if...then" proposition as I begin this examination of the origin, nature, and destiny of the soul. Her argument—one that far too few scientists (or science writers) are even willing to consider—is that **if** the supernatural exists, **then** there is truth beyond the range of scientific explanation. The available evidence **does** establish, in fact, that the supernatural exists and that there **is** "truth beyond the range of scientific explanation." As famed NASA astrophysicist (and self-proclaimed agnostic) Robert Jastrow put it: "That there are what I or anyone would call supernatural forces at work, is now, I think, a scientifically proven fact" (1982, p. 18). While I will not present such evidence in this book, I have done so elsewhere in a rather extensive fashion (see, for example, Thompson, 1995a, 1995b, 2000; Thompson and Jackson, 1982, 1992). The existence of the supernatural (i.e., God) may be doubted by some and ridiculed by still others, but that does not alter the evidence that establishes its reality.

Thus, whenever questions of spiritual importance are under consideration—as they are when discussing the existence, origin, nature, and destiny of the soul—the only reliable source of information must by necessity be the One Who is the Originator and Sustainer of the soul. God, as Creator of all things physical and spiritual (Genesis 1:1ff., Exodus 20:11), and Himself a Spirit Being (John 4:24), is the ultimate wellspring of the soul. The Bible, then, as God's inspired Word (2 Timothy 3:16-17; 2 Peter 1:20-21), must remain the preeminent authority on this subject. In the great long ago, the psalmist wrote: "The sum of thy word is truth; and every one of thy righteous ordinances endure forever" (119:160). Speaking as a member of the Godhead, Christ said: "Sanctify them in truth; thy word is truth" (John 17:17).

We—if we wish to build and sustain a rock-solid faith—need to know the truth about the soul. Thus, we must examine that Word in an in-depth fashion and be prepared to accept what it says. Only then can we obtain the answers to the many questions on this vital topic that have perplexed and plagued humans for millennia.

Definition of the Soul

If you and I were in the midst of a conversation and I mentioned the word "banana," likely you would have absolutely no difficulty understanding my meaning. Your thought processes immediately would conjure up a long fruit—with a yellow outer covering and a light beige, inner soft body—that grows on trees and is useful as food for both humans and animals. But were I to ask you to define the term "foil," without seeing the word in context you could not possibly know what I meant. I might be referring to:

(1) a noun used to define a fencing sword; (2) a noun that indicates a thin, shiny metal used by cooks in kitchens all over the world; or (3) a verb used as a synonym for "defeat." However, if I were to say, "I covered the turkey with foil prior to placing it in the oven," you then would know immediately what I had in mind.

The same is true of the definition of the word "soul." Minus its context, it is difficult, if not impossible, to define accurately. Speaking from the vantage point of a language scholar who had studied the Hebrew and Greek texts for over sixty years, the late Guy N. Woods once suggested that "...there is no pat and easy answer to the question, 'What is the soul?'" (1980, 122[6]:163). Why is this the case? First, the word "soul" in modern English usage is represented by various words in the Hebrew and Greek languages in which the Bible originally was written. Second, those Hebrew and Greek words can have a number of different meanings in their original contexts. Robert Morey has noted:

> These terms are not technical words in the sense that they have one consistent meaning throughout Scripture. They display unity and diversity by being synonymous at times when referring to the immaterial side of man, and at other times, referring to different functions or ways of relating. It is obvious that we should not impose 20th-century standards of consistency and linguistic preciseness to a book which was written thousands of years ago... (1984, p. 44).

Third, the matter of the progressive nature of God's revelation to man must be considered (see Motyer, 2001, p. 17). While it certainly is true that the Lord possesses a constant, unchanging nature (Malachi 3:6; James 1:17), His revelation of that nature and His will for mankind was a progressive process that was adapted to man as he matured spiritually through the ages. This explains why, in the course of human history, God sometimes tolerated in man both attitudes and actions that were less than what the divine ideal intended. This, however, does not mean that the Holy God vacillates in His ethics or morality; rather, it simply means that—because of

His infinite love—He dealt gently and compassionately with man in the particular state of spiritual maturation in which He found him at the time (cf. Acts 14:15-16 and 17:30-31). As God progressively revealed more and more of both His nature and His will, He did so in a manner, and in terms, that fit the occasion. In addressing the failure of some to comprehend and appreciate the importance of this concept, Robert Morey observed that certain words, therefore,

> ...may have a dozen different meanings, **depending on the context and the progressive nature of revelation**. The failure to avoid reductionistic and simplistic definitions is based on the hidden assumption that once the meaning of a word is discovered in a single passage, this same meaning must prevail in every other occurrence of the word.... The resistance to the idea that what soul meant to Moses was probably not what it meant to David or Paul is based on their unconscious assumption that the Bible is one book written at one time. Thus as we approach the biblical term which describes the immaterial side of man, we will not attempt to develop artificial definitions based upon the absolutizing of the meaning of a word in a single passage but recognize that a contextual approach will reveal a wide range of meanings (1984, pp. 44-45, emp. added).

The word "soul" does indeed enjoy a "wide range of meanings." In order to understand those meanings, it is necessary to examine how the word is employed within the various contexts in Scripture where it appears.

Use of the Word "Soul" in Scripture

The word for "soul" in the Bible (Hebrew *nephesh* [from *naphash*, to breathe]; Greek *psuche*) is used in at least four different ways (see Arndt and Gingrich, 1957, pp. 901-902; Thayer, 1958, p. 677). First, the term is employed simply as a synonym for a person. Moses wrote: "All the souls (*nephesh*) that came out of the loins of Jacob were seventy souls (*nephesh*)" (Exodus 1:5; cf. Deuteronomy 10:22). In legal matters, the word soul often was used to denote an individual. The Lord told Moses: "Speak unto the children of Israel, saying, 'If a soul (*nephesh*) shall sin through ignorance against any of the commandments of the Lord concerning things which ought not to be done'..." (Leviticus 4:2). When Jacob was speaking of himself in Genesis 49:6, he used the expression, "O my soul (*nephesh*)"—which meant simply "me." Numbers 9:6 records that "there were certain men, who were unclean by reason of the dead body (*nephesh meth*) of a man, so that they could not keep the Passover on that day" (cf. Numbers 6:6 and Ecclesiastes 9:5). In the New Testament, the word *psuche* is employed in the same manner. In Acts 2:41, Luke recorded that "there were added unto them in that day about three thousand souls (*psuchai*)." In Peter's first epistle, when he addressed the topic of the Genesis Flood he referred to the fact that "few, that is eight souls (*psuchai*), were saved by water" (3:20). In each of these instances, actual people—individually or collectively—were under discussion.

Second, the word soul is used to denote the form of life that man possesses in common with animals and that ceases to exist at death. In their widely used *Hebrew and English Lexicon of the Old Testament*, Brown, Driver, and Briggs noted that *nephesh* often is employed to mean "life principle" (1907, p. 659). In the King James Version, *nephesh* is translated as "soul" in the Old Testament 472 times, as "life" 118 times, and as "creature" 8 times; *psuche* is translated as "soul" in the New Testament 59 times and as "life" 39 times (Morey, 1984, pp. 45,55). In addressing the use of the word "soul" in such passages as Genesis 2:7 and 1:20, Woods wrote:

> ...the word **soul** from the Hebrew *nephesh* occurs, for the first time in the sacred writings, at Genesis 1:20, where it is assigned to fish, birds, and creeping things. (See also, another similar usage in Genesis 1:30.) As thus used, it is clear that the soul in these passages does not refer to anything peculiar to the constitution of man. It signifies, as its usage denotes, and the lexicons affirm, **any creature that breathes**, in all of these early occurrences in the book of Genesis. Nor

is it correct to conclude that the phrase **breath of life** in the statement of Moses ("And the Lord God formed man of the dust of the ground, and breathed into his nostrils the breath of life; and man became a living soul") sums up, or was designed to denote the **whole** constitution of man. The word "life" here is, in the Hebrew text, plural, literally **breath of lives** (*nishmath khay-yim*). It occurs, in similar form, in three other instances in the early chapters of Genesis (6:17; 7:15; 7:22). In the first of these the phrase is *ruach khay-yim*; in the second the same; in the third, *nishmath-ruach khay-yim*, and out of the four instances where the phrase, the **breath of lives**, occurs in our translation the last three are applied to the beasts, birds and creeping things. It follows, therefore, that the phrase "breath of life" does not designate anything peculiar to man. And in view of the fact that the word "soul," from the Hebrew *nephesh*, is similarly extended to include the animal world, birds and creeping things, it may not be properly limited to man... (1985b, 127:691, emp. and parenthetical comment in orig.).

In Genesis 1:20,24, and 30, God spoke of the *nephesh hay-yah*—literally "soul breathers" or "life breathers" (often translated as "living creatures" or "life"—cf. Leviticus 11:10; grammatically the phrase is singular but it bears a plural meaning). The writer of Proverbs stated in regard to animals: "A righteous man regardeth the life (*nephesh*) of his beast; But the tender mercies of the wicked are cruel" (12:10). Hebrew scholar Hugo McCord therefore noted:

> Then the translators realized that the first meaning of *nephesh* is "breath," and so Genesis 1:20,24,30 and Genesis 2:7 all fit together in understanding Moses as saying that all animals and man too are breathers. Breathers, coupled with *hayyah*, "living," the translators thought, would be well translated, in the case of animals, as "living creatures," and in the case of man as a "living being" (1995, 23:87-88).

In Exodus 21:23, Moses commanded: "But if any harm follow, then thou shalt give life (*nephesh*) for life (*nephesh*)." He later wrote that "the life (*nephesh*) of the flesh is in the blood" (Leviticus

17:11,14). Blood often is said to be the seat of life because when blood is shed, death ensues (cf. Deuteronomy 12:23). In speaking of God's retribution upon the Egyptians during the time of the Exodus, the psalmist wrote: "He spared not their soul (*nephesh*) from death, but gave their life over to the pestilence" (78:50). In this particular instance, the Egyptians' souls represented their physical life and nothing more. Ezekiel later observed: "The soul (*nephesh*) that sinneth, it shall die" (18:20).

In the New Testament, the principle is the same. Christ observed in regard to humans: "Therefore I say unto you, be not anxious for your life (*psuche*), what ye shall eat, or what ye shall drink; nor yet for your body" (Matthew 6:25). God told Joseph: "Arise and take the young child and his mother, and go into the land of Israel: for they are dead that sought the young child's life" (*psuche*, Matthew 2:19). In the book of Revelation, John spoke of the fact that "there died the third part of the creatures which were in the sea, even they that had life (*psuchas*); and the third part of the ships was destroyed" (8:9; cf. 16:3, *psuche*). Many a follower of Christ was said to have risked his or her life (*psuche*) for the Lord. In Acts 15:25-26, Luke recorded that Barnabas and Paul were "men that have hazarded their lives (*psuchas*) for the name of our Lord Jesus Christ." Earlier, John recorded Peter as saying to the Lord: "I will lay down my life (*psuchen*) for thee" (John 13:37-38). In Philippians 2:30ff., Paul spoke of "Epaphroditus, my brother and fellow-worker and fellow-soldier...hazarding his life (*psuche*) to supply that which was lacking in your service toward me." And in Luke 14:26, one of the conditions of discipleship was to hate one's own life (*psuche*)—that is, to be willing to deny oneself to the point of losing one's life for Christ (cf. Luke 9:23; Revelation 12:11).

Third, the idea of the soul is used to refer to the varied emotions or inner thoughts of a man—a fact that explains why *nephesh* is translated "heart" (15 times) or "mind" (15 times) in the Old Testament (KJV) and why *psuche* is translated as "heart" (1 time) and "mind" (3 times) in the New. Man was called to love God with all his heart and with all his soul (*nephesh*; Deuteronomy 13:3b). The soul (*nephesh*) is said to weep (Job 30:16; Psalm 119:28) and to be exercised in patience (Job 6:7-11). From the soul (*nephesh*) originate knowledge and understanding (Psalm 139:14), thought (1 Samuel 20:3), love (1 Samuel 18:1), and memory (Lamentations 3:20). In His discussion with a lawyer, Jesus said: "Thou shalt love the Lord thy God with all thy heart, and with all thy soul (*psuche*), and with all thy mind" (Matthew 22:37). In Acts 4:32, Luke recorded how, on one occasion, "the multitude of them that believed were of one heart and soul (*psuche*)." In a similar fashion, "soul" also is employed to refer to the lower, physical nature of mankind. In his first letter to the Christians at Corinth, Paul wrote that "the **natural man** receiveth not the things of the Spirit of God" (2:14). In addressing the intent of this passage, Woods noted that the phrase "natural man" is literally

> **the soulish man**, since the adjective "natural" [*psuchikos* —BT] translates a form of the Greek word for soul, which may be expressed in English as **psychical**. Thus, this usage is supported by etymology and required by the context. See, especially, Paul's teaching in 1 Corinthians 1:18-28 and 2:6-16 (1980, 122:163, emp. in orig.).

Fourth, the word soul is used in Scripture to designate the portion of a person that is immortal and thus never dies. As early as the book of Genesis, the Bible sets forth such a concept. For example, in commenting on Rachel's untimely death at the birth of her son, Moses wrote: "And it came to pass, as her soul (*nephesh*) was departing (for she died), that she called his name Ben-oni: but his father called him Benjamin" (Genesis 35:18). On one occasion while the prophet Elijah was at the house of a widow in the city of Zarephath, the woman's son fell ill and eventually died. But the text indicates that Elijah "cried unto Jehovah..., 'O Jehovah my God, I pray thee, let this child's soul (*nephesh*) come into him again'" (1 Kings 17:21). When the psalmist prayed to Jehovah for forgiveness, he cried: "O Jehovah, have mercy upon me: heal my soul (*nephesh*); for I have sinned against thee" (41:4). In his discussion of the ultimate fate of those who dared to trust in earthly riches rather than in the supreme power of the God of heaven, the psalmist lamented that such people were "like the beasts that perish.... But God will redeem my soul (*nephesh*) from the power of Sheol" (49:15).

Many years later, Christ warned His disciples: "And be not afraid of them that kill the body, but are not able to kill the soul: but rather fear him who is able to destroy both soul (*psuche*) and body in hell" (Matthew 10:28). During His discussion with the Sadducees in Matthew 22, the Lord quoted from Exodus 3:6 where God said to Moses: "I **am** the God of Abraham, and the God of Isaac, and the God of Jacob." Christ then went on to state (22:32): "God is not the God of the dead, but of the living"—a fact that the Sadducees' opponents, the Pharisees, already accepted as true (cf. Acts 23:8). Yet when God spoke with Moses (c. 1446 B.C.) about the patriarchs Abraham, Isaac, and Jacob, those three men had been dead and in their tombs for literally hundreds of years.

Since from Christ's own words we know that "God is not the God of the dead but of the living," the point is obvious. Abraham, Isaac, and Jacob still must have been living. But how? The solution to the seeming problem, of course, lies in the fact that while their **bodies** had died, their immortal **souls** had not. When the apostle John was allowed to peer into the book "sealed with seven seals" (Revelation 5:1), he "saw underneath the altar the souls (*psuchas*) of them that had been slain for the word of God" (Revelation 6:9). Each of these passages is instructive of the fact that there is within man a soul that never dies.

Use of the Word "Spirit" in Scripture

During his tenure as associate editor of the *Gospel Advocate*, Guy N. Woods penned a "Questions and Answers" column in which he dealt with difficult Bible questions, topics, or passages. When one querist wrote to ask: "What is the difference between the soul and the spirit of man?," Woods responded as follows:

Though it is characteristic of most people today to use these terms interchangeably, the scriptures very definitely differentiate them. "For the word of God is living, and active, and sharper than any two-edged sword, and piercing even to the dividing of **soul** and **spirit**, of both joints and marrow, and quick to discern the thoughts and intents of the heart" (Hebrews 4:12). Since the sacred writers provided for "the dividing of soul and spirit," in those instances where they differ, so ought we and so we must if we are to entertain biblical concepts of these words.

The word "spirit," when denoting the human entity (from the Greek word *pneuma*), is a specific term and designates that part of us which is not susceptible to death and which survives the dissolution of the body (Acts 7:59). It is infused in us directly from God and is not a product of human generation (Hebrews 12:9). "Soul," from the Greek word *psuche*, however, is a generic word and its meaning must be determined, in any given instance, from the context in which it appears (1980, 122:163, emp. added, parenthetical item in orig.).

In my above discussion on the use of the word "soul" in Scripture, I examined the various ways in which the Hebrew and Greek terms for soul are employed. I now would like to examine the various ways in which the Hebrew and Greek terms for "spirit" are employed within the sacred text.

The Hebrew term for "spirit" is *ruach* (from *rawah*, to breathe). In their *Hebrew and English Lexicon of the Old Testament*, Brown, Driver, and Briggs noted that *ruach* has nine different meanings, depending on the specific context. *Ruach* may refer to: (1) the Holy Spirit; (2) angels, both good and evil; (3) the life principle found within both man and animals; (4) disembodied spirits; (5) breath; (6) wind; (7) disposition or attitude; (8) the seat of emotions; and (9) the seat of mind and will in men (1907, pp. 924-925). In the Old Testament of the King James Version, *ruach* is translated variously as the Spirit of God (i.e., Holy Spirit) 105 times, man's spirit 59 times, spirit (an attitude or emotional state) 51 times, spirits (angels) 23 times, wind 43 times, and several other items (Morey, 1984, p. 51).

The word *ruach*, like *nephesh*, has a wide range of meanings. First, it seems originally to have referred to the wind, which was viewed as being invisible and immaterial (Gen. 8:1). Second, since God is invisible and immaterial like the wind, He is described as "spirit" (Isa. 63:10). Third, since the angels of God are invisible and immaterial, they are called "spirits" (Ps. 104:4, KJV; cf. Heb. 1:14). Fourth, since the life principle which animates man and animals is invisible and immaterial, it is also called "spirit" (Gen. 7:22). In this sense it was viewed as the "breath" of life which departs at death. Fifth, since man has an invisible and immaterial self or soul which transcends the life principle by its self-consciousness, man's "mind" or "heart" is called his "spirit" (Ps. 77:6; Prov. 29:11, KJV). The invisible side of man which is called "spirit" cannot be reduced to the mere principle of physical life or the breath of the body because man's transcendent self is contrasted to those things in such places as Isa. 42:5. Also, man's self-awareness as a cognitive ego obviously transcends the life principle which operates in animals. At death, this transcendent ego or disincarnate mind is called a "spirit" or a "ghost" (Job 4:15). This is parallel to *rephaim* or disembodied spirit (Job 26:5). Thus at death, while the life principle or breath of life ceases to exist in man or animals, the higher self or spirit of man ascends at death to the presence of God (Ps. 31:5; Eccles. 12:7).... Sixth, since attitudes and dispositions such as pride, humility, joy, or sorrow are invisible and immaterial, they are described as being someone's "spirit" (Prov. 11:13; 16:18). The Holy Spirit is described as the "sevenfold Spirit" in the sense that He gives people the disposition, attitude, or spirit of wisdom, understanding, counsel, might, knowledge, fear and holiness (Isa. 11:2; cf. Rom. 1:4; Rev. 3:1) [Morey, pp. 52-53].

The Greek term for "spirit" is *pneuma* (from *pneo*, to breathe). In their *Greek-English Lexicon of the New Testament and Other Early Christian Literature*, language scholars Arndt and Gingrich noted that *pneuma* has seven different meanings, depending on the specific context. *Pneuma* may refer to: (1) wind or air; (2) that which gives life to the body; (3) disincarnate souls; (4) human personality or ego which is the center of emotion, intellect, and will; (5) a state of mind or disposition; (6) an independent, immaterial being such as God or angels; and (7) as God—as in the Holy

Spirit of God, the spirit of Christ, etc. (1957, pp. 680-685). In his *Greek-English Lexicon of the New Testament,* Thayer provided five definitions for *pneuma* (1958, pp. 520-524). In the King James Version of the New Testament, *pneuma* is translated variously as Spirit (Holy) 165 times, Ghost (Holy) 88 times, spirits (good/evil, angels) 55 times, spirit (man's) 45 times, spirit (attitude) 22 times, spirits or ghosts (man's disincarnate soul) 7 times, spiritual (adjectival use) 23 times, life and wind 1 time each (Morey, pp. 60-61).

> The word *pneuma* in its various forms is found 406 times in the New Testament.... First, the New Testament writers carry on the precedent set by the translators of the Septuagint by using the Greek words for wind such as *animas* instead of *pneuma.* The only instance where *pneuma* definitely refers to the wind is in John 3:8 where there is a poetic play upon the sovereign movement of the divine Spirit and the wind. Second, *pneuma* refers to the life principle which animates the body. This is actually a very rare usage in the New Testament. For example, the false prophet who accompanied the Antichrist in the last days will make an idol "alive" (Rev. 13:15). Third, *pneuma* is used to describe the immaterial nature of God and angels (John 4:24; Heb. 1:14). Christ defined a "spirit" or "ghost" as an immaterial being (Luke 24:39). Fourth, *pneuma* refers to the disposition which characterizes a person, such as pride, humility, fear, etc. (1 Pet. 3:4). Fifth, *pneuma* is used to describe the disincarnate spirit or soul of man after death (Matt. 27:50; Luke 24:37,39; John 19:30; Acts 7:59; Heb. 12:23; 1 Pet. 3:19).... Sixth, man's transcendent self, or ego, is also called *pneuma* because of its immaterial and invisible nature (1 Cor. 2:11). It is described as the center of man's emotions, intellect and will (Mark 8:12; Mark 2:8; Matt. 26:41). Since man's *pneuma* transcends his mere physical life, it is frequently contrasted to his body, or flesh (Matt. 26:41; Mark 14:38; Luke 24:39; John 3:6; 6:63; 1 Cor. 5:5; 7:34; 2 Cor. 7:1; Gal. 5:17; 6:8,9; James 2:26). It is man's *pneuma* which ascends to God at death (Acts 7:59) [Morey, pp. 61-62].

Since *ruach* and *pneuma* both derive from roots meaning "to breathe," it should not be surprising that on occasion they are used synonymously, as the information in Table 1 on the following page documents.

SPIRIT	REFERS TO	SOUL
Genesis 6:17; 7:15; Ecclesiastes 3:19	Breath	Job 41:21
Genesis 7:22	Animal/Human Life	Genesis 9:4; 37:21 Matthew 2:20; 6:25
Ecclesiastes 12:7; 1 Corinthians 5:5	Entities Separate from the Body	Isaiah 10:18; Matthew 10:28
Mark 2:8; 1 Corinthians 2:11; 14:15	Seat of Man's Intellect	Hebrews 12:3; Philippians 1:27
Genesis 41:8; Proverbs 16:18; 17:22; Mark 8:12; Acts 18:25; 1 Corinthians 4:21; 2 Corinthians 2:13	Feelings and Emotions	Exodus 23:9; Psalm 42:1-6; Proverbs 12:10; Matthew 26:38; Luke 2:35; Acts 4:32; 17:16; 2 Peter 2:8
Genesis 1:2; 6:3; Matthew 12:18; John 4:24	God's Nature	Leviticus 26:11; Matthew 12:18; Hebrews 10:38
Psalm 51:10,17; Luke 1:46-47; John 4:24; Romans 1:9	Man's Place of Inner Worship and Reverence Toward God	Psalms 42:1-2,4-6; 103:1; 146:1; Matthew 22:37
Psalm 31:5; Ecclesiastes 12:7; Zechariah 12:1; Luke 8:55; 23:46; Acts 7:59; 1 Corinthians 5:5	Part of a Person that Lives on after Death of the Body	Genesis 35:18; 1 Kings 17:21-22; Psalms 41:4; 49:15; Micah 6:7; Matthew 10:28; Hebrews 10:39; James 1:21; 5:20; 1 Peter 1:9,22; 3 John 2; Revelation 6:9

Writing in the *International Standard Bible Encyclopedia* about both the similarities and the differences between the Old Testament words *nephesh* and *ruach* as compared to their New Testament counterparts *psuche* and *pneuma*, J.I. Marais noted:

> In the NT *psuche* appears under more or less similar conditions as in the OT. The contrast here is as carefully maintained as there. It is used where *pneuma* would be out of place; and yet it seems at times to be employed where *pneuma* might

have been substituted. Thus in Jn. 19:30 we read: "Jesus gave up His *pneuma* to the Father," and, in the same Gospel (Jn. 10:15), "Jesus gave up His *psuche* for the sheep," and in Mt. 20:28 He gave His *psuche* (not His *pneuma*) as a ransom... (1956, 5:2838).

While the "spirit" (*pneuma*) is recognized as man's individual possession (i.e., that which distinguishes one man from another and from inanimate nature), on occasion the same may be said of the soul (*psuche*; cf. Matthew 10:28 and Revelation 6:9-11). The *pneuma* of Christ was surrendered to the Father in death; His *psuche* was surrendered, His individual life was given, "a ransom for many." His life "was given for the sheep." In Acts 2:27, Luke quoted Psalm 16:10 regarding Christ's physical death: "Because thou wilt not leave my soul unto hades, neither wilt thou give thy Holy One to see corruption." The word that Luke used for "soul" is *psuche*, which is employed here not only as the Greek counterpart to the Hebrew *nephesh*, meaning body, but representing specifically a *nephesh meth*—a dead body (cf. Numbers 6:6, 9:6, and Ecclesiastes 9:5). Thus, Christ's body was not abandoned to hades.

Hades is used in Scripture to refer to at least three different places: (a) the general abode of the spirits of the dead, whether good or evil (Revelation 1:18; 6:8; 20:13-14); (b) a temporary place of punishment for the wicked dead (Luke 16:23; Revelation 20:13); and (c) the grave (1 Corinthians 15:55; cf. Acts 2:27). In Psalm 16:10 (the passage quoted by Luke in Acts 2:27), the writer stated: "Thou wilt not leave my soul (*nephesh*) to sheol." In the Old Testament, sheol also is used to refer to three different places: (a) the unseen abode for spirits of the dead (Job 14:13-15; Ezekiel 26:20; Jonah 2:2); (b) a temporary place of punishment for the wicked dead (Psalm 9:17); and (c) the grave (Davidson, 1970, p. 694; Harris, et al., 1980, 2:892; cf. Numbers 16:30-37 where the conclusion of the rebellion of Korah [and those sympathetic with him] against Moses is described in these words: "The earth opened its mouth, and swallowed them up, and their households, and all the men that appertained unto Korah, and all their goods. So they, and all that appertained to them, went down alive into sheol."). In Acts 2:27 (hades) and Psalm 16:10 (sheol), the context seems to require the latter usage—i.e., the grave. Thus, both David and Luke were making the point (to paraphrase): "You will not leave my body in the grave, nor will you allow your Holy One to see decay." In fact, just four verses later the inspired writer referred back to David's declaration and commented that "he foreseeing this spake of the resurrection of the Christ, that neither was he left unto hades, nor did his flesh see corruption" (2:31).

In referring to the death of the physical body, Solomon wrote that "the living know that they shall die: but the dead know not anything" (Ecclesiastes 9:5). The psalmist addressed the same point when he wrote: "The dead praise not Jehovah, Neither any that go down into silence" (115:17) and "His breath goeth forth, he returneth to his earth; in that very day his thoughts perish" (146:4). When Christ yielded up His soul/life (*psuche*; cf. *nephesh*, Psalm 16:10), His dead body was headed for the grave and therefore was in the condition that it could "know not anything" and "praise not Jehovah." [The spirit (*pneuma*) that had vacated the body was alive and well in Paradise (Greek *paradeisos*, Luke 23:43). Paul addressed this principle when he said that Christ's disciples always should be "of good courage, and willing rather to be **absent from the body**, and to be **at home with the Lord**" (2 Corinthians 5: 8; cf. 1 Thessalonians 4:14).] Woods observed:

> Death, mortality, corruptibility, decay, destruction are never affirmed of the spirit. It is, in the nature of the case, impossible for a spirit to die. The scriptures affirm deathlessness of the angels; and the angels do not die because they are angels, but because they are spirits (1985b, 127:692).

Yet it also is impossible for a soul to die (Matthew 10:28; Revelation 6:9-11).

However, as Hebrews 4:12 documents, there are times when the words spirit and soul are **not** used synonymously. The word spirit sometimes refers to wind or air (Genesis 3:8; 8:1; John 3:

8); the word soul does not. The word spirit sometimes refers to demons (Mark 5:2; Luke 9:39); the word soul does not. The word soul sometimes refers to both the inner and outer man (i.e., a whole person; Exodus 1:5; Ezekiel 18:20; Acts 2:41; Romans 13:1); the word spirit does not. The word soul sometimes refers to a corpse (Numbers 5:2; 6:6; Psalm 16:10; Acts 2:27); the word spirit does not. The word soul on one occasion refers to an odor, fragrance, or perfume (Isaiah 3:20); the word spirit does not.

Thus, while it is true that on some occasions the words "soul" and "spirit" are used interchangeably, in other instances they are employed in a non-synonymous fashion. As Woods observed, under certain conditions within Scripture "lexically, logically, and actually these terms differ and must not be confused" (1985b, 127: 692). In any study of these two terms as they occur within God's Word, the context and intent of the writers are the deciding factors that must be considered and respected.

CHAPTER 7

THE ORIGIN, NATURE, AND DESTINY OF THE SOUL—[PART II]

Biblical teaching regarding man acknowledges that he is composed of two distinct parts—the physical and the spiritual. We get an introduction to the origin of the **physical** portion as early as Genesis 2:7 when the text states: "Jehovah God formed man of the dust of the ground, and breathed into his nostrils the breath of life; and man became a living soul (*nephesh chayyah*)." It is important to recognize both what this passage is discussing and what it is not. Genesis 2:7 **is** teaching that man was given **physical life**; it is **not** teaching that man was instilled with an **immortal nature**. The immediate (as well as the remote) context is important to a clear understanding of the intent of Moses' statement. Both the King James and American Standard Versions translate *nephesh chayyah* as "living soul." The Revised Standard Version, New American Standard Version, New International Version, and the New Jerusalem Bible all translate the phrase as "living being." The New English Bible translates it as "living creature."

The variety of terms employed in our English translations has caused some confusion as to the exact meaning of the phrase "living soul" or "living being." Some have suggested, for example, that Genesis 2:7 is speaking specifically of man's receiving his immortal soul and/or spirit. This is not the case, however, as a closer examination of the immediate and remote contexts clearly indicates. For example, the apostle Paul quoted Genesis 2:7 in 1 Corinthians 15:44-45 when he wrote: "If there is a **natural body**, there is also a **spiritual body**. So also it is written, 'The first man Adam became a living soul.' The last Adam became a life-giving spirit." The comparison/contrast offered by the apostle between the first Adam's "natural body" and the last Adam (Christ) as a "life-giving spirit" is absolutely critical to an understanding of Paul's central message (and the theme of the great "resurrection chapter" of the Bible, 1 Corinthians 15), and must not be overlooked in any examination of Moses' statement in Genesis 2:7.

There are six additional places in the Old Testament where similar phraseology is employed, and in each case the text obviously is speaking of members of the animal kingdom. In Genesis 1:24, God said: "Let the earth bring forth living creatures (*nephesh chayyah*) after their kind." Genesis 1:30 records that God provided plants as food "to every beast of the earth, and to every bird of the air, and to everything that creeps on the earth, everything that has the breath of life (*nishmath chayyah*)." When the Genesis Flood covered the Earth, God made a rainbow covenant with Noah and with every living creature (*nephesh chayyah*) that was in the ark with Him (Genesis 9:12). God pledged that He would remember the covenant that He made with every "living creature" (*nephesh chayyah*; Genesis 9:12), and therefore He never again would destroy the Earth by such a Flood. The rainbow, He stated, would serve as a reminder of that "everlasting covenant" between God and every living creature (*nephesh chayyah*, Genesis 9:15). The final occurrence of the phrase is found in Ezekiel's description of the river flowing from the temple in which every living creature (*nephesh chayyah*) that swarms will live (47:9).

Additionally, the Bible declares: "For that which befalleth the sons of men befalleth beasts; even one thing befalleth them: as the one dieth, so dieth the other; yea, they have all one breath; and man hath no preeminence above the beasts" (Ecclesiastes 3:19). Does this mean, therefore, that man possesses only a material nature and has no immortal soul/spirit? No, it does not! In speaking to this very point, Jack P. Lewis wrote:

> It would seem that arguments which try to present the distinctiveness of man from the term "living soul" are actually based on the phenomena of variety in translation of the KJV and have no validity in fact. Had the translators rendered all seven occurrences by the same term, we would have been aware of the fact that both men and animals are described by it. To make this observation is not at all to affirm that the Old Testament is materialistic. We are concerned at this time only with the biblical usage of one term. Neither is it to deny a distinction in biblical thought between men and other animals when one takes in consideration the whole Old Testament view. Man may perish like the animals, but he is different from them. Even here in Genesis in the creation account, God is not said to breathe into the animals the breath of life; animals are made male and female; there is no separate account of the making of the female animal; they are not said to be in God's image and likeness; they are not given dominion. Man is the crown of God's creation (1988, p. 7).

When Dr. Lewis suggested that "man may perish like the animals," he captured the essence of the passage in Ecclesiastes 3:19. It is true that both men and beasts ultimately die, and that in this regard man "hath no preeminence above the beasts." Yet while both creatures are referred to as *nephesh chayyah*, the Scriptures make it clear that God did something special in reference to man. Genesis 1:26-27 records: "And God said, Let us make man **in our image, after our likeness**…. And God created man in his own image, in the image of God created he him; male and female created he them." Nowhere does the Bible state or imply that animals are created in the image of God. What is it, then, that makes man different from the animals?

The answer, of course, lies in the fact that man possesses an immortal nature. Animals do not. God Himself is a spirit (John 4:24). And a spirit "hath not flesh and bones" (Luke 24:39). In some fashion, God has placed within man a portion of His own essence —in the sense that man possesses a spirit that never will die. The prophet Zechariah spoke of Jehovah, Who "stretcheth forth the heavens, and layeth the foundation of the earth, and formeth the spirit (*ruach*) of man within him" (12:1). The Hebrew word for "formeth," *yatsar*, is defined as to form, fashion, or shape (as in a potter working with clay; Harris, et al., 1980, 1:396). The same word is used in Genesis 2:7, thereby indicating that both man's physical body and his spiritual nature were formed, shaped, molded, or fashioned by God. The authors of the *Theological Wordbook of the Old Testament* noted:

> The participial form meaning "potter" is applied to God in Isa. 64:7 where mankind is the work of his hand. When applied to the objects of God's creative work, the emphasis of the word is on the forming or structuring of these phenomena. The word speaks to the **mode of creation** of these phenomena only insofar as the act of shaping or forming an object may also imply the **initiation of that object** (Harris, et al., 1:396, emp. added).

As the Creator, God "initiates" the object we know as man's immortal nature (i.e., his soul or spirit). Solomon, writing in the book of Ecclesiastes, noted that "the dust returneth to the earth as it was, and the spirit returneth unto **God who gave it**" (12:7, emp. added). Man's physical body was formed of the physical dust of the Earth. Would it not follow, then, that his spiritual portion would be formed from that which is spiritual? When the writer of Hebrews referred to God as "the Father of our spirits" (12:9), he revealed the spiritual source of the soul—God.

When Does Man Receive His Immortal Nature?

When does man receive his soul/spirit? In one of the most illustrative passages within the Bible on this topic, James wrote: "The body apart from the spirit is dead" (2:26). This brief but important observation—offered by inspiration on the part of the Bible writer—carries tremendous implications. Without the presence of the spirit (*pneuma*), the physical body cannot live. There is, however, an important corollary to James' assessment. If the body is living, **then the spirit** (*pneuma*) **must be present!**

But when does life actually begin? The answer, quite simply, is that it begins **at conception**. When the male and female gametes join to form the zygote that eventually will grow into the fetus, it is at that very moment that the formation of a new body begins. It is the result of a **viable** male gamete joined sexually with a **viable** female gamete which has formed a zygote that will move through a variety of important stages.

The first step in the process—which eventually will result in the highly differentiated tissues and organs that compose the body of the neonatal child—is the initial mitotic cleavage of that primal cell, the zygote. At this point, the genetic material doubles, matching copies of the chromosomes move to opposite poles, and the cell cleaves into two daughter cells. Shortly afterwards, each of these cells divides again, forming the embryo. [In humans and animals, the term "embryo" applies to any stage after cleavage but before birth (see Rudin, 1997, p. 125).]

As the cells of the embryo continue to divide, they form a cluster of cells. These divisions are accompanied by additional changes that produce a hollow, fluid-filled cavity inside the ball, which now is a one-layer-thick grouping of cells known as a blastula. Early in the second day after fertilization, the embryo undergoes a process known as gastrulation in which the single-layer blastula turns into a three-layered gastrula consisting of ectoderm, mesoderm, and endoderm surrounding a cavity known as the archenteron. Each of these layers will give rise to very specific structures. For example, the ectoderm will form the outermost layer of the skin and other structures, including the sense organs, parts of the skeleton, and the nervous system. The mesoderm will form tissues associated with support, movement, transport, reproduction, and excretion (i.e., muscle, bone, cartilage, blood, heart, blood vessels, gonads, and kidneys). The endoderm will produce structures associated with breathing and digestion (including the lungs, liver, pancreas, and other digestive glands) [see Wallace, 1975, p. 187].

Within 72 hours after fertilization, the embryo will have divided a total of four times, and will consist of sixteen cells. Each cell will divide before it reaches the size of the cell that produced it; hence, the cells will become progressively smaller with each division. By the end of the first month, the embryo will have reached a length of only one-eighth of an inch, but already will consist of millions of cells. By the end of the ninth month, if all proceeds via normal channels, a baby is ready to be born. As one biologist (and author of a widely used secular university biology textbook) noted:

> As soon as the egg is touched by the head of a sperm, it undergoes violent pulsating movements which unite the twenty-three chromosomes of the sperm with its own genetic complement. From this single cell, about 1/175 of an inch in diameter, **a baby** weighing several pounds and composed of trillions of cells will be delivered about 266 days later (Wallace, 1975, p. 194, emp. added).

Is it alive? Of course it is alive. In fact, herein lies one of the most illogical absurdities of arguments set forth by those who support and defend abortion. They opine that the "thing" in the human womb is not "alive." If it is not alive, why the need to abort it? **Simply leave it alone!** Obviously, of course, from their perspective that is not an option because, as everyone admits, in just nine months that growing, vibrant, developing fetus results in a **living human baby**. The truth of the matter is that human life begins at conception and is continuous, whether intrauterine or extrauterine, until death.

In 1981, the United States Senator John East presided over extensive hearings covering a period of eight days, in which 57 expert witnesses gave testimony, concerning Senate Bill #158, the "Human Life Bill." In the final report of the Senate Subcommittee on Separation of Powers, prepared for and presented to the Senate

Judiciary Committee of the 97th Congress, the following conclusion can be found: "Physicians, biologists, and other scientists agree that conception marks the beginning of the life of a human being—a being that is alive and is a member of the human species. There is overwhelming agreement on this point in countless medical, biological, and scientific writings" (see East, 1981). On pages 7-9 of the report prepared by the subcommittee headed by Senator East, thirteen medical textbooks were listed, each of which stated categorically that the life of an individual human begins at conception. On pages 9-10 of the report, the testimony of some of the preeminent witnesses who appeared before the subcommittee was listed. Professor J. Lejeune of Paris (who discovered the chromosome pattern of Down's Syndrome), said: "Each individual has a very neat beginning at conception." Professor M. Matthews-Roth of Harvard University said: "It is scientifically correct to say that individual human life begins at conception." Professor H. Gordon of the famed Mayo Clinic in Rochester, New York testified: "It is an established fact that human life begins at conception." Consider the following scientific facts regarding the living nature of the zygote and fetus, as discussed by Moore and Persaud in their classic medical school textbook, *The Developing Human* (1993).

(1) The baby's heart forms by the end of the third week after conception, with contractions beginning on days 21-22 (p. 65); on days 22-23, the neural tube begins to develop (p. 385).

(2) By the age of two months, the heart beats so strongly that a doctor actually can listen to it with a Doppler stethoscope (p. 6), and by the end of the fifth week the heart is fully partitioned (p. 312).

(3) At 40 days after fertilization, electrical waves (as measured by an electroencephalogram) can be recorded within the baby's brain, indicating brain activity (Hamlin, 1964, 190 [2]:112-114). Brain waves are readily apparent.

(4) Around days 26-27, the respiratory system begins to form, including the larynx, trachea, bronchii, and lungs (pp. 226-236).

(5) Early in the fourth week, the liver, gallbladder, and bilary duct system have formed (pp. 237-244).

(6) By the age of two months, "the embryo has distinct human characteristics" (p. 87). Everything is "in place"—feet, hands, head, organs, etc. Upon close examination, fingerprints are evident. Although less than an inch long, the embryo has a head with eyes and ears, a simple digestive system, kidneys, liver, a heart that beats, a bloodstream of its own, and the beginning of a brain.

(7) The unborn child hiccups, sucks his or her thumb, wakes, and sleeps.

(8) The unborn child responds to touch, pain, cold, sound, and light.

Is the child alive? Do you know any **dead** creature that attains such marvelous accomplishments?

But is the fetus growing in the uterus actually **human**? It is the result of the union of the **human** male gamete (spermatozoon) and the **human** female gamete (ovum)—something that certainly guarantees its humanness. [The *Washington Post* of May 11, 1975 contained an "Open Letter to the Supreme Court"—signed by 209 medical doctors—which stated: "We physicians reaffirm our dedication to the awesome splendor of **human life—from one-celled infant to dottering elder.**"]

And how, exactly, does God view this unborn yet fully human child? He said to the prophet Jeremiah: "Before I formed thee in the belly, I knew thee, and **before thou camest forth out of the womb**, I sanctified thee" (Jeremiah 1:5, emp. added). Jehovah knew the prophet—even while he was *in utero*—and viewed him as a living person. Further, God already had "sanctified" Jeremiah. If his mother had aborted the baby, she would have killed someone that God recognized as a living person.

The same concept applied to the prophet Isaiah who wrote in the book that bears his name:

> Listen, O isles, unto me, and hearken ye peoples, from afar; **Jehovah hath called me from the womb**; from the bowels of my mother hath he made mention of my name.... And now, saith Jehovah that **formed me from the womb** to be his servant... (Isaiah 49:1,5, emp. added).

Jehovah not only viewed Isaiah as a person prior to his birth, but even called him by name.

David, writing in Psalm 139:13-16, provided one of the clearest and most compelling discussions on the nature and importance of life *in utero* when he wrote:

> For thou didst form my inward parts: Thou didst cover me in my mother's womb. I will give thanks unto thee; For I am fearfully and wonderfully made: Wonderful are thy works; And that my soul knoweth right well. My frame was not hidden from thee, When I was made in secret, And curiously wrought in the lowest parts of the earth. Thine eyes did see mine unformed substance; And in thy book they were all written, Even the days that were ordained for me, When as yet there was none of them.

The phrases, "I was made in secret" and "curiously wrought in the lowest parts of the earth," refer to the psalmist's development in the womb (see Young, 1965, p. 76). Notice also that David employed the pronouns "me," "my," and "I" throughout the passage in reference to his own prenatal state. Such usage clearly shows that David was referring to himself, and one cannot talk about himself without having reference to a living human being. The Bible thus acknowledges that David was a human being while he inhabited his mother's womb (and prior to his birth).

Job, who was undergoing a terrible life crisis, cursed the day he was born when he said: "Why did I not **die from the womb**? Why did I not give up the ghost when my mother bore me?" (3:11). It is clear that if the fetus had **died** in the womb, prior to that it must have been **living**. Something (or someone) cannot die if it (or they) never lived. It also is of interest to observe that in Job 3:13-16, the patriarch listed several formerly-living-but-now-dead people with whom he would have had something in common **if** he had died *in utero*. Included in the list—along with kings and princes—was the child who experienced a "hidden untimely birth" (i.e., a miscarriage). Job considered the miscarried child to be in the same category as others who once lived but had died. Obviously, the Holy Spirit (Who guided the author of the book of Job in what he wrote) considered an unborn fetus as much a human being as a king, a prince, or a stillborn infant.

In the Old Testament, even the accidental termination of a pregnancy was a punishable crime. Consider Exodus 21:22—"If men strive together, and hurt a woman with child, so that her fruit depart, and yet no harm follows; he shall be surely fined, according as the woman's husband shall lay upon him...but if any harm follows, then thou shalt give life for life." The meaning of the passage is this: If the child was born prematurely as the result of this accident, but "no harm follows" (i.e. the child survived), then a fine was to be exacted; however, if "harm follows" (i.e., either mother or child died), then the guilty party was to be put to death. Look at it this way. Why would God exact such a severe punishment for the accidental **death** of an unborn child—if that child were not **living**?

The same understanding of the fetus as a living child is found within the pages of the New Testament. The angel Gabriel told Mary that "Elisabeth thy kinswoman, she also hath conceived **a son** in her old age" (Luke 1:36, emp. added). Please note that the conception resulted in neither an "it" nor a "thing," but in **a son**. In Luke 1:41,44, the Bible states (in speaking of Elisabeth, who was pregnant with John the Baptist) that "the babe leaped in her womb." The word for "babe" in these passages is the Greek term *brephos*, and is used here for an unborn fetus. The same word is used in both Luke 18:15 and Acts 7:19 for young or newborn children. It also is used in Luke 2:12,16 for the newborn Christ-child. *Brephos* therefore can refer to a young child, a newborn infant, or even an unborn fetus (see Thayer, 1958, p. 105). In each of these cases a living human being must be under consideration because the same word is used to describe all three.

The fact that the zygote/embryo/fetus is living (an inescapable conclusion supported by both weighty scientific and biblical evidence) thus becomes critically important in answering the question, "When does man receive his immortal nature?" When James observed that "the body apart from the spirit is dead" (2:26), the corollary automatically inherent in his statement became the fact that **if the body is living, then the spirit must be present**. Since at each stage of its development the zygote/embryo/fetus is living, it must have had a soul/spirit instilled at conception. No other view is in accord with the biblical and scientific evidence.

CHAPTER 8

THE ORIGIN, NATURE, AND DESTINY OF THE SOUL—[PART III]

It is one thing to suggest that man possesses a soul or spirit. It is another to suggest that he receives such at conception. And it is still another to suggest that the soul/spirit survives the death of the physical body. [Since I previously documented the fact that on occasion within Scripture the words "soul" and "spirit" may be used synonymously, in order to avoid complicating the subject matter unnecessarily from this point on, I will employ them as such, rather than continuing to use the somewhat cumbersome "soul/spirit" designation.] As I mentioned in chapter 6, there are a number of different views regarding the immortal nature of the soul.

Among those who accept the existence of the soul, there are some who are quite willing to believe that all men have such a spirit residing within them, but who are quite unwilling to believe that such is immortal, preferring to believe instead that this spiritual part is **purely temporal** (and thus lives only as long as our corporeal nature exists). Conversely, there are some who posit the idea that all humans not only possess an immortal soul, but that the souls of

all people (regardless of their actions on Earth) will survive the death of the physical body in order to ultimately inhabit the heavenly realm with God. Others believe that while all men do indeed possess a soul, **only the soul of the faithful child of God** has an immortal nature. That is to say, the souls of those who die outside of Christ are not immortal and perish when the body dies, while the soul of the Christian goes on into eternity. Still others believe that the souls of **both** the faithful child of God **and** the person outside of Christ are immortal—thereby surviving the death of the physical body in order to eventually inhabit either heaven (a place of eternal reward) or hell (a place of eternal punishment). Who is correct? What is the truth of the matter?

"Temporal" Souls?

Concerning the position that all men possess a soul, but that such is purely temporal and incapable of surviving the physical death of the body, Gilbert Thiele, a professor at Concordia Seminary in St. Louis, Missouri, wrote:

> We think it is consequently fair to say, to put it very bluntly, that when a man dies he is dead. The Bible when examined in its length and breadth knows of no disembodied condition in which man lives, temporarily, and certainly not permanently; it knows of neither a temporary nor a permanent human immortality as such (1958, p. 18).

Such a position, however, "to put it very bluntly," is indefensible in light of the multifarious teachings of Scripture. There are too many passages (e.g., Acts 7:59, Revelation 6:9, Matthew 10:28, et al.—discussed previously) which teach that the soul does, in fact, partake of an immortal nature. More will be said on this later in this book.

Universalism

The idea that all humans possess an immortal soul, and that each and every one of those souls will survive the death of the physical body in order to inhabit the heavenly realm with God (regardless of their actions on Earth), is known as **universalism**. According to this view, all people will be saved; none will be lost. Advocates of this theory teach that since God is love (1 John 4:8), as well as a Sovereign Who desires mercy rather than sacrifice (Matthew 9:13), then divine punishment must be viewed as merely remedial. God's loving, longsuffering nature, they suggest, cannot tolerate the loss of even one of His creatures since He is "not willing that any should perish" (2 Peter 3:9).

This view may be somewhat unusual, but it is by no means new. Origen, a well-known, third-century preacher (c. A.D. 185-254), was among the first to espouse it, and he has been joined by a parade of the famous (and not so famous) in the days since. The great poet, Alfred Lord Tennyson, in his poem, *In Memoriam*, advocated universalism. Scottish theologian and University of Glasgow divinity professor, William Barclay, was one of the concept's most ardent twentieth-century defenders. In his book, *The Plain Man Looks at the Apostles' Creed*, he wrote:

> It seems to us that if God is the God who is the God and Father of our Lord Jesus Christ, and if the total impression of the Gospel is true, we may dare to hope that when time ends God's family will be complete, for surely we must think in terms, not of a king who is satisfied with a victory which destroys his enemies, but of a Father who can never be content when even a single child of his is outside the circle of his love (1967, p. 239).

When you stop to think about it, it should not be at all surprising that such a view should receive widespread support. After all, it is a most comforting position. In his book, *How Can a God of Love Send People to Hell?,* British author John Benton addressed the inherent appeal of universalism when he wrote:

> I am sure that there is a part in all of us which would like to believe that that was true. If not, we are in danger of becoming very hard and unloving people indeed. We sympathize with the emotions which draw some people in the direction of universalism. But, in all honesty, it is impossible to interpret Jesus as teaching universalism (1985, p. 38).

I agree wholeheartedly with both parts of Benton's assessment. First, surely there is a twinge of desire in every human heart that would **like** to see everyone end up in heaven on the Day of Judgment. What an invigorating and refreshing belief—to entertain the hope that not a single human would lose his or her soul to the netherworld, but instead would walk the golden streets of heaven with God throughout all eternity. Second, however, in all honesty, it **is** impossible to interpret Jesus as teaching universalism. No amount of wishful thinking on our part can avoid the force of His arguments, or those of His inspired writers, on the subject of the final destination of those who live in rebellion to Heaven's will in the here and now.

Generally speaking, there are two distinct views regarding the mechanics of ultimate, universal salvation. First, there is the idea that entails the "remedial suffering" of which I spoke earlier. Prominent theologian Carl F.H. Henry referred to this notion when he wrote: "Hell itself is transformed from the ultimate state of the lost into a means of grace—a neo-Protestant purgatory of sorts" (1967, p. 27). Second, there is the idea known as "transcendentalism," which one writer expressed as follows:

> This idea held that every soul is a part of the "oversoul" of the universe. To use a common metaphor, man is a spark of the universal flame and will eventually return to it to be absorbed into the One Soul of all time.... Hell, according to this nebulous theory, is a training school for fragments of the Eternal Self which must be disciplined into final merger. The soul of man is only a spark of the divine flame and will finally be reabsorbed into it (Woodson, 1973, p. 60).

In both views, "hell" becomes simply a repository of the souls of people who need either: (a) a "second chance"—a fact brought to their attention by a little temporary "remedial suffering"; or (b) a brief period of disciplining/chastising to help them "shape up before they ship out" to the eternal joys of heaven. Such fanciful theories, of course, are not found within Scripture. Rather, they represent little more than wishful thinking on the part of those who, like universalists, hope to avoid the eternality of Hell that is associated in the Bible with God's divine mode, and term, of punishment. Anyone who suggests that repentance, reparation, and redemption are possible **after death** (as both of these ideas plainly teach) simply does not understand the bulk of the Bible's teaching on such matters. The writer of the book of Hebrews wrote: "It is appointed unto men once to die, and after this cometh judgment" (9:27). The Lord Himself explained in Matthew 25:31-46 exactly what would happen to the wicked (whom He termed "goats," as opposed to the righteous, whom He labeled "sheep") on that great Judgment Day: "And these shall go away into **eternal punishment**, but the righteous into **eternal life**" (v. 46). Not much comfort for the universalist in these passages, is there?

In order to bolster their belief system, on occasion universalists have appealed to passages of Scripture that refer to God's concern for "all" men, or which show that the gift of life has been given to "all" people. Numerous statements from Paul, for example, have been quoted in potential support of universalism, including: (a) Romans 5:18 ("through one act of righteousness the free gift came unto **all** men to justification of life"); (b) Romans 11:25-26 ("**all** Israel shall be saved"); (c) 1 Corinthians 15:22 ("in Christ **all** shall be made alive"); and (d) 2 Corinthians 5:14 ("the love of Christ constraineth us; because we thus judge, that one died for **all**"). In his book, *Eternal Hope*, liberal theologian Emil Brunner wrote:

> That is the revealed will of God and the plan for the world which He discloses—a plan of **universal salvation**, of gathering all things into Christ. We hear not one word in the Bible of a dual plan, a plan of salvation and its polar opposite. The will of God has but one point, it is unambiguous and positive. It has one aim, not two (1954, p. 182, emp. added).

John A.T. Robinson, a bishop in the Church of England, wrote in a similar vein:

In a universe of love there can be no heaven which tolerates a chamber of horrors, no hell for any which does not at the same time make it hell for God. He cannot endure that—for that would be the final mockery of His nature—and He will not (1949, p. 155).

Brunner and Robinson, however, are dead wrong. It is clear—when the passages from Paul's inspired pen are examined in their appropriate context—that they are not teaching the false concept of universalism. While the apostle taught that the Gospel of Christ is **universally available,** he did not teach that the Gospel would be **universally accepted!** In fact, he taught quite the opposite. In 2 Thessalonians 1:8, Paul referred to the fact that one day the Lord would return "from heaven with the angels of his power in flaming fire, rendering vengeance to them that know not God, and to them that **obey not the gospel** of our Lord Jesus." Interestingly, in the very next verse he wrote that such people "shall suffer punishment, **even eternal destruction from the face of the Lord** and from the glory of his might." Not much support here for universalism either, is there?

Universalism is an erroneous view that must be rejected, not only because it contradicts plain Bible teaching on the eternal fate of the wicked, but also because it makes a mockery of Christ's commission to His followers (whether in His day or in ours) as presented in Matthew 28:19-20. His command was: "Go ye therefore, and make disciples of all the nations, baptizing them into the name of the Father and of the Son and of the Holy Spirit: teaching them to observe all things whatsoever I commanded you." But, as Benton has pointed out:

> If everyone is saved, then Jesus' commission to his followers to preach the gospel and make disciples is pointless. People are going to be saved anyway. Universalism suffers from fatal defects. It is an alluring theory, but it does not fit the New Testament. Christianity is founded on the teachings of Christ and if we want to know what Christianity stands for, we must be prepared to face squarely what Jesus taught (1985, p. 38).

Indeed we must! But suggesting that all men everywhere will be saved—regardless of the lives they lead or the obedience to God's Word that they do or do not render—is tantamount to saying that Christ erred when He said that at His Second Coming He will "render unto every man **according to his deeds**" (Matthew 16:27, emp. added). If universalism is true, He likewise was mistaken when He taught that "every idle word that men shall speak, they shall give account thereof in the day of judgment. For by thy words thou shalt be justified, and by thy words **thou shalt be condemned**" (Matthew 12:36-37, emp. added). Similarly, Paul was wrong when he reminded first-century Christians: "So then each one of us shall give account of himself to God" (Romans 14:12).

True, universalism is an "alluring theory"—no doubt due in large part to the fact that it stresses only the goodness of God and none of His other equally important traits. Paul, however, "shrank not from declaring the **whole counsel** of God" (Acts 20:27, emp. added). Rather, he proclaimed: "Behold then the goodness and severity of God: toward them that fell, severity; but toward thee, God's goodness, if thou continue in his goodness: otherwise thou also shalt be cut off" (Romans 11:22). As David Brown observed:

> One of the great obligations of the church in getting lost men to see the error of their ways and obey the gospel is to preach the truth of the Bible regarding Hell and who is going there. To preach only the goodness of God is to omit part of the whole counsel of God (1999, p. 166).

From the beginning of the Old Testament (e.g., Deuteronomy 4:2) to the end of the New (e.g., Revelation 22:18), the injunctions against altering, adding to, or deleting from God's Word are serious indeed. Universalism—as a doctrine that alters, adds to, and deletes from God's Word—should be (in fact, must be!) rejected.

Annihilation for the Wicked/ Eternity in Heaven for the Righteous?

It hardly should surprise or shock us that atheists, agnostics, and infidels of every stripe have long rejected the notion (associated with the concept of an immortal soul) of an unending penalty for wickedness. First, they reject the idea of the existence of the soul itself and, second, they find the idea of eternal punishment utterly abhorrent. As Brown noted: "One should not think it strange when men imagine doctrines that release them from the eternal consequences of a sinful life. What doctrine of the Bible has escaped corruption in the fertile imagination of rebellious men?" (1999, p. 161). Prominent British atheistic philosopher Antony Flew stated:

> I must confess that this subject of the doctrine of hell is one about which I find it very difficult to maintain my supposed national British calm and reserve. But let me, with what restraint I can muster, say that if anything can be known to be monstrously, inordinately wrong and unjust, it is the conduct of which this God is said to assume. If anything can be known to be just quite monstrously, inordinately, unquestionably unjust and evil, it is the conduct of a Being creating conscious creatures, whether human or animal, in the full knowledge, and with the intention, that these creatures should be maintained by His sustaining power eternally in infinite and unlimited torment. I speak of this with what little restraint I can muster because, if anything seems clear to me about good and evil, just and unjust, it is clear to me that this is monstrous (1977, pp. 84-85).

The famous nineteenth-century American agnostic, Robert G. Ingersoll (1833-1899), wrote:

> This idea of hell was born of ignorance, brutality, fear, cowardice, and revenge. This idea testifies that our remote ancestors were the lowest beasts. Only from the dens, lairs, and caves, only from the mouths filled with cruel fangs, only from hearts of fear and hatred, only from the conscience of hunger and lust, only from the lowest and most debased could come this cruel, heartless, and bestial of all dogmas... (1990, p. 4).

Ingersoll then went on to say:

> The idea of hell is born of revenge and brutality. I have no respect for any human being who believes in it. I have no respect for any man who preaches it. I dislike this doctrine. I hate it, despise, and defy it. The doctrine of hell is infamous beyond words (as quoted in Stacey, 1977, p. 59).

In his widely circulated essay, *Why I Am Not a Christian*, English agnostic philosopher Bertrand Russell commented: "I must say that I think all this doctrine, that hell-fire is a punishment for sin, is a doctrine of cruelty. It is a doctrine that put cruelty into the world and gave the world generations of cruel torture..." (1967, p. 18).

But what about those who believe in God and who accept as genuine the existence of the soul? Some among that number believe that while all men do indeed possess a soul, **only that of the faithful child of God has an immortal nature**. That is to say, the souls of those who die outside of Christ are not immortal and thus perish when the body dies, while the soul of the Christian goes into eternity (i.e., heaven). Others believe that the souls of **both** the faithful child of God **and** the person outside of Christ are immortal—thereby surviving the death of the physical body in order to eventually inhabit either a place of eternal reward (heaven) or a place of eternal punishment (hell). Which position is correct?

To be sure, there have been those who have taught that **only** the souls of the faithful are immortal, while those of the unfaithful perish at their physical death (a concept known as annihilationism). And again, this is not a new doctrine. In the July 1852 issue of *Christian Magazine*, a popular preacher from Nashville, Tennessee, Jesse B. Ferguson, asked:

> Is Hell a dungeon dug by Almighty hands before man was born, into which the wicked are to be plunged? And is the salvation upon the preacher's lips a salvation from such a Hell? For ourself, we rejoice to say it, we never believed, and upon the evidence so far offered, never can believe it (1852, p. 202).

In an article titled "Fire, Then Nothing" written in *Christianity Today* 135 years later, denominational scholar Clark Pinnock suggested that the souls of the wicked are annihilated at physical death (1987). In his book, *The Fire That Consumes*, Edward W. Fudge taught the same concept when he wrote: "The wicked, following whatever degree and duration of pain that God may justly inflict, will finally and truly die, perish and **become extinct for ever and ever**" (1982, p. 425, emp. added). Interestingly, Fudge's book drew rave reviews from certain quarters.

John N. Clayton, a self-proclaimed former-atheist-turned-Christian who lectures frequently on Christian evidences, and who is known chiefly for his numerous compromises of the Genesis account of creation, edits a small, bi-monthly journal titled *Does God Exist?* In the September/October 1990 issue, he reviewed *The Fire That Consumes* and said:

> One of the most frequent challenges of atheists during our lectures is the question of the reasonableness of the concept of hell. Why would a loving, caring, merciful God create man as he is, **knowing** that man would sin, reject God, and be condemned to eternal punishment? I have had to plead ignorance in this area because I had no logical answer that was consistent with the Bible.... I have never been able to be comfortable with the position that a person who rejected God should suffer forever and ever and ever (1990a, p. 20, emp. in orig.).

Clayton first described Fudge's book as "an exhaustive, scholarly study of the subject of hell," then confidently affirmed that it "will open many new viewpoints to any thinking reader," and finally concluded by saying: "**I recommend this book highly** to the serious student of the Bible who is not afraid to have some traditions challenged" (pp. 20-21, emp. added). Strangely, in the 1990 edition of his book, *The Source*, Clayton recommended Fudge's volume as one that contained "reasonably accurate **scientific** material"—even though the book deals solely with **theological** matters (1990b, pp. 190-191). At his weekend seminars on Christian evidences, Mr. Clayton routinely makes available a handout in which he recommends certain books that he believes would be of benefit to each of the seminar participants. Fudge's book is included on that handout. And, in the 1991 edition of the *Teacher's Guide* that accompanies his *Does God Exist? Christian Evidences Interme-diate Course*, Clayton offered the following suggestion in regard to lesson number six:

> **One approach that is very useful**, although somewhat controversial, is Edward Fudge's book *The Fire That Consumes*. Fudge deals with the subject of this lesson and takes the position that hell is the destruction of the soul (1991, p. 25, emp. added).

In April 1988, while speaking on the subject of "A Christian Response to the New Age Movement" at the annual Pepperdine University lectures in Malibu, California, best-selling author F. LaGard Smith asked the members of his audience:

> I also wonder if you feel as uncomfortable as I do in our traditional view of hell. Do you readily accept the traditional view of hell that says God sort of dangles you over the fires that burn day and night?... Is that what hell is all about? Haven't you struggled with the idea of how there can be a loving God and anywhere in his presence permit that to exist? Doesn't it seem like cruel and unusual punishment? (1988).

In that same lecture, Smith strenuously argued that God will "destroy it [the soul—BT]. Not punish it. Not dangle it. Not torture it. **Destroy it**!" (1988). Three years later, in October 1991, Wayne Jackson (as editor of the *Christian Courier*) wrote LaGard Smith to ask him about his position on the destiny of the souls of the wicked. Within a week, Smith replied via a five-page, handwritten letter in which he admitted that he believed in "the possibility that part of the ultimate punishment of the wicked is total destruction of their souls" (as quoted in Jackson, 1993, p. 65; see Jackson, 1998b, 33: 35 for a discussion of, and response to, Smith's subsequent claim that he has been "misunderstood" in regard to his views on the annihilation of the soul).

Another advocate of the view that the souls of the wicked will be annihilated is Alan Pickering who, in the 1980s, presented seminars around the country under the title of "Sharpening the Sword."

In December of 1986, he spoke at the Central Church of Christ in Stockton, California and advocated the view that the souls of the wicked, after a limited period of punishment, will cease to exist. As he had done with LaGard Smith, Wayne Jackson (who resides in Stockton) wrote Pickering to inquire if the material available on audio tape from his lectures did, in fact, accurately represent his views. In a subsequent telephone conversation a few days later, Mr. Pickering acknowledged that it did, and even went so far as to state that the concept of eternal conscious punishment for the wicked was a "slap in the face of God." He then challenged Wayne to a public debate on the matter—a challenge he later retracted when his offer was accepted (see Jackson, 1987a, 23:31).

In addition to those mentioned above, well-known creationist Robert L. Whitelaw defended the annihilationist position in his booklet, *Can There be Eternal Life Apart from Christ?*, when he wrote of those who die outside of Christ:

> Yet nowhere among all the pillars of theological orthodoxy ...do we find a work of solid exegesis proving the notion of man's innate immortality to be the teaching of the Bible, based on the whole counsel of Scripture.... Search Scripture as you will, there is no hint of any other kind of life or existence beyond Judgment Day for any being, human or demonic.... We have shown that nowhere in Scripture does God describe the state of lost mankind after Judgment Day as "life," "living," or even unconscious existence (1991, pp. 2,11).

The list of prominent religionists who in the past have supported, and who continue to support, the annihilationist position could be extended with ease. What, then, should be our response to this curious dogma?

At the outset, we should acknowledge clear biblical instruction that the soul of the faithful child of God will enjoy eternity forever in heaven. Such a concept is established beyond doubt in both the Old and New Testaments. As early as the book of Genesis, we read that Abraham "was gathered to his people" (25:8). Obviously, this cannot mean that Abraham was buried with his ancestors since "his people" were buried in Ur of the Chaldees and in Haran. Abraham, on the other hand, was buried in the cave of Machpelah (25: 9). The same words were used of Aaron (Numbers 20:24,26) and Moses (Numbers 27:13; 31:2; Deuteronomy 32:50). Certainly, in their individual cases this cannot possibly have reference to their interment in some sort of family tomb or burial plot. Gesenius, in his *Hebrew-Chaldee Lexicon to the Old Testament,* noted that "this being gathered to one's people, or fathers, is expressly distinguished both from death and from burial" (1979, p. 67).

When David's son (born as a result of his adultery with Bathsheba) died shortly after birth, the shattered sovereign said:

> While the child was yet alive, I fasted and wept: for I said, "Who knoweth whether Jehovah will not be gracious to me, that the child may live?" But now he is dead, wherefore should I fast? Can I bring him back again? **I shall go to him**, but he will not return to me (2 Samuel 12:22-23, emp. added).

Amidst his much suffering, the patriarch Job said:

> But as for me I know that my Redeemer liveth, and at last he will stand upon the earth: And after my skin, even this body, is destroyed, **then without my flesh shall I see God**; Whom I, even I, shall see, on my side, and mine eyes shall behold, and not as a stranger (Job 19:25-27, emp. added).

When Elijah raised the widow's son from the dead (1 Kings 17: 21-22), Scripture states:

> And he stretched himself upon the child three times, and cried unto Jehovah, and said, "O Jehovah my God, I pray thee, let this child's soul come into him again." And Jehovah hearkened unto the voice of Elijah; and the soul of the child came into him again, and he revived.

Because of the fact that we have access to later revelation, such as that contained in James 2:26 which states that "the body apart from the spirit is dead," we understand that in 1 Kings 17 the word soul (*nephesh*) is employed to speak of the immortal nature of the young man (i.e., his soul/spirit). His body was dead due to the fact that his spirit had departed. Elijah prayed that it be returned, and it was

—a fact that certainly precludes its annihilation. In His discussion with Martha concerning life after death, Jesus said: "I am the resurrection, and the life: he that believeth on me, though he die, yet shall he live; and **whosoever liveth and believeth on me shall never die**" (John 11:25-27, emp. added; cf. Revelation 6:9).

On one occasion while Saul was serving as king of Israel, the Philistines were amassing for war, "and when Saul saw the host of the Philistines, he was afraid, and his heart trembled greatly. And when Saul inquired of Jehovah, Jehovah answered him not" (1 Samuel 28:5). Saul, therefore—in violation of both God's law (Deuteronomy 18:10) and Israelite law (1 Samuel 28:9)—sought out a "medium" whom he hoped could "conjure up" Samuel's long-departed spirit (1 Samuel 28:3 records that "Samuel was dead, and all Israel had lamented him, and buried him in Ramah"), from whom he intended to seek counsel and comfort. The medium (known as "the witch of Endor") somehow contacted Samuel and quickly expressed her great fear at the sight of his disembodied spirit (1 Samuel 28:12). Samuel's response documents the fact that he did not relish a call back to this world: "Why hast thou disquieted me, to bring me up?" (28:15). If his immortal nature had been annihilated at his death, how, then, was he able to return (and even to complain about having to do so!)? Remember also that the spirits of Moses and Elijah not only joined Christ on a mountaintop in Palestine, but spoke to Him as well (Luke 9:30-31). If those spirits had ceased to exist at their owners' demise, how could they have done either?

That death is **not** total annihilation is clear from the words of Christ in John 5:28-29: "The hour cometh in which **all** that are in the tombs shall hear his voice, and **shall come forth**." In Luke 8:55, the account is recorded of Christ raising Jairus' daughter from the dead. The text reads as follows: "And her spirit (*pneuma*) returned, and she rose up immediately." If her spirit had been annihilated, it hardly could have "returned." And, at the risk of repeating myself, I would like to point out that Christ's discussion with the Sadducees (as recorded in Matthew 22) must not be overlooked in this context. On that occasion, the Lord quoted from Exodus 3:6 where God had said to Moses: "I am the God of Abraham, and the God of Isaac, and the God of Jacob." Yet as Christ went on to state (and as the Sadducees accepted as true), "God is not the God of the dead, but of the living" (22:32). Abraham, Isaac, and Jacob had been dead and in their graves for many years. Since we know from Christ's own words (and the inability of the Sadducees to offer any rebuttal whatsoever) that "God is not the God of the dead, but of the living," the point is obvious. Abraham, Isaac, and Jacob still must have been living. How so? The answer, of course, lies in the fact that while their bodies had died, their souls had not. And since their immortal nature lived on, it could not have been annihilated at their physical demise.

On one occasion during Jesus' earthly ministry, He discussed the importance of the soul with His disciples when He said: "For what shall it profit a man, if he shall gain the whole world, and lose his own soul? Or what shall a man give in exchange for his soul?" (Mark 8:36-37). Indeed, if the immortal nature of man is annihilated at the death of the body, what was Christ's point? Would not a man benefit by exchanging "annihilation" for the "whole world"?

What did Christ mean, then, when He warned: "Be not afraid of them that kill the body, but are not able to kill the soul: but rather fear him who is able to destroy both soul and body in hell" (Matthew 10:28)? As D.M. Lake observed, at the very least this "does imply a transcendental reality that is in some cases independent of the body. This seems to be the force of Jesus' statement [in] Matthew 10:28" (1976, 5:497). The "destruction" of which Jesus spoke was described by the apostle John as the "second death."

> The devil that deceived them was cast into the lake of fire and brimstone, where are also the beast and the false prophet; and they shall be tormented day and night **for ever and ever**.... And they were judged every man according to their works. And death and Hades were cast into the lake of fire. This is the second death, even the lake of fire (Revelation 20: 10-14, emp. added).

The eternal nature of that second death is evident from John's description of the wicked men who "shall drink of the wine of the wrath of God...and shall be tormented with fire and brimstone... and **the smoke of their torment goeth up for ever and ever; and they have no rest day and night**" (Revelation 14:10-11, emp. added).

Furthermore, the position that **only** the souls of the faithful are immortal, while those of "lost mankind" are annihilated at their physical death, is both terribly wrong and squarely at odds with the teachings of God's Word. The Scriptures plainly indicate that the disobedient are to be subjected to eternal punishment. In Matthew 25:46, Jesus said that the wicked would "go away into **eternal** punishment, but the righteous into eternal life." In his second epistle to the Christians at Thessalonica, Paul wrote specifically of "them that know not God" and "obey not the gospel of our Lord Jesus Christ" as those "who shall suffer punishment, even **eternal** destruction from the face of the Lord and from the glory of his might" (1:8-9). In addressing this point, Wayne Jackson wrote:

> There is, however, no punishment, or suffering, apart of consciousness. And yet, consciousness (knowledge, awareness) is a characteristic of the spirit (1 Cor. 2:11). One must necessarily infer, therefore, that the spirit (our soul) of man will exist in an eternal conscious state. Jesus once said regarding the traitor Judas that it would have been better for that man had he never been born (Mark 14:21). If Judas did not exist before his earthly life, and yet was to be annihilated eventually, how does the Lord's statement make sense? How is nonexistence better than non-existence? (1991, 27:19).

Additionally, the New Testament account (recorded in Luke 16) that describes Christ's discussion of two men who died under different circumstances merits serious consideration here. One, Lazarus, went to Abraham's bosom (a synonym for paradise). The other, an unnamed rich man, found himself in the portion of hades where, he exclaimed, "I am tormented in this flame" (16:22-24). Thus, the spirits of the two men, upon leaving their bodies, were alive, conscious, and even able to converse—although they were in two significantly different places. One was "comforted," one was "tormented," and a great gulf separated them (Luke 16:26). When the rich man requested that Lazarus be allowed to return to Earth to warn his five siblings not to follow him to such a terrible place, Abraham denied his request and responded: "If they hear not Moses and the prophets, neither will they be persuaded **if one rise from the dead**" (16:31). The key phrase here, of course, is "**if** one rise from the dead." Abraham did not say that such was **impossible**; rather, he indicated that it was **inappropriate**. There is a vast difference in the two. Lazarus **could** have returned, but was not allowed to do so. The simple fact of the matter is that Abraham's spirit, Lazarus' spirit, and the rich man's spirit all continued to exist beyond the grave. That the rich man found himself in a place (and state) of torment demolishes the idea that the souls of the wicked do not survive this life. That the souls of the wicked endure torment "for ever and ever, and have no rest day and night" (Revelation 14:10-11) demolishes the idea that the souls of the wicked are annihilated at any point following the death of the physical body.

Some, of course, have lamented that since the account in Luke 16 is "only" a parable, neither its message nor its implications may be taken literally. Such a notion, however, overlooks several important points regarding the nature of the text itself. First, notice that Christ referred to two of the three people **by name**. He mentioned both Abraham and Lazarus. As Tim Rice has observed:

> Those of the "parable" philosophy who disparage of an eternal hell's existence think that the rich man was a fictional character. They even ignore the fact that Lazarus' name is the **only proper name ever used in a parable** (if this be a parable). The key to the question of whether this account is strictly imagery is not just the consideration of the rich man or Lazarus, but Abraham! In Matthew 22:32, Jesus Himself claimed that Abraham continued to live in the spiritual realm. The narrative of the rich man and Lazarus places Lazarus in the presence of a literal Old Testament figure, Abraham, who was existing in some realm at that time (1987, 15[1]:6, emp. added, parenthetical comment in orig.).

Second, what, exactly, was Christ's point in relating this account? Was He attempting to deceive His hearers? Was He merely trying to "scare" them into submission to Heaven's will? Rice inquired:

> If the covetous do not really enter a realm where they can think, remember, and where they desire relief and are bound from salvation by a great gulf, why would Jesus con his hearers by discussing such a realm? The thrust of his narrative was to make his hearers avoid the position in which the rich man found himself, i.e., torment (15[1]:6).

Third, compare the condition of the rich man (as depicted by Jesus) with a similar passage also from the lips of the Lord. That covetous fellow described his horrible fate when he remarked: "I am tormented in this **flame**" (Luke 16:24, emp. added). In Matthew 25:41, the Lord said to those who were doomed: "Depart from me, ye cursed, into the eternal **fire** which is prepared for the devil and his angels." Acknowledging what Christ taught in Matthew 25, upon what basis could we draw the conclusion that He was teaching anything different in Luke 16? Was He not attempting to warn His hearers in both instances of a **literal** place where they (**literally!**) did not want to go?

Fourth, Jesus was not in the habit of using the "abstract" in His parables. Rather, He used substantive examples of events that were based on the everyday lives of His audience. When He presented for His audience's consideration the parables of the sower (Matthew 13:3-23), the tares (Matthew 13:24-30), or the lost coin (Luke 15:8-10), He was speaking about things that literally could have happened. Similarly, the things He discussed in the account of the rich man and Lazarus could have happened, since additional passages (e.g., Matthew 25, Jude 7, et al.) confirm the existence of a spirit realm such as the one described by the Lord in Luke 16. As Rice has noted: "Even if this account **were** a parable, the realm described is real" (15[1]:6, emp. in orig.). David Brown reasoned in a comparable fashion.

If, for the sake of argument, we admit that Luke 16:19-31 is a parable, annihilationists can get no solace from such an admission. Why is this the case? It is because all parables teach the truth. Now, what is the truth taught in the case of the "Rich man and Lazarus"? At death wicked men go into torment, and saved men into a place of comfort and rest. However, we do not admit that the passage is a parable. It bears no marks of a parable. Quite the contrary when the passage is analyzed. Please note that Jesus emphatically declared in no uncertain terms, "There was a certain rich man...." Question: Was there? Jesus answers, "There was...." Our Lord declared in no uncertain terms, "...there was a certain beggar named Lazarus...." Question: Was there? Jesus answers, "There was...." These two men lived on earth, died, and according to their conduct on earth, went to their respective places in the hadean world to await the end of the world, the resurrection, and the Judgment. Our Lord selected them to teach us a lesson regarding what transpired at death for the wicked and the blest (1999, pp. 170-171, emp. in orig.).

In a similar vein, Daniel Denham remarked:

The absurdity of the argument is also seen in that as a "parable," it would **still** teach the same thing: for a parable by definition draws the force of its imagery from the reality of the action or thing with which the similitude is made. It is the fact of and reality of sowing crops, for instance, that provides the substance for the Lord's lesson in the Parable of the Sower, and it was the common rites of matrimony upon which the Lord drew for emphasis and color in the Parable of the Wise and Foolish Virgins. To use the account of Luke 16:19ff. as a parable (granting for the moment it is such) would not be possible, except that first such a condition of things ascribed therein to Hades did, in fact, exist!

Another thing about parables is that the truth displayed by the story is always greater in degree and importance than the story itself due to the consequences entailed. Planting seeds indeed was necessary for one to have crops to harvest, but how much more important is the planting of the Word of God? It is far worse not to be ready when the Master comes, than to be one of the foolish maids who are left knocking at the barred door of an earthly wedding! It would be far worse to be in the spiritual plight of the Pharisees than to be the Rich Man in Hades (1998, p. 621, emp. and parenthetical comment in orig.).

Furthermore, there are several other important points that practically leap off the pages of Scripture, and that need to be examined in this particular context. First, those who argue for the ultimate annihilation of the souls of the wicked apparently have failed to comprehend both the abominable, repulsive nature of man's sin against God and the inestimable, unspeakable price Heaven paid to redeem rebellious man from its clutches. Second, they appear not to have grasped the necessity or purpose of punishment in God's grand plan. Third, they evidently have overlooked (or ignored) the straightforward teaching of the Scriptures on the eternal fate of the wicked. And fourth, they seem to have missed the telling fact that every single argument made against the existence of an eternal hell likewise can be leveled against the existence of an eternal heaven. Each of these deserves close scrutiny.

CHAPTER 9

THE ORIGIN, NATURE, AND DESTINY OF THE SOUL—[PART IV]

Of all the living beings that dwell on planet Earth, one solitary creature was made "in the image of God" (Genesis 1:26-27). Mankind was not created in the physical image of God, of course, because God, as a Spirit Being, has no physical image (John 4:24; Luke 24:39; Matthew 16:17). Rather, mankind was fashioned in the spiritual, rational, emotional, and volitional image of God (Ephesians 4:24; John 5:39-40; 7:17; Joshua 24:15; Isaiah 7:15). Humans are superior to all other creatures on Earth. No other living being has been given the faculties, capacities, potential, capabilities, or worth that God instilled in each man and woman. Indeed, humankind is the peak, the pinnacle, the apex of God's creation. In its lofty position as the zenith of God's creative genius, mankind was endowed with certain responsibilities. Men and women were to be the stewards of the entire Earth (Genesis 1:28). They were to glorify God in their daily existence (Isaiah 43:7). And, they were to consider it their "whole duty" to serve the Creator faithfully throughout their brief sojourn on this planet (Ecclesiastes 12:13).

Unfortunately, however, as the first man and woman, Adam and Eve used their volitional powers—and the free moral agency based on those powers—to rebel against their Maker. Finite man made some horribly evil choices, and thereafter found himself in the spiritual state designated biblically as "sin." The Old Testament not only pictures in vivid fashion the entrance of sin into the world through Adam and Eve (Genesis 3), but also alludes to the ubiquity of sin throughout the human race when it says: "There is no man that sinneth not" (1 Kings 8:46). Throughout its thirty-nine books, the Old Covenant discusses over and over sin's presence amidst humanity, as well as its destructive consequences. The great prophet Isaiah reminded God's people:

> Behold, Jehovah's hand is not shortened that it cannot save; neither his ear heavy that it cannot hear: but your iniquities have separated between you and your God, and your sins have hid his face from you, so that he will not hear (Isaiah 59: 1-2).

The New Testament is no less clear in its assessment. The apostle John wrote: "Every one that doeth sin doeth also lawlessness; and sin is lawlessness" (1 John 3:4). Thus, sin is defined as the act of transgressing God's law. In fact, Paul observed that "where there is no law, neither is there transgression" (Romans 4:15). Had there been no law, there would have been no sin. But God **had** instituted divine law. And mankind freely chose to transgress that law. Paul reaffirmed the Old Testament concept of the universality of sin when he stated that "all have sinned, and fall short of the glory of God" (Romans 3:23).

As a result, mankind's predicament became serious indeed. The Old Testament prophet Ezekiel lamented: "The soul that sinneth, it shall die" (18:20a). Once again, the New Testament writers reaffirmed such a concept. Paul wrote: "Therefore, as through one man sin entered into the world, and death through sin; and so death passed unto all men, for that all sinned" (Romans 5:12). He then added that "the wages of sin is death" (Romans 6:23). Years later,

James would write: "But each man is tempted when he is drawn away by his own lust, and enticed. Then the lust, when it hath conceived, beareth sin: and the sin, when it is full-grown, bringeth forth death" (James 1:15-16). As a result of mankind's sin, God placed the curse of death on the human race. While all men and women must die **physically** as a result of Adam and Eve's sin, each person dies **spiritually** for his or her own sins. Each person is responsible for himself, spiritually speaking. The theological position which states that we inherit the guilt of Adam's sin is utterly false. We do not inherit the **guilt**; we inherit the **consequences**. In Ezekiel 18: 20, the prophet went on to say:

> The son shall not bear the iniquity of the father, neither shall the father bear the iniquity of the son: the righteousness of the righteous shall be upon him, and the wickedness of the wicked shall be upon him.

The reality of sin is all around us, and its effects permeate every aspect of our lives. Disease and death were introduced into this world as a direct consequence of man's sin (Genesis 2:17; Romans 5:12). Many features of the Earth's surface that allow for such tragedies as earthquakes, tornadoes, hurricanes, violent thunderstorms, etc., can be traced directly to the Great Flood of Noah's day (which came as the result of man's sin; Genesis 6:5ff.). The communication problems that man experiences, due to the multiplicity of human languages, are traceable to ambitious rebellion on the part of our ancestors (Genesis 11:1-9). Man generally is without the peace of mind for which his heart longs (just consider the number of psychiatrists in the Yellow Pages!). Isaiah opined: "They have made them crooked paths; whosoever goeth therein doth not know peace" (59:8; cf. 57:21). By sinning, man created a yawning chasm between himself and God (Isaiah 59:2). In his intriguing book, *Created in God's Image*, Anthony Hoekema addressed this chasm when he wrote:

Sin is always related to God and his will. Many people consider what Christians call **sin** mere imperfection—the kind of imperfection that is a normal aspect of human nature. "Nobody's perfect," "everybody makes mistakes," "you're only human," and similar statements express this kind of thinking. Over against this we must insist that, according to Scripture, sin is always a transgression of the law of God.... Sin is therefore fundamentally opposition to God, rebellion against God, which roots in hatred to God.... [T]hough fallen man still bears the image of God, he now functions wrongly as an image-bearer of God. This, in fact, makes sin all the more heinous. Sin is a perverse way of using God-given and God-reflecting powers (1986, pp. 169,171, emp. in orig.).

Earlier, in chapter 3 of this book, I quoted British writer C.S. Lewis, who expressed this point in a vividly poignant manner via a personal letter to one of his friends. Lewis wrote:

[I]ndeed the only way in which I can make real to myself what theology teaches about the heinousness of sin is to remember that every sin is the distortion of an energy breathed into us.... We poison the wine as He decants it into us; murder a melody He would play with us as the instrument. We caricature the self-portrait He would paint. Hence all sin, whatever else it is, is sacrilege (1966, pp. 71-72).

Unless remedied, this rebellion, this sacrilege, will result in man's being unable to escape what the Son of God Himself called the "judgment of hell" (Matthew 23:33)—the end result of which is eternal separation from God throughout all eternity (Revelation 21:8; 22:18-19).

The key phrase in the above discussion, of course, is **unless remedied**. The question then becomes: Has Heaven provided such a remedy? Thankfully, the answer is "yes." One thing is certain, however. God had no **obligation** to provide a means of salvation for the ungrateful creature that so haughtily turned away from Him, His law, and His beneficence. The Scriptures make this apparent when they discuss the fact that angels sinned (2 Peter 2:4; Jude 6), and yet "not to angels doth he give help, but he giveth help to the seed of Abraham" (Hebrews 2:16). The rebellious creatures that once inhabited the heavenly portals were not provided a redemptive plan. But man was! Little wonder, then, that the psalmist was moved to ask: "What is **man**, that thou art mindful of **him**?" (8:4, emp. added).

Why would God go to such great lengths for mankind when His mercy was not even extended to the angels that once surrounded His throne? Whatever answers may be proffered, there can be little doubt that the Creator's efforts on behalf of sinful man are the direct result of pure, unadulterated love. As a God of love (1 John 4: 8), He acted out of a genuine concern, not for His own desires, but rather for those of His creation. And let us be forthright in acknowledging that Jehovah's love for mankind was completely **undeserved**. The Scriptures make it clear that God decided to offer salvation—our "way home"—even though we were ungodly, sinners, and enemies (note the specific use of those terms in Romans 5: 6-10). The apostle John rejoiced in the fact that: "Herein is love, not that we loved God, but that He loved us" (1 John 4:10). God's love is universal, and thus not discriminatory in any fashion (John 3:16). He would have **all men** to be saved (1 Timothy 2:4)—**if they would be** (John 5:40)—for He is not willing that **any** should perish (2 Peter 3:9). And, further, Deity's love is unquenchable (read Romans 8:35-39 and be thrilled!). Only man's wanton rejection of God's love can put him beyond the practical appropriation of Heaven's offer of mercy and grace.

Did God understand that man would rebel, and stand in eventual need of salvation from the perilous state of his own sinful condition? The Scriptures make it clear that He did. Inspiration speaks of a divine plan being set in place even "before the foundation of the world" (Ephesians 1:4; 1 Peter 1:20). After man's initial fall, humankind dredged itself deeper and deeper into wickedness. When approximately a century of preaching by the righteous Noah failed to bring mankind back to God, Jehovah sent a global flood to purge the Earth (Genesis 6-8). From the faithful Noah, several generations later, the renowned Abraham descended, and, through him, the Hebrew nation. From that nation, the Messiah—God-incarnate—one day would come.

Some four centuries following Abraham, the Lord, through His servant Moses, gave to the Hebrews the written revelation that came to be known as the Law of Moses. Basically, this law-system had three purposes. First, its intent was to define sin and sharpen Israel's awareness of it. To use Paul's expression in the New Testament, the Law made "sin exceeding sinful" (Romans 7:7,13). Second, the law was designed to show man that he could not save himself via his own effort, or as a result of his own merit. The Law demanded perfect obedience, and since no mere man could keep it perfectly, each stood condemned (Galatians 3:10-11). Thus, the Law underscored the need for a **Savior**—Someone Who could do for us what we were unable to do for ourselves. Third, in harmony with that need, the Old Testament pointed the way toward the coming of the Messiah. He was to be Immanuel—"God with us" (Matthew 1:23). Jehovah left no stone unturned in preparing the world for the coming of the One Who was to save mankind.

One of God's attributes, as expressed within Scripture, is that He is an absolutely **holy** Being (cf. Isaiah 6:3 and Revelation 4:8). As such, He simply cannot ignore the fact of sin. The prophet Habakkuk wrote: "Your eyes are too pure to look on evil; you cannot tolerate wrong" (1:13). Yet, another of God's attributes is that He is absolutely **just**. Righteousness and justice are the very foundation of His throne (Psalm 89:14). The irresistible truth arising from the fact that God is both holy and just is **that sin must be punished!** If God were a cold, vengeful Creator (as some infidels wrongly assert), He simply could have banished mankind from His divine presence forever, and that would have been the end of the matter. But the truth is, He is not that kind of God! Our Creator is loving (1 John 4:8), and "rich in mercy" (Ephesians 2:4). When justice is meted out, we **receive what we deserve**. When mercy is extended, we **do not receive what we deserve**. When grace is bestowed, we **receive what we do not deserve**.

Thus, the problem became: How could a loving, merciful God pardon a wickedly rebellious humanity? Paul addressed this very matter in Romans 3. How could God be just, and yet a justifier of sinful man? The answer: He would find someone to stand in for us —someone to receive **His** retribution, and to bear **our** punishment. That "someone" would be Jesus Christ, the Son of God. He would become a substitutionary sacrifice, and personally would pay the price for human salvation. Paul wrote: "Him who knew no sin he made to be sin on our behalf that we might become the righteousness of God in him" (2 Corinthians 5:21). In one of the most moving tributes ever written to the Son of God, Isaiah summarized the situation as follows:

> Surely he hath borne our griefs, and carried our sorrows; yet we did esteem him stricken, smitten of God, and afflicted. But he was wounded for our transgressions, he was bruised for our iniquities; the chastisement of our peace was upon him; and with his stripes we are healed. All we like sheep have gone astray; we have turned everyone to his own way; and Jehovah hath laid on him the iniquity of us all.... He bare the sin of many, and made intercession for the transgressors (53:4-6,12).

Paul reminded the first-century Christians in Rome:

> Scarcely for a righteous man will one die: for peradventure for the good man some one would even dare to die. But God commendeth his own love toward us, in that, while we were yet sinners, Christ died for us (Romans 5:7-8).

Jehovah's intent was to extend grace and mercy freely—on the basis of the redemptive life and death of His Son (Romans 3:24ff.). Though part of the Godhead, Christ took upon Himself the form of a man. He came to Earth as a human being (John 1:1-4,14; Philippians 2:5-11; 1 Timothy 3:16), and thus shared our full nature and life-experience. He even was tempted in all points exactly as we are, yet He never yielded to that temptation and sinned (Hebrews 4:15).

There was no happy solution to the justice/mercy dilemma. There was no way by which God could remain just (justice demands that the wages of sin be paid), and yet save His Son from death. Christ was abandoned to the cross so that mercy could be extended to sinners who stood condemned (Galatians 3:10). God could not save sinners by fiat—upon the ground of mere authority alone —without violating His own attribute of divine justice. Paul discussed God's response to this problem in Romans 3:24-26:

> Being justified freely by his grace through the redemption that is in Christ Jesus; whom God set forth to be a propitiation, through faith, in his blood...for the showing of his righteousness...that he might himself be just and the justifier of him that hath faith in Jesus.

Man's salvation was no arbitrary arrangement. God did not decide merely to consider man a sinner, and then determine to save him upon a principle of mercy. Sin placed man in a state of antagonism toward God. Sinners are condemned because they have violated God's law, and because God's justice cannot permit Him to ignore sin. Sin could be forgiven only as a result of the vicarious death of God's Son. Because sinners are redeemed by the sacrifice of Christ, and not because of their own righteousness, they are sanctified by the mercy and grace of God. Our sins were borne by Jesus on the cross. Since Christ was tested, tempted, and tried (Isaiah 28:16), and yet found perfect (2 Corinthians 5:21; 1 Peter 2: 22), He alone could satisfy Heaven's requirement for justice. He alone could serve as the "propitiation" (i.e., an atoning sacrifice) for our sins. Just as the lamb without blemish that was used in Old Testament sacrifices could be the (temporary) propitiation for the Israelites' sins, so the "Lamb of God" (John 1:29) could be the (permanent) propitiation for mankind's sins.

In the death of the Lamb of God, divine justice was satisfied; in the gift of Christ, Heaven's mercy and grace were extended. When humans became the recipients of heaven's grace, the unfathomable happened. God—our Justifiable Accuser—became our Vindicator.

He extended to us His wonderful love, as expressed by His mercy and grace. He paid our debt so that we, like undeserving Barabbas (Matthew 27:26), might be set free. In this fashion, God could be just and, at the same time, Justifier of all who believe in and obey His Son. By refusing to extend mercy to Jesus as He hung on the cross, God was able to extend mercy to mankind—**if** mankind was willing to submit in obedience to His commands.

The Necessity and Purpose of Punishment

But what if God does not exist? Or what if He does, but mankind **is unwilling to submit to Him**? What then? First, of course, if there is no Creator, if everything ultimately springs from natural causes and this life is all there is, what would it matter **how** man acts? If he is merely the last in a long chain of evolutionary accidents, why should his conduct be of any concern at all? The late, eminent evolutionist of Harvard University, George Gaylord Simpson, considered this point and concluded:

> Discovery that the universe apart from man or before his coming lacks and lacked any purpose or plan has the inevitable corollary that the workings of the universe cannot provide any automatic, universal, eternal, or absolute ethical criteria of right and wrong (1951, p. 180).

Matter—in and of itself—is impotent to evolve any sense of moral consciousness. If there is no purpose in the Universe, as Simpson and others have asserted, then there is no purpose to morality or ethics. But the concept of a purposeless morality, or a purposeless ethic, is irrational. Unbelief therefore must contend, and, in fact, does contend, that there is no ultimate standard of moral/ethical truth, and that, at best, morality and ethics are relative and situational. [Morality is the character of being in accord with the principles or standards of right conduct. Ethics generally is viewed as the system or code by which attitudes and actions are determined to be either right or wrong.] That being the case, who could ever suggest (correctly) that someone else's conduct was "wrong," or that a man "ought" or "ought not" to do thus and so? The simple fact of the matter is that infidelity cannot explain the origin of morality and ethics. If there is no God, man exists in an environment where "anything goes." Russian novelist Fyodor Dostoevsky, in *The Brothers Karamazov* (1880), had one of his characters (Ivan) say that in the absence of God, everything is allowed. French existential philosopher Jean Paul Sartre later wrote:

> Everything is indeed permitted if God does not exist, and man is in consequence forlorn, for he cannot find anything to depend upon either within or outside himself.... Nor, on the other hand, if God does not exist, are we provided with any values or commands that could legitimize our behavior (1961, p. 485).

Sartre contended that **whatever** one chooses to do is right, and that value is attached to the choice itself so that "we can never choose evil" (1966, p. 279). Thus, it is impossible to formulate a system of ethics by which one objectively can differentiate "right" from "wrong." Agnostic British philosopher Bertrand Russell admitted as much when he wrote in his *Autobiography:*

> We feel that the man who brings widespread happiness at the expense of misery to himself is a better man than the man who brings unhappiness to others and happiness to himself. I do not know of any rational ground for this view, or, perhaps, for the somewhat more rational view that whatever the majority desires (called utilitarian hedonism) is preferable to what the minority desires. These are truly ethical problems but I do not know of any way in which they can be solved except by politics or war. All that I can find to say on this subject is that **an ethical opinion can only be defended by an ethical axiom, but, if the axiom is not accepted, there is no way of reaching a rational conclusion** (1969, 3: 29, emp. added).

If there is no objective ethical axiom—no moral right or wrong —the concept of violating any kind of "law" becomes ludicrous, and punishment therefore would be futile. If no law or standard has been violated, with what justification may punishment then be enacted?

Yet the concepts of moral right or wrong, and ethical obligation, are experienced by all men to a greater or lesser degree. Although Simpson argued that "man is the result of a purposeless and materialistic process that did not have him in mind," he was forced to admit that

> good and evil, right and wrong, concepts irrelevant in nature except from the human viewpoint, become **real and pressing features** of the whole cosmos as viewed morally because **morals arise only in man** (1951, p. 179, emp. added).

Some have objected, of course, and have suggested that there are serious differences in various cultures regarding what is perceived as right and wrong. Charles Baylis, in an article on "Conscience" in *The Encyclopedia of Philosophy,* mentioned this objection and called attention to such differences as those between conscientious objectors to war versus volunteers, and cannibals versus vegetarians (1967, 1/2:190). This misses the point, however. C.S. Lewis observed that even though there may be differences between moralities, those differences have not "amounted to anything like a total difference" (1952, p. 19). They clearly would not, as Baylis suggested, "differ radically." As Lewis went on to remark, a totally different morality would consist of something like (to choose just two examples) a country where people were admired for running away from battle, or a person who felt proud for double-crossing those who had been kindest to him. Yet as Thomas C. Mayberry noted: "There is broad agreement that lying, promise breaking, killing, and so on, are generally wrong" (1970, 154:113). Atheistic philosopher Kai Nielsen even admitted that to inquire, "Is murder evil?," is to ask a self-answering question (1973, p. 16). Why is this the case? In his book, *Does God Exist?*, A.E. Taylor wrote:

> But it is an undeniable fact that men do not merely love and procreate, they also hold that there is a difference between right and wrong; there are things which they **ought** to do and other things which they **ought not** to do. Different groups

of men, living under different conditions and in different ages, may disagree widely on the question whether a certain thing belongs to the first or the second of these classes. They may draw the line between right and wrong in a different place, but at least they all agree that there is such a line to be drawn (1945, p. 83).

Paul wrote in Romans 2:14-15:

For when the Gentiles, which have not the law, do by nature the things contained in the law, these, having not the law, are a law unto themselves: which show the work of the law written in their hearts, their conscience also bearing witness, and their thoughts meanwhile accusing or else excusing one another.

Although the Gentiles (unlike their Jewish counterparts) had no **written** law, they nevertheless had a law—a **moral** law—and they felt an obligation to live up to that law. Their conscience testified in regard to certain moral obligations in agreement with the law—urging them to do right and discouraging them from doing wrong.

But why was this the case? How is it that "morals arise only in man" and thus become "real and pressing features" of the Cosmos? Why did the Gentiles feel an obligation to uphold a certain ethical law? Who, or what, was the source of that law "written in their hearts"? The answer to such questions, of course, can be found only in the acknowledgment that the Creator of the Cosmos and the Author of that ethical law are one and the same—God!

Because of Who He is (Sovereign Creator), and because of what He has done (redeemed sinful man), He has the right to establish the moral/ethical laws that men are to follow, and to establish the punishment for any violation of those laws that might occur. I repeat: If there were no law, then there could be no sin—since where there is no objective standard there can be no right or wrong. If there is no sin, then there is no moral responsibility incumbent upon man. But if no moral responsibility is required of us, why, then, do we find courts and prisons spanning the globe?

Punishment for infractions of this moral/ethical code, however, can take any one of three forms—preventative, remedial, or retributive. Preventative punishment is a penalty exacted in order to deter others from acting in a similar unlawful fashion (e.g., soldiers who refused to obey a legitimate order from a superior officer being court-martialed). Remedial punishment is intended as a penalty to evoke improvement in the person(s) being punished (e.g., an employer requiring an employee to remain after his shift is over because of being a slacker on the job). Retributive punishment is a penalty meted out because, quite simply, it is deserved (e.g., a student being suspended from school for verbally abusing a teacher).

All three types of punishment are biblical in nature. Preventative punishment was evident in the deaths of Ananias and Sapphira after they lied about their donation to the church (Acts 5; note specifically verse 11: "And great fear came upon the whole church, and upon all that heard these things."). Remedial punishment can be observed in passages like Hebrews 12:6-7, where the writer told the saints:

> For whom the Lord loveth he chasteneth, and scourgeth every son whom he receiveth. It is for chastening that ye endure; God dealeth with you as with sons; for what son is there whom his father chasteneth not?

Retributive punishment is evident in God's instructions to Noah after the Flood: "Whoso sheddeth man's blood, by man shall his blood be shed, for in the image of God made he man." Granted, at times the various types of punishment may (and often do) overlap. Forcing disobedient soldiers to endure a court-martial, and then sending them to prison, not only will have a beneficial effect on others (preventative punishment), but hopefully will deter those who broke the law from ever doing so again (remedial punishment).

In employing retributive punishment, however, God will "pay back" the wicked. Paul, in referring to God's words in Leviticus 19:18 and Deuteronomy 32:35, reminded the first-century Christians who were undergoing severe persecution: " 'Vengeance is mine;

I will repay,' saith the Lord" (Romans 12:19). In writing his second epistle to the Christians at Thessalonica, Paul assured them that God was just, and that

> It is a righteous thing with God to recompense affliction to them that afflict you, and to you that are afflicted rest with us, at the revelation of the Lord Jesus from heaven with the angels of his power in flaming fire, rendering vengeance to them that know not God, and to them that obey not the gospel of our Lord Jesus: who shall suffer punishment, even eternal destruction from the face of the Lord and from the glory of his might (2 Thessalonians 1:6-9).

When the writer of the book of Hebrews cried out, "It is a fearful thing to fall into the hands of the living God" (10:31), he was attempting to warn us against having to endure the retributive punishment of God. The famous British preacher, Charles Spurgeon, once said:

> When men talk of a little hell, it is because they think they have only a little sin, and they believe in a little Savior. But when you get a great sense of sin, you want a great Savior, and feel that if you do not have him, you will fall into a great destruction, and suffer a great punishment at the hands of the great God (as quoted in Carter, 1988, p. 36).

Those who suggest that no "good God" ever could condemn people's souls to eternal punishment obviously have failed to grasp the "great sense of sin" of which Spurgeon spoke. Nor do they understand the horrible price Heaven paid to offer sanctification, justification, and redemption to sinful mankind. As Paul stated the matter in Romans 5:10:

> But God commendeth his own love toward us, in that, while we were yet sinners, Christ died for us. Much more then, being now justified by his blood, shall we be saved from the wrath of God through him. For if, while we were enemies, we were reconciled to God through the death of his Son, much more, being reconciled, shall we be saved by his life.

As Jesus hung on the cross dying for sins that He did not commit —in order to pay a debt that He did not owe, and a debt that we could not pay—He raised His voice and implored: "My God, my

God, why hast thou forsaken me?" (Matthew 27:46). One writer described Christ's words as "among the most shocking in Scripture" (Peterson, 1995, p. 214). Why? The word "forsaken" is defined as to "abandon, desert," and is used here of "being forsaken by God" (Bauer, et al., 1979, p. 215). Imagine the Son of God—abandoned, deserted, and forsaken **by His own Father** in order to pay the price for **our** sins!

Christ suffered the wrath of God so that mankind would not have to endure that wrath. In the Garden of Gethsemane, as Peter drew his sword to defend his Lord, Jesus turned to him and asked: "The cup which the Father hath given me, shall I not drink it?" (John 18:11). What, exactly, was this "cup"? And why did it bring such anguish to Christ's soul? The Old Testament provides the answer. In Jeremiah 25:15ff., the weeping prophet wrote:

> For thus saith Jehovah, the God of Israel, unto me: "Take this cup of the wine of wrath at my hand, and cause all the nations, to whom I send thee, to drink it. And they shall drink, and reel to and fro, and be mad, because of the sword that I will send among them."

When the evil nations to whom Jeremiah spoke drank of the "cup of God's wrath," they were destroyed—never to rise again—because God's anger at their evil ways was so intense (vss. 26-27). The psalmist referred to the same cup of wrath when he wrote:

> But God is the judge: He putteth down one, and lifteth up another. For in the hand of Jehovah there is a cup, and the wine foameth; it is full of mixture, and he poureth out of the same. Surely the dregs thereof, all the wicked of the earth shall drain them, and drink them (75:7-9).

Peterson observed in regard to these two passages:

> This is the cup from which our holy Savior recoiled. A cup for "all the wicked of the earth" (Ps. 75:8), this cup, full of the wine of God's wrath (Jer. 25:15), should never have touched Jesus' sinless hands. That is why he was "overwhelmed with sorrow to the point of death" (Matt. 26:38) and prayed three times for the Father to take it away. On the cross the

son of God drank to the dregs the cup of God's wrath for
sinners like you and me.... And he did so willingly! (1995,
p. 216).

At the cross, we catch a glimpse of the enormity of our sin and
its offense to God. Christ—forsaken by His Father—suffered the retributive punishment that should have been ours. We deserved it;
He did not. At the cross, we stare deeply into the vast chasm of human sin, and within it we see nothing but that which is vile and dark.
But it is also at the cross where we stare deeply into the mysterious,
unfathomable, incomprehensible love of God, and within it see a
holy and righteous Sovereign Who, while abandoning and desert-
ing His own Son, stubbornly refused to abandon and desert us. As
Peterson went on to say:

> Viewed in the light of the Father's everlasting love for him,
> Jesus' cry of abandonment in Matthew 27:46 is almost im-
> possible to understand. **The eternal relations between
> Father and Son were temporarily interrupted!** The
> preceding verse hints at this when it tells us that darkness
> covered the land of Israel from noon until 3 p.m.; **a pro-
> found judgment was taking place** (1995, p. 214, emp.
> added).

Elizabeth Browning set these eternal truths into poignant poetic
form when she wrote:

> Yea, once Immanuel's orphaned cry his universe hath shaken.
> It went up single, echoless, "My God, I am forsaken!"
> It went up from the Holy's lips amid His lost creation,
> That, of the lost, no son should use those words of desolation.

Once again, I say: Those who claim not to understand how God
could send sinful men into eternal punishment simply do not comprehend either the abominable, repulsive nature of man's rebellious crime against God or the inestimable, unspeakable price that
Heaven paid to redeem rebellious man from Satan's clutches. Guy
N. Woods wrote:

> Those who would palliate the punishment or seek to short-
> en its duration by pointing to the love, long-suffering, and
> patience of God, ignore other attributes of deity, and disre-

gard the fact that his goodness is evidenced just as much in his characteristics of justice and truth as in his love and long-suffering. As a matter of fact, love and long-suffering are valid only when the principles of justice and truth are also operative in the divine government. To promise punishment and then to unilaterally cancel it is impossible to One who is not only the God of love but also the God of truth! He will not do so because he cannot do so, and maintain his character. God cannot impeach his own veracity, since "it is impossible for God to lie" (Hebrews 6:18). Were he to cease to be just and truthful, he would cease to be good. The effort to emphasize some of the attributes of the great Jehovah to the neglect of others, or to array some against others, is to compromise the divine character (1985a, 127:278).

I must confess that in my most private and contemplative moments, I have reflected on the meaning and seriousness of the moving passage found in Hebrews 10:28-29.

A man that hath set at nought Moses' law dieth without compassion on the word of two or three witnesses. Of **how much sorer punishment**, think ye, shall he be judged worthy, **who hath trodden under foot the Son of God**, and hath counted the blood of the covenant wherewith he was sanctified an unholy thing, and hath done despite unto the Spirit of grace?

And in those same private, contemplative moments, I confess that I also have wondered (viewing this matter from what is, admittedly, a purely human standpoint—as the proud, earthly father of two precious, irreplaceable, sons): If I gave "only" one of **my** sons' lives (God had "only" one!) in order to save a wicked wretch who was my enemy in the first place—and that enemy then not only spurned the unique, exquisite, priceless gift of my son's blood, but mocked the supreme sacrifice that both my son and I had gone to such great lengths to make on his behalf—what kind of retributive punishment would **I** devise for such a one?

CHAPTER 10

THE ORIGIN, NATURE, AND DESTINY OF THE SOUL—[PART V]

As one examines the various means through which men have attempted to circumvent the idea of the existence of hell, it is evident that there is no shortage of such theories. From universalism on the one hand to annihilationism on the other, men have done their best to disgorge the concept of eternal punishment from their minds. Some even have suggested that the only "hell" men experience is that of their own making here on Earth. Such a notion is standard fare in the vernacular of our day. For example, people speak of the fact that "war is hell." They complain that, as they endure the vicissitudes of life, they are "going through hell." As John Benton noted:

> When people's personal lives go wrong, when they get caught up in bitterness and anger, when perhaps there is vicious language and even violence in the family home, we sometimes speak of people creating "hell on earth...." The psychological agony of guilt or the deep pain of bereavement are spoken of colloquially as being "like hell" (Benton, 1985, p. 42).

In his book, *Hell and Salvation*, Leslie Woodson observed: "The reference to man's hard lot in life as 'going through hell' has become so commonplace that the modern mind has satisfied itself with the assumption that hell is nothing more" (1973, p. 30).

Believe whatever we will, say whatever we please: the simple fact is that none of these descriptions fits the biblical description of hell. And certainly, Jesus never spoke of hell in such a fashion. When He warned us to "fear Him who is able to destroy both soul and body in hell" (Matthew 10:28) and spoke of those who "shall go away into **eternal** punishment" (Matthew 25:46), He was not referring to some sort of temporary earthly misery resulting from war, bereavement, or the like. Furthermore, the idea that "hell" is represented by whatever "pangs of guilt" we may experience from time to time during this life is a foolish assertion indeed. As one writer summarized the matter:

> [I]t is a well-known fact that the more one sins the more callous he may become until he has "seared his conscience as with a hot iron" (II Tim. 4:2). **If this theory is true then it follows that the righteous suffer greater punishment than the wicked**. A wicked person can destroy his "hell" by searing his conscience. However, a righteous man will be sensitive to sin and will feel the pangs of guilt when he sins. And, the more devout he is the more sensitive he is about sin. Again, **if this theory is true the worse a man is the less he will suffer**. To escape hell one simply would plunge himself into unrestrained sin and harden his heart. Obviously this doctrine is false (Ealey, 1984, p. 22, emp. added).

As the book of Job makes clear, on occasion the righteous do suffer terribly, while the wicked seem to prosper mightily. At times, the psalmist even grew envious of the prosperity of the wicked, and wondered if it really was to his benefit to strive to be righteous (Psalm 73:2-5,12-14). Absolute justice is a rarity in the here and now, but is guaranteed at the Judgment yet to come (Matthew 25:31-46). We would do well to remember that the "Judge of all the Earth" **will** "do that which is right" (Genesis 18:25). We also should remember:

> It is significant that the most solemn utterances on this subject fall from the lips of Christ himself. In the New Testament as a whole there is a deep reserve on the nature of the punishment of the lost, though of course the act of final judgement is prominent. But with Christ himself the statements are much more explicit (Carson, 1978, p. 14).

The urgent question then becomes: What did Christ and His inspired writers teach regarding hell? What does the Bible say on this extremely important topic?

The word "hell" (which occurs 23 times in the King James Version of the Bible) translates three different terms from the Greek New Testament—*hades, tartaros,* and *géenna.* While each has a different meaning, on occasion the KJV translators chose to translate each as "hell." Was this an error on their part? Considering the way the word was used in 1611, no, it was not. Robert Taylor addressed this point when he wrote:

> Hell in 1611 referred to the place of the unseen, the place that was beyond human eyesight, the place that was covered. In that day men who covered roofs were called hellers—they put coverings on buildings or covered them (1985, p. 160).

According to Brown, "this was a correct rendering in 1611 because the word 'Hell' in Elizabethan English also meant an unseen place (e.g., Matthew 16:18; Luke 16:23; Acts 2:27,31; et al.)" [1999, p. 171].

The actual origin of the Greek *hades* (transliterated as hades in the English) is not well known. Some scholars have suggested that it derives from two roots: *a* (a negative prefix depicting "not") and *idein* (a word meaning "to see"). Therefore, according to *Thayer's Greek-English Lexicon, hades* would evoke the idea of "not to be seen" (1958, p. 11). W.E. Vine advocated the view that *hades* meant "all receiving" (1991, p. 368). The exact meaning of the term, however, must be determined via an examination of the context in which it is used. *Hades* occurs eleven times in the Greek New Testament. On ten occasions (Matthew 11:23; 16:18; Luke

10:15; 16:23; Acts 2:27,31; Revelation 1:18; 6:8; 20:13-14) the KJV translates it as "hell." [In such occurrences, most recent versions (e.g., the ASV, NKJV, et al.) transliterate the Greek as "hades."] Once (1 Corinthians 15:55), *hades* is translated as "grave."

The Greek *tartaros* is the noun (translated into English via the Latin *tartarus*, cf. ASV footnote on 2 Peter 2:4) from which the verb *tartarosas* (aorist participle of *tartaroo*) derives. Ralph Earle observed that the term signified "the dark abode of the wicked dead" (1986, p. 447). Originally, it seems to have carried the idea of a "deep place"—a connotation that it retains in both Job 40:15 and 41:23 in the Septuagint. The Greek poet Homer wrote in his *Iliad* of "dark Tartarus...the deepest pit" (8.13). The word *tartaros* occurs only once in the Greek New Testament (2 Peter 2:4), where it is translated "hell" ("God spared not angels...but cast them down to hell"). In writing of this singular occurrence, R.C.H. Lenski remarked: "The verb does not occur elsewhere in the Bible; it is seldom found in other writings. The noun 'Tartarus' occurs three times in the LXX [Septuagint—BT], but there is no corresponding Hebrew term. The word is of pagan origin..." (1966, p. 310).

The Greek *géenna* is the predominant term used in the New Testament to depict hell. The word "represents the Aramaic expression *ge hinnom*, meaning 'Valley of Hinnom' (Neh. 11:30; cf. Josh. 15:8), and for this reason the word is commonly transliterated into English as *Gehenna* " (Workman, 1993, p. 496). Several sites have been suggested for the "valley of Hinnom" (or Valley of the Son of Hinnom, Vos, 1956, 2:1183; Earle, 1986, p. 447), but most authorities now believe that it was located on the south side of Jerusalem. In the Bible, the valley is mentioned first in Joshua 15:8. Centuries later, the apostates of Judah used it as a place to offer child sacrifices to the pagan god Molech (2 Chronicles 28:3; 33:6). When good king Josiah ascended the throne and overthrew idolatry, he "defiled" the place called Topheth (a name signifying something to be abhorred and spit upon) in the Valley of Hinnom (2 Kings 23:10). The valley came to be reviled for the evil that had occurred there, and eventually turned into a smoldering garbage dump that served the entire city of Jerusalem. Years later, it even was used as a potter's field (as is evident from the many rock tombs that are known to rest at its lower end). A perpetual fire was kept burning to prevent the spread of contagion, and worms and maggots performed their unseen, unsavory tasks amidst the debris and decay (see Morey, 1984, p. 87; cf. Foster, 1971, pp. 764-765). J. Arthur Hoyles graphically described the grisly goings-on:

> Here the fires burned day and night, destroying the garbage and putrefying the atmosphere from the smell of rotten flesh or decaying vegetation. In time of war the carcasses of vanquished enemies might mingle with the refuse, thus furnishing patriotic writers with a clue as to the destiny of their own persecutors. They were destined to be destroyed in the fires that were never quenched (1957, p. 118).

By the second century B.C., the term *géenna* began to appear in Jewish literature as a symbolic designation for the place of unending, eternal punishment of the wicked dead. As Gary Workman noted:

> It is natural, therefore, that when the New Testament opens *Gehenna* would be the primary term for hell. It is so recorded eleven times from the lips of Jesus and is also used once by James. It was not to the literal Valley of Hinnom outside Jerusalem that they referred, nor anything similar to it, but rather to "the *Gehenna* of fire" in a realm beyond the grave. Both Jewish and Christian historians confirm that the prevailing view of Jews at the time of Christ (except the Sadducees who denied even the resurrection) was that of eternal punishment for the wicked. And since Jesus never attempted to correct Pharisaic thinking on the duration of *Gehenna*, as he did with eschatological errors of the Sadducees (Matt. 22:29), this is weighty evidence for the meaning he intended to convey by his use of the term (1993, pp. 496-497).

The word *géenna* occurs twelve times in the Greek New Testament. In nine of these (Matthew 5:29-30; 10:28; 23:15,33; Mark 9:43,45; Luke 12:5; James 3:6—KJV), it is translated as "hell."

Three times it is translated as "hell fire" (Matthew 5:22; 18:9; Mark 9:47—KJV). David Stevens has pointed out: "It is also significant that eleven of the twelve times that the word *gehenna* is used, it is used by the Lord himself! Thus, it is evident that what we know about *gehenna*, we learn from the Lord himself" (1991, 7[3]:21).

There exists a diversity of views regarding the usage of these terms in Scripture. For example, some scholars have suggested that hades (or the Old Testament *sheol*) is simply a generic term for **the abode of the dead, whether good or evil**, while they await the final Judgment—a view with which I concur. Thus, hades is composed of two compartments: (1) the abode of the spirits of the righteous (known either as paradise—Luke 23:43, or Abraham's bosom—Luke 16:22); and (2) the abode of the spirits of the wicked (Tartarus—2 Peter 2:4, or "torment"—Luke 16:23) [Davidson, 1970, p. 694; Denham, 1998, p. 609; Harris, et al., 1980, 2:892; Jackson, 1998b, 33:34-35; Stevens, 1991, 7[3]:21; Thayer, 1958, p. 11; Zerr, 1952, 5:17].

On the other hand, some scholars suggest that hades should not be used as an umbrella term to refer to the general abode of the dead. Rather, they suggest that after death, there exists: (1) the grave for the physical body (*sheol*, physical abyss, physical hades); (2) the abode of the spirits of the righteous (paradise, Abraham's bosom, the "third heaven"); and (3) the abode of the spirits of the wicked (Tartarus, spiritual abyss, spiritual hades) [McCord, 1979, 96[4]:6]. Still others have advocated the belief that hades, gehenna, and Tartarus are synonyms representing exactly the same thing —"the place of all the damned" (Lenski, 1966, p. 310).

There is one thing, however, on which advocates of each position agree wholeheartedly, and on which the biblical text is crystal clear: after death and the Judgment, gehenna (hell) will be the ultimate, final abode of the spirits of the wicked. But what, exactly, will hell be like?

Hell is a Place of Punishment for Bodies and Souls of the Disobedient Wicked

The Scriptures speak with clarity and precision on the topic of hell as a place of punishment appointed for the disobedient wicked. In his Revelation, John spoke of the fact that Satan would be "cast into the lake of fire and brimstone" and "tormented day and night for ever and ever" (Revelation 20:10). But Satan is not the only one mentioned by John in that context. The "beast" and the "false prophet" also will suffer the same fate. Gary Workman observed that these two terms represent "humans spoken of collectively as allies of the devil. It is 'they'—all of them—who are tormented forever.... Whatever the fire will do for Satan and his demons, it will also do for humans who join them there" (1992, 23[3]:34). Workman therefore concluded:

> It is said that the lost will be "cast" (*ballo*) into hell (Matt. 5:29) or into "the furnace of fire" (Matt 13:42; cf. 18:8-9) as a "prison" (Matt. 18:30). The devil will be "cast" into the lake of fire to be tormented (Rev. 20:10), and so will people who follow him (v. 15).... The compound word for "cast" is *ekballo*. Thus it is said that the wicked will be "cast out" (Luke 13:28) into outer darkness (Matt. 8:12; 22:13; 25:30). Does this mean snuffed out of existence? No, for if "cast forth" (Matt. 8:12) means annihilation, the same word translated "cast out" in reference to demons four verses later must also mean the same thing (v. 16). But Jesus did not annihilate demons; instead, he sent them away (v. 31). When the devil was "cast out" at the cross (John 12:31), was he annihilated? When he was "cast" into the abyss or bottomless pit (Rev. 20:3), did he cease to exist? No, and neither will the lost (1992, 23[3]:33).

The psalmist wrote by inspiration: "The wicked shall be turned into hell, and all the nations that forget God" (9:17). Jesus taught that at Judgment, the wicked will "depart" into punishment "prepared for the devil and his angels" (Matthew 25:41; cf. Matthew 25:46 where Jesus employed the Greek term *kolasis,* which means punishment, torment, suffering, and chastisement [see Brown, 1999,

p. 173]). When John described those who would join the devil in hell's horrible abyss, he referred to "the fearful, and unbelieving, and abominable, and murderers, and fornicators, and sorcerers, and idolaters, and liars" (Revelation 21:8). Paul said that those who inhabit hell with Satan will be those who "know not God" and who "obey not the gospel of Christ" (2 Thessalonians 1:7-9).

In discussing gehenna in the *International Standard Bible Encyclopedia*, Geerhardus Vos addressed the verses that deal with hell, and then stated: "In all of these it designates the place of eternal punishment of the wicked, generally in connection with the final judgment.... Both body and soul are cast into it" (1956, 2:1183). E.M. Zerr commented: "*Gehenna* is the lake of unquenchable fire into which the whole being of the wicked (body, soul and spirit) will be cast after the judgment" (1954, 5:17, parenthetical item in orig.). Hell is indeed described as a place of punishment and suffering (Matthew 25:46; Revelation 14:11) that involves both body and soul (Matthew 10:28). It is a place of sorrow and trouble (Psalm 116:3), contempt and shame (Daniel 12:2), affliction (Jonah 2:2), and torment and anguish (Luke 16:23-24). It is a place of "outer darkness" (Matthew 8:12; 25:30) that Jude described as "blackness of darkness" (13) and that Peter referred to as "pits of darkness" (2 Peter 2:4) because those who inhabit it will be removed from the source of light (2 Thessalonians 1:9).

Hell is a Place of Conscious Sorrow, Torment, Pain, and Suffering

From such vivid descriptions, it is quite evident that the wicked will be in a state of **consciousness**. In fact, John wrote that Satan and his human cohorts would be "cast **alive** into the lake of fire that burneth with brimstone" (Revelation 19:20). That is to say, the Bible definitely teaches "**the persistence of personality** after physical death" (Warren, 1992, p. 32, emp. added). In addressing this point, Guy N. Woods offered the following assessment:

If the Bible is a credible document—and of course it is—**conscious suffering is to be the lot of the wicked in the world to come**. The punishment the Righteous Judge will administer at that last great day is pain inflicted because of sin; it is inseparably associated with disobedience, and it is the action of the divine government for the violation of its laws. Some seek to soften the impact of the penalty by advancing the notion that the punishment threatened will be limited to remorse or conscience, unhappy memories of neglected opportunities, hopelessness and despair. These are doubtless to be some of the **consequences** of eternal punishment, but not the **penalty**. One convicted of murder does not, by deep remorse from his horrible crime, thereby cancel the penalty which has fallen upon him because of his felonious act. He must still expiate his crime (Romans 6:23).

Many men and women today languish in lonely cells deeply regretful of their unsociable behavior and who would give the world to go back in time and cancel the act or acts which brought them to their present painful state. But bitter regrets alone will not discharge the debt they owe. A well-known warden of famous Sing-Sing prison many years ago wrote of walking slowly down the corridors of that formidable fortress at the midnight hour and of hearing the sobbing of distraught men separated from their loved ones and friends in the free world, some of whom would never enter it again (1985a, 127:278, first emp. added; last two in orig.).

When Christ described hell as a place of "weeping and gnashing of teeth" (Matthew 22:13), He overtly emphasized the fact that its inhabitants will endure **conscious** sorrow. Hell is a place of such terrible suffering (2 Thessalonians 1:9) that the apostle John referred to it as the "second death" (Revelation 20:14-15; 21:8). Benton summarized this well:

Hell is to be shut out from all joy, light and life. It is to be deprived of the good things you have tasted in life, but never appreciated. It is to be shut out of God's presence, cut off from all that is good and wholesome. It is to be cut off from all love, all peace, all joy for ever. Jesus explains that once people realize this, once they realize what they have missed, the effect upon them will be devastating. "There will be weeping and gnashing of teeth." It is an unspeakably sombre picture. Men seldom weep, but in hell men weep uncontrollably.

Jesus speaks of the place being totally characterized by tears. The Greek in which the New Testament was written includes the definite article in Jesus' words. It is not just "weeping" in hell; it is "**the** weeping." It is as if Jesus is saying that every connotation of what is involved when people shed tears on earth is summed up in the total distress of hell. All the tears of earth are just a preview to the sobs of hell. Here, in this life, men and women weep, but **the** weeping awaits.... In hell people do not just weep; they gnash their teeth. Having been shut out of the presence of God into the eternal blackness, permanently deprived of all that is wholesome and good, in bitter anger men and women grind their teeth in speechless rage. As they realize that once and for all, "I've been shut out!" they are overcome with a sense of eternal loss which leads to a depth of anger and fury that they find impossible to express in words. What an awful picture is contained in the words of Jesus! (1985, pp. 47-48, emp. in orig.).

In addressing the consciousness of those in hell, Wayne Jackson wrote:

Punishment implies **consciousness**. It would be absurd to describe those who no longer exist as being "punished." The wicked will be "tormented" with the fire of Gehenna (cf. Rev. 14:10-11). Torment certainly implies awareness (cf. Rev. 9: 5; 11:10) [1998b, 33:35, emp. in orig.].

And torment there will be! When, in Revelation 20:10, John wrote of this torment, he employed the Greek word *basanisthesontai*, the root of which (*basanizo*) literally means "to torment, to be harassed, to torture, to vex with grievous pains" (Thayer, 1958, p. 96; cf. Matthew 8:6 regarding the one "tormented" [*basanizomenos*] with palsy).

Previously, John spoke of those who inhabit hell as experiencing the "wine of the wrath of God, which is prepared unmixed in the cup of his anger" (Revelation 14:10). Imagine—experiencing the undiluted wrath of God! In the next verse, John lamented: "The smoke of their torment [notice: **not** the smoke of their annihilation!—BT] goeth up for ever and ever." Little wonder, then, that the writer of Hebrews referred to the second death as "a sorer punishment" than any mere physical death (10:29).

Hell is a Place of Unquenchable Fire and Undying Worms

Earlier I made the point that eleven of the twelve times where the word gehenna is employed in the New Testament, it was Christ Who was doing the speaking. In one of those instances (Mark 9: 43) He spoke of it as "unquenchable fire" (Greek *asbestos*—denoting something that cannot be extinguished; see Bagster, 1970, p. 54), and then five verses later described hell as a place "where their worm dieth not" (v. 48). In his *Greek-English Lexicon*, Joseph Thayer described fire as a metaphor for "the extreme penal torments, which the wicked are to undergo after their life on earth" (1958, p. 558). Gary Workman suggested:

> This double metaphor, used originally of temporal punishments in Isaiah 66:24, was used by Jesus to describe the future punishment in resurrection bodies. God once intervened with the laws of nature so that a bush "burned" (Ex. 3:2) but was "not burnt" (v. 3, same Hebrew word—*ba'ar*). Though it was on fire, it was "not consumed" (v. 2). In like manner God will suspend the natural laws of the temporal realm when people enter the eternal realm. Shadrach, Meshach and Abednego walked around in a fiery furnace without being burned up by the flames that consumed their enemies because God arranged for the fire to have "no power upon their bodies" (v. 27). In eternity God will arrange for the wicked to burn in the flames of hell while continuing to exist, just as they do right now in Hades (Luke 16:19-31). Their fate will be "everlasting burnings" (Isa. 33:14).... Our Lord could not have indicated an eternity of torment any clearer. The isolation and the fire did not **stop** their agony, but **caused** it (1992, 23[3]: 31, emp. in orig.).

The second part of the metaphor used by the Lord concerned the fact that in hell "their worm (Greek, *skolex*, depicting a creature that feeds on dead animal or human remains) dieth not"—a fitting description in light of the fact that the Valley of Hinnom outside Jerusalem was well known for the flesh-eating maggots that feasted daily upon the rotting refuse of that eerie, other-worldly place. In their widely used *Greek-English Lexicon,* Arndt and Gingrich remarked that the never-dying worm is used as a symbol of the unending "torment of the damned" (1957, p. 765). Greek scholar A.T. Robertson said that the phrase "is thus a vivid picture of eternal punishment" (1930, 1:346). Thayer recorded that the phrase referred to the fact that "their punishment after death will never cease" (1958, p. 580). Did the Lord mean what He said? Oh yes —He meant that, and more! As John Benton commented:

> This is a picture which suggests that in hell there is an eternal dissolution which never ceases.... Perhaps the nearest illustration we can use from our present experience is that of a sleepless night caused by worry. There is something upon your mind that causes you deep anxiety. The prospect of it scares you and drains you of all energy. The worry gets you nowhere and yet you cannot stop worrying about it. You feel as if you are falling apart as a person. You cannot be at peace or feel settled in yourself. It is as if something just keeps gnawing and gnawing away at you, something with which you just cannot come to terms. Jesus, with a love in his heart, does not want us to go there, warns us of the place where the "worm does not die." Hell is a place with which no one will ever be able to come to terms....
>
> The description of hell which emerges from Jesus' teaching is fearful. It is the most horrendous thing we can ever imagine. Knowing the character of Jesus, we cannot for a moment suppose that he merely intended to play upon people's fears in telling us such things. If Jesus was ignorant upon these profound subjects he had no right to set out such a dreadful picture to torment people's imaginations. Still less would he be justified in telling us such things if, being perfectly aware of the true nature of life after death, he knew that there was no such place as hell. It will not do to think that Jesus was using the ends to justify the means—to paint a terrible picture of hell simply in order to scare people into living a moral life, or into believing in him as a Saviour. **Jesus was not that kind of man**. Jesus was always a man of love and truth. He would not set out a picture if he had not been completely sure of it and he certainly would not tell lies. **Knowing the character of Jesus, we have got to say that he was simply**

> **being straight with us**.... Jesus said in the Sermon on the Mount: "You have heard that it was said...but I tell you...." Jesus saw the consequences of sin as terrifying. He saw sin as leading people to this place of indescribable misery and so again he is shockingly urgent and direct in his warnings (1985, pp. 55-56,51, emp. added).

In His account of the rich man and Lazarus in Luke 16, the Lord employed the vivid imagery of fire when He depicted the rich man as begging for relief because he was in agony in its clutches (vss. 23-24). Benton went on to state:

> [W]e must reject the idea that because it is picture language, it holds no meaning and no fear for us. Let nobody think that it is only symbolical and therefore not so terrible. Rather, we should realize that **if the symbol, the mere picture, is already awe-inspiring, how horrible must the actual reality be!** Surely, if anything is clear, it is that Jesus does not want us to toy with the possibility that hell might be bearable. A symbol representing something is never greater than the thing itself (p. 52, emp. added).

Those who attempt to portray the account in Luke 16 as merely allegorical or metaphorical are wasting their considerable efforts. As John Blanchard has reminded us: "In common communication the thing being symbolized is always greater than the symbol.... [E]ven if we can prove that hell's 'fire' and 'worm' are metaphorical we shall not have removed one iota of their horror or terror" (1993, p. 141). While considering the Lord's comments in Luke 16, Wayne Jackson asked: "If the condition of the rich man in hades was one of 'anguish' (*odunao*—'to suffer pain'), though it involved only the soul, does it seem likely that the ultimate punishment of Gehenna, which involves both body and soul, would entail **less**?" (1998b, 33:35, emp. in orig.). Surely it was this very point that the Lord was attempting to emphasize to His hearers. Who—in their right mind—would go **voluntarily** to a fiery place of punishment, sorrow, torment, pain, and suffering that they knew was best described as one where "the [flesh-eating] worm dieth not"?

Hell is Eternal in Nature

Surely, one of the most horrific aspects of hell is its eternal nature. Throughout the Bible, words like "eternal," "forever and forever," "unquenchable," and "everlasting" are used repeatedly to describe the duration of the punishment that God will inflict upon the wicked. Some, of course, have objected that "eternal" punishment simply is not acceptable since, on the face of it, it is "too long." Gary Ealey responded to such an objection when he wrote:

> If it is argued that "everlasting" punishment is too long or severe, we again reply that such a conclusion is based upon our inability to fully appreciate the ugliness of sin. How do you determine the hideousness of an act? Do you do so on the basis of the time involved in performing the act itself? If a man in a football stadium filled with people fired a machine gun for thirty seconds and kills 100 people, should he be punished for 100 seconds? Would you double that? Triple it? Would you sentence him to life imprisonment or to execution? Clearly, only God can determine what is the just punishment for sin (1984, p. 25).

As the "Judge of all the earth" (Genesis 18:25), God alone has the right to determine the nature and duration of whatever punishment is due to the wicked. And He has decreed that such punishment will be eternal in nature (Matthew 25:46; Revelation 14:10-11). That might not agree with our mind-set, or appeal to our sensitivities, but it is God's word on the matter nevertheless.

I once heard of a newspaper in Detroit, Michigan that published a story about a man who (ironically) had been transferred from Hell, Michigan to a city by the name of Paradise. The headline read: "Man Leaves Hell for Paradise!" Such an event might occur in **this** lifetime, but you may rest assured that it will not happen in the **next** (Luke 16:19-31). When Dante, in his *Inferno*, depicted the sign hanging over hell's door as reading, "Abandon all hope, ye who enter here," he did not overstate the case.

Others have objected to the concept of **eternal** punishment because of such passages as Mark 12:9 (where Jesus foretold in a parable that God would "destroy" those who killed His beloved Son) and Matthew 10:28 (where Jesus told His disciples to fear Him who was able to "destroy" both soul and body in hell). But the belief that the soul will be annihilated is based, not on an understanding, but on a **mis**understanding, of the passages in question. In addition to referring to destruction, the Greek word *apollumi* employed in these two portions of Scripture (and approximately 90 more times elsewhere in the New Testament) also can mean "lose," "perish," or "lost." As Vine pointed out: "The idea is not extinction but ruin, loss, not of being, but of well-being" (1991, p. 211). Thayer defined *apollumi* as it appears in Matthew 10:28 as "to devote or give over to eternal misery" (1958, p. 64). In speaking of the idea of eternal punishment as expressed in Matthew 25:46, biblical commentator Adam Clarke wrote:

> But some are of opinion that this punishment shall have an end: this is as like as that the glory of the righteous shall have **an end**: for the same word is used to express the **duration** of the punishment, *kolasin aionion*, as is used to express the duration of the state of glory: *zoen aionion*. I have seen the best things written in favour of the final redemption of damned spirits; but I never saw an answer to the argument against that doctrine, drawn from this verse, but what sound learning and criticism should be ashamed to acknowledge. The original word *aion* is certainly to be taken here in its proper grammatical sense, **continued being**, *aieion*, **never ending**. Some have gone a **middle** way, and think that the wicked shall be **annihilated**. This, I think, is contrary to the text; if they go **into punishment**, they **continue** to **exist**; for that which **ceases** to **be**, **ceases** to **suffer** (n.d., 5:244, emp. in orig.).

Granted, it would be more comforting for the wicked to believe that at the end of this life they simply will be punished "for a little while" and then "drop out of existence," rather than having to face the stark realization of an eternal punishment in the fires of hell. But comforting or not, the question must be asked: Is such a belief in compliance with biblical teaching on this subject?

While it is true that, on rare occasions in Scripture, words such as "everlasting" and "forever" may be used in a non-literal sense (i.e., the thing being discussed is not strictly eternal—e.g. Exodus 12:14 and Numbers 25:13), they **never** are used in such a sense when describing hell. The word *aionios* occurs some seventy times in the Greek New Testament where it is translated by such English terms as "eternal" or "everlasting" (e.g., "eternal fire," Matthew 18: 8, 25:41, Jude 7; "eternal punishment," Matthew 25:46; "eternal destruction," 2 Thessalonians 1:9; and "eternal judgment," Hebrews 6:2). In his *Expository Dictionary of New Testament Words,* Vine wrote of *aionios*:

> Moreover, it is used of persons and things which are in their nature, endless, as, e.g., of God (Rom 16:26); of His power (I Tim. 6:16), and of Him (I Peter 5:10); of the Holy Spirit (Heb. 9:14); of the redemption effected by Christ (Heb. 9: 12), and of the consequent salvation of men (5:9); ...and of the resurrection body (II Cor. 5:1), elsewhere said to be "immortal" (I Cor. 15:53), in which that life will be finally realized (Matt. 25:46; Titus 1:2) [1966, p. 43].

Thayer stated that *aionios* means "without end, never to cease, everlasting" (1958, p. 112).

In his inspired discussion about the coming fate of false teachers, Jude assured the first-century Christians that those who perverted the truth **would** be punished. To illustrate his point, he reached back to Sodom and Gomorrah (Genesis 19:24-25) as an example of those "suffering the punishment of eternal fire" (v. 7). G.L. Lawlor commented on Jude's illustration as follows:

> Jude says these cities, their sin, and their terrible destruction lie before us as an example, *deigma.* Better, perhaps, the word might be rendered "sign," that is, to show us the meaning and significance of something, i.e., this awful sin and God's catastrophic judgment. The cities were destroyed by fire and brimstone, but the ungodly inhabitants are even now undergoing the awful torment of everlasting punishment. These cities are an example, they lie before us as a sign, to show the certainty of divine punishment upon an apostasy of life dreadful almost beyond description (1972, p. 70).

But what did Lawlor mean when he said that the inhabitants of Sodom and Gomorrah "are even now undergoing the awful torment of everlasting punishment"? His point is this. The Greek *hupechousai* (rendered "suffering") is a present participle which "shows that they were enduring 'eternal fire' even as Jude wrote! The primary force of the present tense in the Greek, especially as connected with a participial construction as here, is that of **continuous** action" (Denham, 1998, p. 607, emp. added). Greek scholar M.R. Vincent wrote regarding this point: "The participle is present, indicating that they are suffering to this day the punishment which came upon them in Lot's time" (1946, 1:340). Brown remarked: "This grammatical construction simply means that Jude is saying that the inhabitants of the two cities not only suffered, but they continue to suffer. What a warning to those in rebellion to God!" (1999, p. 176).

The Jews (and Jewish Christians) of Jude's day would have understood that point because they knew and understood the significance attached to gehenna. Alfred Edersheim, who stood without equal as a Hebrew/intertestamental period scholar, devoted an entire chapter of his monumental work, *The Life and Times of Jesus the Messiah*, to the rabbinical and New Testament evidence on the subject of eternal punishment. His conclusion was that the Jews in the time of Christ understood gehenna as referring to a place of eternal, conscious torment for the wicked (1971, pp. 791-796). Eminent religious historian Phillip Schaff (1970, 2:136) reported that, except for the Sadducees (who believed in neither a resurrection for the righteous nor the wicked), the Jews of Christ's day consistently held to a view of personal, eternal, conscious punishment—a truly important point for the following reason.

During His ministry, Jesus was quite outspoken against those things that were wrong or misleading. In Matthew 22:23-33 He chastised the Sadducees severely regarding their erroneous views about the lack of a future existence. Yet, as noted earlier, He **never opposed** the Jewish concept of eternal punishment of the soul.

Had the Jews been in error regarding the afterlife, surely the Son of God would have corrected them in as public a manner as He did on so many other points of Scripture. Instead, He **repeatedly reaffirmed** such a concept. His silence speaks volumes!

No Hell...No Heaven

When Christ spoke to the people of His day about the ultimate fate of humanity in eternity, He stated that the wicked would "go away into everlasting (*aionios*) punishment, but the righteous into eternal (*aionios*) life." As Denham has pointed out: "The word rendered 'eternal' is the same Greek word *aionios*, rendered earlier as 'everlasting'" (1998, p. 615). The Lord's double use of the term *aionios* is critically important in this discussion. J.W. McGarvey addressed this fact when he wrote:

> Whatever this Greek word means in the last clause of this sentence it means in the first; for it is an invariable rule of exegesis, that a word when thus repeated in the same sentence must be understood in the same sense, unless the context or the nature of the subject shows that there is a play on the word. There is certainly nothing in the context to indicate the slightest difference in meaning, nor can we know by the nature of the subject that the punishment spoken of is less durable than the life. It is admitted on all hands that in the expression "everlasting life" the term has its full force, and therefore it is idle and preposterous to deny that it has the same force in the expression "everlasting punishment." The everlasting punishment is the same as the everlasting fire of verse 41. The punishment is by fire, and its duration is eternal (1875, pp. 221-222).

There can be absolutely no doubt that the Lord intended to teach two specific states of conscious future existence. In fact, as James Orr observed in the *International Standard Bible Encyclopedia*: "The whole doctrine of the future judgment in the NT presupposes survival after death" (1956, 4:2502). Writing in *The New International Dictionary of New Testament Theology*, Joachim Guhrt stated that since "God's life never ends, i.e., that everything belonging to him can also never come to an end,...even perdition must be called *aionios*, eternal" (1978, pp. 830,833). In this same vein, Guy N. Woods commented: "Our heavenly Father is described as 'the everlasting God' (Romans 16:26). Hell will be the inhabitation of the wicked so long as God himself exists" (1985a, 127: 278). George Ladd thus noted:

> The adjective *aionios* does not of itself carry a qualitative significance, designating a life that is different in kind from human life. The primary meaning of the word is temporal. It is used of fire, punishment, sin, and places of abode; and these uses designate **unending duration** (1974, p. 255, emp. added).

But that is only half of the Lord's message. Orr went on to say: "Here precisely the same word is applied to the punishment of the wicked **as to the blessedness of the righteous**.... Whatever else the term includes, it connotes duration" (1956, 4:2502, emp. added). When he discussed the definition and meaning of the word *aionios* in *The Theological Dictionary of the New Testament,* Herman Sasse noted that when the word is used "as a term for eschatological expectation," if it conveys "eternity" for the rewards of the righteous it also must convey "the sense of 'unceasing' or 'endless'" (1964, 1:209). Therefore, "however long then the righteous will experience the blessedness of **eternal** life is just how long the wicked will suffer **everlasting** punishment..." (Denham, 1998, p. 615, emp. in orig.).

In his intriguing book, *Hell on Trial—The Case for Eternal Punishment*, Robert Peterson wrote the following under the chapter titled "The Case for Eternal Punishment": "Jesus places the fates of the wicked and the righteous side by side.... The parallelism makes the meaning unmistakable: the punishment of the ungodly and the bliss of the godly both last forever" (1995, p. 196). Gary Workman spoke to this very point when he observed:

New Testament writers used *aion* and *aionios* 141 times when speaking of eternity to convey the idea of unceasing, endless, and perpetual. If the word means "without end" when applied to the future blessedness of the saved, it must also mean "without end" when describing the future punishment of the lost (1992, 23[3]:33).

Benton elaborated:

The same word *aionios*, "eternal," is used to describe both heaven and hell. If we take the position that hell is capable of termination then, to be consistent, we must believe that the same is true of heaven. But, from the rest of the Bible, that is plainly not the case. Heaven is **for ever**. We must stay with the plain meaning of the word "eternal." Both heaven and hell are without end (1985, p. 55, emp. in orig.).

These writers are correct. The fact that Christ made a special point of repeating *aionios* in the same sentence requires that we "stay with the plain meaning of the word." Hoekema therefore concluded:

The word *aionios* means without end when applied to the future blessedness of believers. It must follow, unless clear evidence is given to the contrary, that this word also means without end when used to describe the future punishment of the lost.... It follows, then, that the punishment which the lost will suffer after this life will be as endless as the future happiness of the people of God (1982, p. 270).

Those who argue against an eternal hell must be provided with teaching to help them realize that whatever arguments they make against the eternal abode of the wicked apply with equal force to the eternal abode of the righteous. Perhaps it is the realization of the unscriptural implications of such a position that elicits such righteous indignation on the part of those who accept Christ's instruction on the nature of eternity—because they realize that suggestions intended to limit the nature of hell have a correspondingly similar effect on heaven. For example, two short years after Edward Fudge published his book, *The Fire That Consumes* (in which he advocated the doctrine of annihilationism), Robert Morey published *Death and the Afterlife*, a scholarly refutation of Fudge's position that one writer suggested was so well argued that it "took Fudge to the theological woodshed" (Jackson, 1993, p. 64). Later, theologian John Gerstner authored *Repent or Perish*, a huge portion of which also was devoted to examining and refuting Fudge's arguments. [Interestingly, in his book Dr. Gerstner suggested that the masterful manner in which Morey demolished Fudge's arguments might be compared to using a battlefield canon to kill a housefly! (1990, p. 41).]

Those who are willing to accept Christ's teaching on heaven should have no trouble accepting His teaching on hell. Yet some do. Their refusal to accept biblical teaching on the eternal nature of the wicked, however, is not without consequences. John Benton accurately summarized the situation.

> Disregarding the doctrine of eternal damnation tends to make us doubt eternal salvation.... Though Revelation 21-22 proclaims the final fate of the wicked—existence in the lake of fire (21:8) and exclusion from the city of God (22:15)—these chapters trumpet more loudly the final destiny of the redeemed (1995, p. 217).

But does it **really** matter **what** a person believes in this regard? Wayne Jackson answered that question when he wrote:

> Those who contend that the wicked will be annihilated are in error. But is the issue one of importance? Yes. **Any theory of divine retribution which undermines the full consequences of rebelling against God has to be most dangerous** (1998b, 33:35, emp. added).

Since both heaven and hell are described via the same, exact terminology in Scripture, once the instruction of the Lord and His inspired writers on the subject of an eternal hell has been abandoned, how long will it be before the Bible's instruction on the eternal nature of heaven likewise is abandoned? Have we not witnessed the effects of this type of thinking before? Those who started out to compromise the first chapter of Genesis eventually compromised other important facets of biblical doctrine as well (e.g., biblical miracles, Christ's virgin birth, the Lord's bodily resurrection, etc.). For many, rejecting the biblical concept of the eternality of hell may well represent the first steps on the slippery slope that eventually will lead to compromise in other areas of Scripture. Surely it would be better by far to echo the heartfelt sentiments of Joshua when he told the Israelites that while they were free to believe whatever they wished, or to act in any manner they chose, "as for me and my house, we will serve Jehovah" (Joshua 24:15).

Conclusion

This chapter has dealt at some length with the concept of the souls of the wicked inhabiting an eternal hell, but has had relatively little to say about the concept of the souls of the righteous inhabiting an eternal heaven. Actually, this should not be all that surprising. The very idea of hell has met with violent opposition—for good reason. No one **wants** to go to hell. Thus, the Good Book's teaching on heaven is accepted far more readily than its teaching on hell.

The simple fact of the matter, however, is that God created man as a dichotomous being who consists of both a body and a soul. When eventually each of us has "shuffled off this **mortal** coil" (to quote Shakespeare), our **immortal** soul will return to God Who gave it (Ecclesiastes 12:7). Infidelity, of course, always has objected strenuously to the concept of "life after death." The very idea seems preposterous to unbelievers—just as it did to King Agrippa in the first century when Paul asked the pagan monarch: "Why is it judged incredible with you, if God doth raise the dead?" (Acts 26:28).

Indeed, why should it be difficult to believe that an omnipotent God could raise the dead? For the God Who created the Universe and everything within it in six days, and Who upholds "all things by the word of his power" (Hebrews 1:3), how difficult could it be to raise the dead? As Blaise Pascal, the famed French philosopher once remarked: "I see no greater difficulty in believing the resurrection of the dead than the creation of the world. Is it less easy to reproduce a human body than it was to produce it at first?" (as quoted in Otten, 1988, p. 40). In commenting on this point, Herman J. Otten, long-time editor of *Christian News*, wrote: "The task will not be ours. Omnipotence and omniscience have assumed it; they will do it, and they will do it well" (1988, p. 40).

Indeed, God will do His part well. Writing in the book of Revelation, the apostle John described in unforgettable language the destiny of the righteous when this world finally comes to an end: "Behold, the dwelling of God is with men. He will dwell with them, and they shall be his people, and God himself will be with them" (21:3, RSV). Thousands of years earlier, God's pledge to Abraham had foreshadowed just such a covenant relationship. Moses recorded: "And I will establish My covenant between Me and you and your descendants after you in their generations, for an everlasting covenant, to be God to you and your descendants after you" (Genesis 17:7, NKJV). Paul spoke of the fact that "if ye are Christ's, then are ye Abraham's seed, heirs according to promise" (Galatians 3:29), and referred to those who serve Christ faithfully as "heirs according to the hope of eternal life" (Titus 3:7). James rejoiced in the fact that those who were "rich in faith" would be "heirs of the kingdom that he promised to them who love him" (James 2:5). The writer of the book of Hebrews spoke of Christ as having become "unto all them that obey him, the author of eternal salvation" (5:9).

No doubt that is exactly what John had in mind when he went on to say in Revelation 21: "He that overcometh shall inherit these things; and I will be his God, and he shall be my son" (vs. 7). God will be Father to the man or woman who demonstrates faith in Him, perseveres to the end, and lives in humble obedience to His divine will. Such is the promise of sonship to believers. God will welcome those who believe in and obey His Son as "heirs of God, and joint-heirs with Christ" (Romans 8:17), and will—according to His promise—bestow upon them all the riches and blessings of heaven.

In the next verse, however, John went on to paint a picture of stark contrast when he described the ultimate end of the impenitent wicked:

> But for the fearful, and unbelieving, and abominable, and murderers, and fornicators, and sorcerers, and idolaters, and all liars, their part shall be in the lake that burneth with fire and brimstone; which is the second death (Revelation 21:8).

What diametric alternatives—enjoying eternal happiness as a son or daughter of God, or enduring eternal pain in "the lake that burneth with fire and brimstone"!

The good news, of course, is that no one **has** to go to hell. When Christ was ransomed on our behalf (1 Timothy 2:4), He paid a debt He did not owe, and a debt we could not pay, so that we could live forever in the presence of our Creator (Matthew 25:46). God takes no joy at the death of the wicked (Ezekiel 18:23; 33:11). Nor should we. As one writer eloquently stated it: "No one who has been snatched from the burning himself can feel anything but compassion and concern for the lost" (Woodson, 1973, p. 32).

As we begin to comprehend both the hideous nature of our sin, and the alienation from God resulting from it, we not only should exhibit a fervent desire to save ourselves "from this crooked generation" (Acts 2:40), but we also should feel just as passionate about warning the wicked of their impending doom (Ezekiel 3:17-19).

CHAPTER 11

ABANDONING FAITH— WHY ARE WE LOSING OUR CHILDREN?

The telephone rings in the middle of the night. The caller weeps uncontrollably. A teenager is...dead. Hearts break; words of comfort flee; advice fails. A funeral takes place; final "good-byes" are whispered in muted tones; classmates mourn; friends grieve. Everyone wants to know—**why**?

The telephone rings in the middle of the night. The caller weeps uncontrollably. A teenager is...dead. Hearts break; words of comfort flee; advice fails. But there will be no funeral or hushed "good-byes." Classmates will not mourn; few friends will grieve. Fewer still will bother to ask, "why?"

What is the difference in these two scenarios? The first describes the **physical** death of a teenager; the second describes a **spiritual** death. The former causes our hearts to ache, and our eyes to mist. But does the latter? The spiritual death has, at least potentially, far greater implications. Suppose, for example, that the teenager who died physically was very much "alive" spiritually. Suppose this child—in humility to the Lord and in submission to His will—had obeyed the biblical commands in regard to becoming a Christian, and had lived faithfully to the very hour of his demise. After the funeral—when all the visitors have left, and the last morsel of food has been put away—as the time comes to turn out the light and lay their heads on pillows of sorrow drenched with tears of grief, what shall comfort those parents at that awful moment? Neither possessions nor station in life shall suffice. Rather, faith in their God and in the truthfulness of His promises will sustain them. With both Hosea (13:14) and Paul (1 Corinthians 15:55), they may raise their voices to heaven in joyful praise, with the anthem on their lips, "O death, where is thy sting? O death, where is thy victory?" They shall be comforted with the full knowledge that this life is so very short (James 4:14), and that at its end they too—if they have lived faithfully—shall inherit the same reward as their child (1 Corinthians 3:8). Their **physical** loss is temporary; a spiritual reunion is promised.

The same cannot be said, however, of a **spiritual** death. If the child in the second scenario chooses to abandon his faith in God and live in rebellion, were he to die in that condition, his last state would be worse than his first. Peter wrote by inspiration:

> For if, after they have escaped the defilements of the world through the knowledge of the Lord and Savior Jesus Christ, they are again entangled therein and overcome, the last state is become worse with them than the first. For it were better for them not to have known the way of righteousness, than, after knowing it, to turn back from the holy commandments delivered unto them (2 Peter 2:20-21).

The Scriptures are clear in addressing the horrible fate that awaits those who live in unbelief (Romans 1:18-32; Revelation 21:8).

Consider the anguish that parents must feel when **their** son or daughter is the one described in the second scenario above. Conservative estimates suggest that we are now losing 50% or more of our young people after they graduate from high school. In many areas, the numbers approach 90% (see Goad, 1981, 98:297). These statistics are not just meaningless strings of numbers about "other folks' kids" when you suddenly awake to the heart-rending fact that it is **your** child or grandchild who is lost. When you are prostrate before God, praying on behalf of that child's soul, the situation is more real and more urgent than you ever thought possible.

One of the most important responsibilities parents face is the protection of their children's souls. As their children grow up, some parents find themselves spending countless hours, and sleepless nights, struggling with problems that occur in the lives of those children. At times, the parents' lives are affected adversely by their children's actions. Similarly, children may have their lives, and their faith, affected adversely by the actions of their parents. The tragic fact remains that when our children lose their faith, we lose our children, and everyone suffers.

There is no loss more saddening, however, than the one that could have been prevented in the first place. In Proverbs 22:6, the writer urged parents to "train up a child in the way he should go," the result being that "even when he is old, he will not depart from it." The thrust of the proverb is that there are things we, as parents, can do to help prevent the loss of a child's soul.

When Christ spoke to the multitudes that thronged to hear Him, He addressed the precious, and safe, nature of a child's soul. In Mark 10:14, Jesus commented that "to such belongeth the kingdom of God." One verse earlier, it is recorded that when Christ observed children being kept from Him, "he was moved with indignation." Jesus placed a premium on the soul of a child, as the discussion in Matthew 18:5-6 plainly indicates.

Should we today do any differently? The psalmist indicated that "children are a heritage of Jehovah; and the fruit of the womb is his reward" (127:3). Our children are, literally, gifts from the Lord. As God's heritage, they are sent to us for safekeeping, which is why we are commanded to rear them "in the nurture and admonition of the Lord" (Ephesians 6:4). The spiritual instruction of a child is not an option. It is not something we do if we have the time or if we find it convenient. God has given us, as parents, the awesome responsibility of introducing our children to His covenant, and of teaching our children His Word. But what is the ultimate goal of this daunting task? Is it not safe to say that our ultimate goal is to see the soul of a child returned to the God of heaven from whom it was sent originally (Ecclesiastes 12:7)?

Is this responsibility sobering and weighty? Yes. Is it at times burdensome or difficult? Yes. But is it impossible to accomplish? No! God never gave a command that we, with His aid and assistance, cannot carry out successfully. Christ, in speaking to the people of His generation, stated that "with God, all things are possible" (Matthew 19:26). He was not suggesting that the illogical could become logical. He did not mean that God could make such things as a round square, or an acceptable sin. In the context, He was making the point that with God's help, obstacles that at first glance appear to us to be insurmountable can, in fact, be overcome. Tasks that seem too arduous can, in fact, be completed.

And so it is with the successful rearing of a child. God has given us as parents the responsibility of ensuring the safety of our children's souls. Fortunately, He also has given us tools equal to the task, and the instruction booklet we are to employ as we go about completing our assignment. The tools include such things as love, parental authority, wisdom, and experience. The instruction booklet is His Word, the Bible. Granted, there may be times when parents use both the tools and the instruction booklet to the best of their ability and still fail because a child employs his or her God-given free will to rebel against heaven's admonition. Samuel and Eli provide just such an example. Both of these men had ungodly children. God condemned Eli, but within the Scriptures there is found no condemnation for Samuel. Why the difference? Both sets of children possessed free will, and both used that free will to rebel. Apparently, however, Samuel attempted, to the best of his ability, to restrain his children, while Eli did not. Let us not condemn dedicated, godly parents who attempt to turn their children unto the paths of righteousness, but who fail through no fault of their own.

At the same time, however, let us not attempt to defend parents who neglect their children, and who thus contribute to their spiritual delinquency.

But **why** are we losing our children, and what can we **do** about it?

Why are We Losing Our Children?

In any given year, more than six million people have their lives altered forever—by becoming parents. Children are intended to be a tremendous blessing. The psalmist echoed this thought when he reminded us that children are indeed "a heritage of Jehovah, and the fruit of the womb is his reward," They can bring such love, joy, and pleasure to a home.

Yet children also bring sobering responsibilities. As one parent put it: "What a responsibility—to know that our children will build a life on what we teach and the love we show them. No wonder parenting is a job that brings more joy and challenge than any other" (Mayhue, 1992, p. 49). But how many of those six million people **prepare** for the challenge of rearing children—in the sense of making the necessary mental and spiritual adjustments to ensure that a child will be reared in the "nurture and admonition of the Lord" (Ephesians 6:4)? In Psalm 127:3, the writer noted that children are "a heritage of Jehovah." In the very next verse, he commented on the nature of that heritage when he observed that "as arrows in the hand of a mighty man, so are the children of youth" (127:4). Here is his point: **children, like arrows, are to be launched toward a singular target**! That target is heaven; we want our children (figuratively speaking) to walk once again in the cool of the Garden with their God. To a great degree, parents (and often grandparents) determine whether or not children reach that target. Our neglect—intentional or accidental—can rob them of that heavenly home. One writer has suggested:

> All across this great land mothers and fathers alike are throwing up their hands in despair and asking, "What has happened to our kids?" or "Where did we go wrong?" ...When we read or hear of a case where a child is physically or sexually abused we become extremely angry. We seek swift and severe punishment of those who are perpetrators of child abuse. Yet, what many parents fail to realize is that they shall stand before God and give an account of abusing their children in a way that is much worse than any physical abuse one could imagine—and that is spiritual abuse! Perhaps the greatest form of abuse is that of neglect. Children must not be neglected when it comes to basic Bible teaching.... Why, you ask? Because the consequences are eternal! (Causey, 1992, p. 12).

Indeed, the consequences **are** eternal. During His earthly ministry, Jesus taught His disciples a lesson on this very point. Matthew (19:13-15), Mark (10:13ff.), and Luke (18:15-17) all record a conversation between Christ and His disciples on the subject of children. He rebuked those disciples who wanted to prevent the children from coming to Him and then warned: "See that you despise not one of these little ones: for I tell you, that in heaven their angels always behold the face of my Father who is in heaven" (Matthew 18: 10). Jesus wanted children near Him. That has not changed. R.W. Lawrence said of this instance: "And so the invitation of Jesus stands clear: 'Parents, relatives, loved ones, friends of the little children: **bring** them to me!' The invitation has never been modified or rescinded" (1976, pp. 22-23, emp. in orig.). It is the task of parents and grandparents to bring these children to Christ—to launch them (as "arrows in the hand of a mighty man") toward the target. If we fail in this task, our children will lose their souls.

That we are failing is evident, else we would not be losing 50-90% of our young people after high school graduation. But **why** are we failing so terribly. Why are we losing so many of our precious offspring? What is it, exactly, that puts a child's soul in harm's way?

We Have Failed to Teach Our Children Spiritual Values

Aside from the obvious responsibility parents have for the salvation of their own souls, there is no greater responsibility than saving the souls of their children. The job of rearing and training children is exactly that—a full-time job. Children cannot be trained properly by parents who approach the task half-heartedly. David Boswell correctly observed:

> As parents we owe certain obligations to our children. We can't let them down. We can't let God down. God expects each and every parent to do his or her part in raising children. The very first responsibility we have as parents is to teach our children of God. Every other responsibility falls before this one.... As parents we also need to know that instilling in our children a faith in God and the Bible, is the best thing we can ever do for them. That early teaching will stay with them the rest of their lives. Impressions are made while they are young (1980, p. 785).

We become upset when a child makes Ds or Fs on a school report card, but may never give it a second thought when that same child fails to study and/or prepare his or her Bible class lesson. Dalton Key lamented this fact when he wrote:

> Our children are important to us. We closely monitor their scholastic and athletic progress. Their knowledge of past events, current events, human events, and human psychology must not be hindered. Their sports achievements must not be hampered. Yet we passively allow the next generation to grow up without the most important knowledge, the most valuable training information of all. Our children know books, but know little about the Book of Books—the Bible (1992b, p. 1).

The prophet Hosea observed that "my people are destroyed for lack of knowledge" (4:6). The truthfulness of that statement has not dimmed across the centuries. Where knowledge is lacking, wisdom always will be in short supply. A generation ago, we taught diligently on such topics as the existence of God, the inspiration of the Bible, the importance of the creation account, the uniqueness and singularity of the church, etc. But ultimately we taught less and less on these matters and, as a result, our children's faith began to rest on shifting sand instead of solid rock. When the winds of tribulation and change came, that faith collapsed and we lost our children to atheism, agnosticism, theistic evolution, denominationalism, and similar errors.

Someone did Their Job Better Than, and Before, We did Ours

Christians always have served God in an anti-Christian environment. That was true in the first century, and it is equally true in the twenty first. Similarly, parents always have had to rear children in such an environment. While parents taught one thing, the world taught another. The key to success was, and is, helping children understand that while Christians exist and function **in** the world, they are not **of** the world (Romans 12:2; James 4:4; 1 John 2:15). Blurring that distinction in the mind of a child has disastrous results.

Somewhere along the way, it appears that we forgot one important point—it is not a matter of **if** our children are going to be taught; it is only a matter of **what** they are going to be taught, and **who** is going to do the teaching. The question is: Who will we allow to do the teaching, and what will they be allowed to teach? The late Rita Rhodes Ward, a public school teacher for more than fifty years, knew from firsthand experience that frequently

> when a Christian mother leads her 6-year-old to the first grade room or her 5-year-old to kindergarten, she leads him from the sheltered environment of the home into the cold, pagan environment of secular humanism. From that day on, the child will be taught two contradictory religions... (1986, 128:520).

Certainly it is not the case that **all** public school teachers are humanists. There are those who approach their job from a Christian perspective. Nevertheless, the public school **environment** often creates an atmosphere of hostility toward the belief system that

Christian parents attempt to instill in their children. In their volume, *The Evolution Conspiracy*, Matrisciana and Oakland included a chapter titled "Children at Risk" in which they suggested that

> traditionally the schoolroom has been an open forum of learning. Today it has become a pulpit for the aggressive conversion of impressionable minds. It is the battlefield where war is being waged against the Judeo-Christian God, His principles, His morality, and the Bible (1991, p. 125).

There is ample evidence that this assessment is correct, and that it has been for quite some time. Dr. C.F. Potter was an honorary president of the National Education Association. In 1930, he authored the book, *Humanism: A New Religion*, in which he made the following statement:

> Education is thus a most powerful ally of Humanism, and every American public school is a school of Humanism. What can a theistic Sunday school's meeting, for an hour once a week, and teaching only a fraction of the children, do to stem the tide of the five day program of humanistic teaching? (p. 128).

At a seminar on childhood education some years ago, Dr. Chester Pierce, professor of education and psychiatry at Harvard University, told those in attendance:

> Every child in America entering school at the age of five is mentally ill, because he comes to school with certain allegiances toward our founding fathers, toward our elected officials, toward his parents, toward a belief in a supernatural Being, toward the sovereignty of this nation as a separate entity. It's up to you teachers to make all of these sick children well by creating the international children of the future (1973, p. 24).

The truth is, some public school teachers have a "hidden agenda," their objective being to destroy our children's faith. This situation represents a real and present danger to a child's spiritual well-being. If we allow atheists, humanists, evolutionists, and infidels to influence our children—and if they do their job better than, and before, we do ours—our children will lose their faith, and we will lose our children.

Parents Have Served as Faulty Role Models

We cannot expect to be taken seriously by our children if we, by our example, leave them with the impression that they are to "do as we **say**, not as we **do**." During his tenure as editor of the *Rocky Mountain Christian*, Roy H. Lanier Jr. penned a timely editorial in which he observed:

> What is happening to our children? Why are many showing little interest in the work of the church? Why are so many quitting the church and Jesus when they leave home? Why are we having all these heartaches?
>
> It is because of a faulty role model by the parents. Children, especially teens, can see through the outer walls of sham and know that something is wrong in their own homes. It may just confuse them; they may not be able to give in detail what the problems are, but they know something is awry. There are many stubborn and rebellious children who do not know why they are so rebellious. They just know something is wrong and they cry out against it with all the abilities at their disposal (1981, 9[8]:2).

Parents cannot live **unrighteously** and expect their children to live **righteously**. We often say, somewhat in jest, "monkey see, monkey do," when children mimic our actions. But behind the humor is a painful lesson—children **do** mimic our actions! The question is: What are they mimicking? Dalton Key provided the answer:

> We read with avid interest the funny page, the sports section, the advice columns, the financial, world, national, and local news items, but can't seem to find the time to open the one book with all the answers for a problem-filled world—the Bible....
>
> Our lives are hectic and schedule-driven. Our days are ruled by clocks and calendars, our joy hinges on time off and free time, yet we foolishly ignore the book of timeless treasure, the volume of divine truth which prepares souls to live beyond life and travel past time into the bliss of endless, heavenly eternity. We are too busy for—the Bible.... Yes, these are the confessions of a world-filled church. Make application where you will, allow the shoe that fits to be worn, let the chips fall where they may.... Let's start putting first things first (1992a, pp. 1-3).

Sometimes we seem not to realize that we teach our children in two ways: (1) by what we **say** through oral instruction; and (2) by what we **do** through physical action. The adage is true: "What you do speaks so loudly I cannot hear what you say." Children cannot (and should not be expected to) "sift" our actions, allowing the inconsistencies to be blown away as chaff before the wind while retaining the consistencies as the grain. That is not their job; it is ours as parents.

Parents' May Have an Incorrect View of God and His Word

As I noted earlier, the prophet Hosea, in speaking for God, lamented that "my people are destroyed for lack of knowledge" (4: 6). Today, God's people still are destroyed for lack of knowledge. Where knowledge is lacking, wisdom always will be in short supply. We cannot teach what we do not know. As parents, we cannot instruct our children in the precepts of the Lord if we do not first know those precepts ourselves. And as a result of our ignorance of God's Word, we inadvertently may place the soul of a child in danger. A specific example comes to mind.

Some time ago, a mother was discussing with me a serious problem in the life of her son. The sixteen-year-old boy had begun to date (with his parents' permission and foreknowledge) a girl that had a widely known (and well-deserved) reputation as being promiscuous, and the relationship had very quickly become sexual in nature. When another concerned parent inquired about what the mother planned to do about the situation, she responded by saying that it always had been her policy to "respect her children's privacy and not interfere in their lives" and to simply "let go and let God." Her point was this: she did not have to act on her child's behalf because God would.

But are those concepts scriptural? In God's divine plan, children were placed in the care of parents so that those parents could offer guidance, instruction, and discipline—and yes, so they could "interfere" in their children's lives from time to time. In Ephesians 6:1, children are commanded to obey their parents. Inherent in that command is the concept of parents giving instructions that are in keeping with God's Word, and that therefore should be obeyed. Three verses later in that same chapter, fathers are admonished to rear their children "in the chastening and admonition of the Lord." The writer of Proverbs noted: "He that spareth his rod hateth his son, but he that loveth him chasteneth him diligently" (13:24). Call it what you will—this is "interfering" in the life of a child. And it is the kind of interference that God not only expects, but commands.

In Proverbs 31, the writer painted a portrait of a godly woman who is described variously as a person who does good, works hard, and "openeth her mouth with wisdom, and the law of kindness is on her tongue; she looketh well to the ways of her household.... Her children rise up and call her blessed" (31:26-38). This hardly is the description of a mother who refuses to "interfere" in the lives of her children. Rather, a careful reading of Proverbs 31:10-31 presents a picture of a woman who is actively involved in the life of her husband and the lives of her children because, besides her own soul, they are her most cherished possessions. A mother who suggests that she is doing her children a favor by "not interfering" in their lives has a terribly warped view of what, according to God's Word, a mother is supposed to do,

Further, nowhere in Scripture is the concept of "let go and let God" presented in regard to the rearing of children. While the slogan may have some legitimacy if it is interpreted to mean that we always should trust God and have faith in Him, it is a gross misinterpretation of Scripture for a parent to use such a concept to suggest, "I do not have to act because God will act for me." It is true that faith is essential to a correct relationship with God (Ephesians 2:8-9). But it also is true that a biblical faith is an obedient, working faith. James addressed the relationship between our faith and our actions when he wrote:

> What doth it profit, my brethren, if a man say he hath faith, but have not works? Can that faith save him?... Yea, a man will say, Thou hast faith, and I have works: show me thy faith apart from thy works, and I by my works will show thee my faith (James 2:14,18).

As God's people, we are commanded to carry out certain duties and assignments. For example, we are to take the Gospel to the lost (Matthew 28:18-20). We are to care for orphans and widows (James 1:27). We are to minister to those in need (Matthew 6:7-12). Each of these is something Christians must do; God will not do them for us. We cannot simply "let go and let God."

The rearing of children falls into that same category. We often hear it said that "God will not do for us what we can do for ourselves." While that exact statement is not found in the Bible, the principle behind it is biblical. God expects us to use the tools He has provided to accomplish the task He has assigned. When a child is placed in our care, it is not as if we as parents are left to our own devices to rear that child. God has given us His Word—containing His instructions—on exactly what we are to do and how we are to go about doing it. While every situation that may arise in the life of a child may not be covered in the Bible by a "thus saith the Lord," the principles contained within God's Word will apply to every conceivable situation. For us simply to sit back and say that we will "let go and let God" is to ignore plain biblical teaching on parental responsibility. And, if we adhere to such a policy, it will spell ultimate doom for the souls of our children.

Parents did not Provide Proper Instruction or Supervision

The wording of the psalmist in speaking of our children as "arrows in the hand of a mighty man" (127:4) was no accident. Each step the archer takes is deliberately calculated. When he sights the goal, draws the bowstring, and sends the arrow on its way, it does not reach its intended target because it was handled in a haphazard fashion. The archer knows exactly where the arrow has been aimed, and he has taken steps to see that it successfully reaches its final target. Each step that we take as parents must be deliberately calculated as well. We must not handle our children's souls in a haphazard fashion. Every action we take must be with the intention of seeing our children reach their final target of a home in heaven with their God. If we do not provide proper instruction, or proper supervision, we will fail in that task.

In Proverbs 29:15, the writer observed that "a child left to himself bringeth shame to his mother." Have we not seen that very scenario acted out over and over again in this day and age? In times past, we as children came home to a house that was brightly lit and that smelled of hot, chocolate chip cookies just out of the oven. We opened the kitchen door on any given day after school and were met by a smiling mother with flour on her cheeks and an apron around her waist. Amazingly, she never was too busy to sit and talk to us, even though we had little of importance to say. As we ate those homemade cookies and looked into that flour-speckled face, we were making memories that would last us a lifetime. And, unbeknownst to us, we also were receiving instruction and supervision that would see us through both the good times and the bad. Our moms used those opportunities to talk to us about God, His will and way in the world, and His plans for our lives. We never even knew what our mothers were doing, but they knew. They were ensuring that their son or daughter was not the "child left unto himself."

How things have changed. Today, all too often children come home, not to a brightly lit house or to the smell of fresh-baked cookies, but to a dark, dank home where their only company is the television set or the Nintendo machine attached to it, and where store-bought cookies are to be found in the cookie jar on the kitchen cabinet. There is no apron-clad mother waiting to hear about the day's activities or to impart instructions to the waiting sponge-like mind of a child. And an opportunity to mold the mind of one so young has been missed yet another day.

Our children may find their souls in danger because we as parents fail to properly instruct and supervise those children. While we should be seizing every possible chance to "expound unto them the way of the Lord more accurately" (Acts 18:26), at times we may forfeit that opportunity. Then, not only is the needed instruction missing, but something else often takes its place. The example I mentioned above of the young man who began dating the girl of questionable moral character can provide some insight.

The parents involved chose not to "interfere" in this aspect of their son's life. As he built a relationship with the admittedly promiscuous young lady, he invited her to his house night after night —with his parents' approval. But the parents rarely were at home because they chose to go to church fellowships, social functions, dinner parties, Bible studies, etc., and thus were not present to provide any adult supervision. By their absence, they placed their son in harm's way. While this may not have been their intention, it was the end result of their actions. Instead of laying down proper guidelines and then providing supervision to ensure that those guidelines were obeyed, they paved the way for their son to lose his moral footing. Rather than being there for their son as his protector, they abandoned him both physically and spiritually. How many times have families seen a child lose his or her moral purity, or had to endure an unexpected pregnancy, because parents failed in their supervisory capacity? In such instances the proverb becomes all too real—"a child left to himself bringeth shame to his mother."

Parental Priorities Are not in Order

Each of us, parent or not, struggles to keep our priorities in order. In His beautiful Sermon on the Mount, Christ addressed the idea of how important it is that we succeed, and reminded us to "seek first the kingdom, and his righteousness, and all these things shall be added unto you" (Matthew 6:33). Sadly, when we fail in keeping our priorities straight, it often is our children who suffer most. This is, in fact, exactly what happened in the case of the young man discussed above. Something became more important than the protection of a son's soul. Eventually, both the child and the parents suffered as a result.

There is an old saying that "nature abhors a vacuum." When we as parents do not seize the God-given prerogative to fill our children's lives with things that are pure and wholesome, the world always stands ready to fill the vacuum. In Matthew 16:26, Jesus asked the question: "For what shall a man be profited, if he shall gain the whole world, and forfeit his soul? Or what shall a man give in exchange for his soul?" To a parent, that passage has a double meaning. While we rightly value highly our own souls—as we are instructed by Scripture to do—we also value highly the souls of our children. Most parents gladly would lay down their own lives to save the lives of their children. Even more so, then, should that kind of sacrifice be apparent when it comes to the soul of a child. No parent who loves the Lord, and who loves his or her children, can bear to think about the soul of even one of those children being lost. And surely, no parent could stomach the fact that such a loss was caused by his or her own parental neglect due to misplaced priorities.

Conclusion

Within each child there is an element of individuality that must be considered, and that cannot be ignored. As parents, we are commanded to train our child "in the way he should go." That phrase does not mean that we are to train our children in the way **we want them to go**. Rather, we are to take into account each child's personality, disposition, and natural talents, and as we do, we then can provide instruction that enables the child to be a spiritual success. It is our God-given duty as parents to study our children, to learn their ways, to know their strengths and weaknesses, and to avoid applying some kind of rigorous standard to each child in an indiscriminate fashion.

Each child possesses a God-given free will. Our job is to instruct our children carefully so that they use that free will properly, in keeping with God's plan for their lives. In John 5:39-40, Jesus told the Pharisees, "Ye search the scriptures, because ye think that in them ye have eternal life: and these are they which bear witness of me; and ye will not come to me that ye may have life." The Pharisees **could have** come to Christ, but they freely **chose** not to. Of interest is the fact that Jesus never violated their freedom of choice. We, as parents, cannot make the choices for our children. We can, however, use parental authority, prayer, biblical instruction, adult supervision, and the wisdom of the ages as found in God's inspired Word to help them make the correct choices in this pilgrimage we call "life."

To lose 50-90 out of every 100 of our youngsters is repulsive. To lose even one is a tragedy; that "one" is someone's precious son or daughter. We must begin immediately to correct this problem. But what can we do?

The following suggestions represent a compendium of ideas that I have gleaned from several authors on how we can keep our children saved (see Goad, 1981; Lanier, 1981; Workman, 1981b; Kearley, 1992; Fulford, 2001).

(1) We must work diligently to impart proper spiritual values to our children while at the same time working just as diligently to give them the evidence upon which they can build their own faith, rather than depending on them to live by ours. We must teach them how they can know God exists (Psalm 46:10), how they can know the Bible is His inspired Word (2 Timothy 3:16-17), how they can know Christ is His only begotten, virgin-born, crucified and resurrected Son (John 3:16; Matthew 1:21-23; Luke 22:33; Mark 16:1-6), the uniqueness and singularity of Christ's church Ephesians 5:22; 1:22-23; Colossians 1:18,24), the moral and ethical systems that God has designed for mankind (Galatians 5:16-24; Philippians 4:8-9), and the value of a single human soul (Matthew 16:26).

(2) We must demonstrate that God, His Word, His Son, and His church are the most important things in our lives. Our priorities must be correct, and we must not veer from those priorities. Our children need to hear us **say** that spirituality matters, and then see us **live** as if it really does.

(3) We must provide a "hothouse" of unselfish love. Our children need to know there is a place where they **always** will be accepted, and where unconditional *agape* love is given freely. We should provide them with a happy home—a place that becomes not only a sort of foyer or vestibule in this life through which they can "peek into" the next, but where we "make memories" that will last them a lifetime. Above all, our children must be able to experience in their present earthly home a foretaste of their future heavenly home.

(4) We need to teach our children to pray and to read their Bibles frequently (2 Timothy 2:15; Acts 17:11; 1 Thessalonians 5:17). Communion with their heavenly Father is important, and study of His Word will enrich their lives and provide them with strength to overcome the temptations of the world (2 Timothy 2:26; 2 Peter 2:9; James 4:7). As Dalton Key observed:

> The Bible is a parent's best friend. The principles of child-rearing sprinkled throughout the Bible are time-tested and true. They are quite literally heaven-sent. And one more thing I know—it is high time we who are parents begin to take parenthood seriously. May we use both the good sense and the Good Book which God has given us as we "bring them up in the nurture and admonition of the Lord" (Ephesians 6:4) (1992a, p. 2).

If we are successful, it will be our reward in that Great Day yet to come to stand beside those children and hear their Master say, "Well, done, good and faithful servant; enter into the joy of your Master." No earthly pleasure ever could compare with that of spending an eternity in heaven with the children we brought into this world—and helped usher into the next.

CHAPTER 12

ABANDONING FAITH—
WHY ARE WE LOSING
OUR ADULTS?

*"For all sad words of tongue or pen, the saddest are these:
'It might have been.'"* —John Greenleaf Whittier

As we make our way through this pilgrimage we call life, each of us faces opportunities and challenges that require not only forethought and decision, but commitment and dedication as well. At times we think carefully, choose wisely, and act forcefully. At times we do not.

While it is true that there exist scenarios in which a personal failure may be due to circumstances beyond our control, often it is true that the responsibility for failure rests solely with the individual. It seems to be a part of human nature that we readily empathize with the person who works hard, gives his best, and yet still fails. But it is just as much a part of human nature that we disdain the person who—in the heat of battle—simply quits, gives up, and walks away. That person will never experience the sweet taste of victory, the joy of success, or the innate pride of having given his all. Truly, the saddest words are, "It might have been."

Nowhere is the truth of this adage more evident than in our relationship with our God. And nowhere is failure more tragic, or the results more permanent. Within the pages of both the Old and New Testaments there are numerous accounts of people—or nations—that simply quit, gave up, and walked away from both their faith and their God. The results nearly always were disastrous to them personally. Sadder still was the effect their personal loss of faith had on family, friends, neighbors, and even future generations. It is a simple fact that many who leave the faith fail to count the high cost of doing so.

Every person familiar with the Old Testament is aware that one of its central themes is that of the evil results of spiritual apostasy. From the beginning of Genesis to the end of Malachi, Heaven's warning was this: faithfulness would bring spiritual life and God's blessings, while unfaithfulness would bring spiritual death and God's wrath. Ezekiel declared: "When the righteous man turneth away from his righteousness, and comitteth iniquity, and dieth therein; in his iniquity that he hath done shall he die" (Ezekiel 18:26).

Moses frequently warned the Israelites of the horrible effects of apostasy (see, for example, Deuteronomy 8:11-14; 4:9; 28:62). God was willing to help them possess the land of Canaan (Exodus 23:30; Deuteronomy 10:22). But on more than one occasion their sins reversed God's promised blessings. Eventually their apostasy caused God to allow them to be dispersed. In fact, no nation has ever been disseminated so completely. The Northern Kingdom was captured and removed from Canaan by the Assyrians c. 722 B.C. These people never would return to Israel as a group, and ended up being scattered around the world. The Southern Kingdom, Judah, was taken into captivity by the Babylonians, and despite the vast number of people exiled, only a remnant would return seventy years later.

Truly, God's people had failed to count the high cost of leaving the faith. That failure even affected generations yet unborn. Moses and the other prophets understood what so many of the general populace did not—obedience is important because it is the only possible demonstration of faith (James 2:18); without faith, no one can please God (Hebrews 11:6), and without obedience, there is no faith (Romans 1:5; 16:26).

Turning to the New Testament, the story remains much the same. During His tenure on Earth, Jesus warned that some, in temptation, would fall away from the faith (Luke 8:13), and even went so far as to note that some branches [disciples] would be pruned from Him as the vine and burned (John 15:1-6). We know that, indeed, some of the early Christians did leave the faith. The apostle Paul observed that Demas forsook him and his own faith, "having loved this present world" (2 Timothy 4:10). Some abandoned Christianity, reverting to their beloved Judaism, and in so doing "fell away" (Hebrews 6:4-6; Galatians 5:4). In fact, it was prophesied that prior to the return of Christ at His second coming, a great apostasy would occur (2 Thessalonians 2:1-12; cf. 1 Timothy 4:1ff., 2 Timothy 4:1ff.).

Paul observed that the things written in the Old Covenant had been penned "for our learning" (Romans 15:4), and that the old law was to be our "schoolmaster" (Galatians 3:24). It should come as no surprise, then, to see Paul catalog in 1 Corinthians 10 a number of instances in which the Israelites apostatized—as a warning to those who would follow so they could avoid making the same mistakes. Through the years that followed, however, there have been those who have ignored the inspired warning, and who subsequently have abandoned the faith. Why is this the case? And what has been the cost?

Why do Adult Christians Leave the Faith?

Were it possible for us today to catalog the reasons why adult Christians leave the faith, no doubt the list would be quite lengthy. Likely, however, included among those reasons would be some, or all, of the following.

First, some fall away because they neglect their own spiritual welfare. The Scriptures are clear regarding the fact that Christians have been provided a "great salvation" that should not be neglected (Hebrews 2:3). When a person does what the Bible commands him to do to be saved, he enters the kingdom (i.e., the church) as a newborn enters an earthly family—in need of milk for sustenance and tender care for survival. The apostle Peter spoke of such people as "newborn babes" who were to "long for the spiritual milk which is without guile, that ye may grow thereby unto salvation" (1 Peter 2:2). Paul discussed those whom he had fed spiritually "with milk, not with meat" because they were not yet ready for such (1 Corinthians 3:2).

But just as the neonatal child eventually grows into adolescence and adulthood, so, too, Christians are to mature in their faith. Peter observed that one of the responsibilities of being a faithful child of God is to "grow in the grace and knowledge of our Lord and Savior Jesus Christ" (2 Peter 3:18). There are those who never would dream of neglecting their **physical** needs (such as food, exercise, and rest) or the welfare of their families (shelter, food, medical treatment, etc.), yet who nevertheless carelessly neglect their **spiritual** needs. They do not attend worship services regularly (Hebrews 10:24-25). They make no effort to cultivate personal habits of diligent study and meditation (2 Timothy 2:15; Psalm 1:2; 1 Thessalonians 5:17). They ignore biblical commands to assist in the salvation of others and thus bear fruit as a Christian (John 15:1-10; Romans 7:4). They fail to sever harmful entanglements with the world (1 Corinthians 15:33; Ephesians 5:11; 2 Timothy 2:4). As a result, they grow disinterested in spiritual matters and eventually drift away completely. No other person or "outside force" caused the loss of their faith; rather, that loss occurred due to their own careless neglect.

Second, some leave the faith as a result of persecution. In His parable of the sower in Matthew 13, the Lord discussed how some of the seed (i.e., the Word of God) fell on rocky soil, which was a thin layer of dirt with a bedrock underneath. He then went on to explain how "he that was sown upon the rocky places, this is he that heareth the word, and straightway with joy receiveth it; yet hath he not root in himself, but endureth for a while; and when persecution ariseth because of the word, straightway he stumbleth" (vss. 20-21). No doubt some are drawn to Christianity because of the "abundant life" it ensures in the here and now (John 10:10), and because of the promise of an eternal life with God in the hereafter (John 3:16). They sometimes fail to realize, however, that "all that would live godly in Christ Jesus **shall** suffer persecution" (2 Timothy 3:12, emp. added). When that persecution arises—from family, friends, or the world—their faith becomes like the seed that fell on the shallow soil with a layer of bedrock underneath. It sprang up quickly, but soon was destroyed by the heat of the midday Sun. Perhaps this is why, in Luke 14:27-32, Christ provided several examples that were intended to emphasize the importance of counting the cost of discipleship. A part of that cost is persecution, as the passage above from 2 Timothy 3:2 makes plain. Failure to realize that, and to endure such persecution, has been responsible for the loss of many an individual's precious faith.

Third, some abandon their faith because they fall prey to false teaching. Faithful Christians must take heed how they hear (Luke 8:18) and must be careful to compare all that they hear to the Word of God (Acts 17:11). In Matthew 22:23-33, Christ vociferously rebuked the Sadducees because of their personal ignorance of the Word of God, and then attributed their manifold errors to such ignorance. In both 1 Timothy 4:1ff. and 2 Timothy 4:1ff., Paul foretold of a time when some would fall away from the faith because they succumbed to the doctrines of false teachers (cf. also 1 John 4:1). In this day and age, when there is a different religious group represented on practically every street corner, and a different televangelist on practically every TV station, it is all the more easy to fall victim to human doctrines that are at variance with the Word of God. Such doctrines have snared many, and have caused them to lose their souls.

While at times the end results of erroneous teaching may not be difficult to recognize, the false teacher is not always easy to identify. There are, however, certain discernible criteria that signal a departure from the Truth (see Miller, 1987). First, the person who teaches error generally is bold to advance his ideas in certain settings, but is strangely silent or evasive in others. When among those sympathetic to his erroneous views, he will not hesitate to advocate them, but when in the presence of those he knows are well versed in the Scriptures, and who therefore could recognize and refute such views, he often will keep them to himself, or even go so far as to deny believing them.

Second, whereas the false teacher once was understood easily, and known for the clarity with which he taught, now he has begun to speak or write in vague terms that employ a "new vocabulary" of his own making. When questioned or challenged, he then claims that he has been "misrepresented," "misunderstood," or "quoted out of context." He has become a chameleon-like character, able to vacillate back and forth between truth and error at will.

Third, as the real nature of the false teacher becomes increasingly evident and the documentation of his error irrefutable, he becomes more overt in his teachings. Soon he associates himself with those whom, in the past, he would have had no association. Others who are well known to teach error suddenly consider him an ally, and actively promote him and his teachings.

Fourth, in time, as more and more faithful Christians rise up to challenge the false teacher, he depicts them as troublemakers who are unreliable barometers of the present spiritual atmosphere. He charges them as being paranoid, narrow-minded, unloving, tradition-bound, stagnant, witch-hunting pseudo-Christians who possess no real love for the Lord or His Word. He urges them to dispense with their Pharisaic legalism, and to cloak themselves with an "irenic" spirit that allows Christians the right to "agree to disagree" about fundamental Bible doctrines, resulting in the misnamed concept known as "unity in diversity."

The damage inflicted by one who teaches error can be almost inestimable. That damage can be minimized, however, if faithful Christians follow the procedures set forth in Scripture for dealing with false teachers (e.g., Romans 16:17; Galatians 6:1; Ephesians 4:14-15; 5:11; 2 Thessalonians 3:6; 2 Timothy 2:25-26; Titus 3:10-11; James 5:19-20; 2 Peter 2:1-2; 1 John 4:1; 2 John 9-11). As Paul explained to Titus, "There are many unruly men, vain talkers and deceivers...whose mouths must be stopped; men who overthrow whole houses, teaching things which they ought not. ...For this cause reprove them sharply, that they may be sound in the faith" (Titus 1:10-11,13).

The sad truth is that all too often people are not willing to handle the Truth aright. When they are challenged regarding the inappropriate and incorrect content of their message, the justification they offer (even if it is not usually verbalized in these exact words—although on occasion it is!) is that "the end justifies the means." Some apparently feel that employing **just** straightforward, unadulterated Bible teaching will not impress people sufficiently to convince them to want to obey God's Word. Add to that the fact that it simply is not popular in our day and age to advocate many biblical truths, and it is clear why the message of the Bible frequently is altered (or ignored).

In every human activity, the process of recognizing, believing, and properly utilizing truth is vitally important. Jesus tried to impress this upon His generation when He said: "Ye shall know the truth, and the truth shall make you free" (John 8:32). The same principle operates even today, two thousand years later. Surely, if **knowing** the truth makes us free, then **not knowing** the truth makes us captives of one sort or another. When we refuse to acknowledge and believe the truth, we become susceptible to every ill-conceived plan, deceptive scheme, and false concept that the winds of change may blow our way. We become slaves to error because we have abandoned the one moral compass—truth—that possesses the ability to show us the way, and thereby to set us free.

The simple fact of the matter, however, is that we are responsible for what we choose to believe. Using the personal volition with which God has endowed us, we may choose freely to believe the truth, or we may choose just as freely to believe error. The choice is up to each individual. And once an individual has made up his mind that he prefers error over truth, God will not deter him, as Paul made clear when he wrote his second epistle to the Thessalonians. In that letter, he spoke of those who "received not the love of the truth" (2:10), and then went on to say that "for this cause God sendeth them a working of error, that they should believe a lie" (2 Thessalonians 2:11). What a horrible thought—to go through life believing a lie!

But what, exactly, was Paul suggesting when he stated that "God sendeth them a working of error, that they should believe a lie"? Was the apostle teaching that God **purposely** causes men to believe error?

No, he most certainly was not. Paul's point in this passage was that because God has granted man personal volition, and because He has provided within the Bible the rules, regulations, and guidelines to govern the use of that personal volition, He therefore will refrain from overriding man's freedom of choice—even when it violates His law. God will not contravene man's decisions or interfere with the actions based on those decisions. The prophet Isaiah had recorded God's words on this subject many years before when he stated:

> Yea, they have chosen their own ways, and their soul delighteth in their abominations: I also will choose their delusions, and will bring their fears upon them; because when I called, none did answer; when I spake, they did not hear: but they did that which was evil in mine eyes, and chose that wherein I delighted not (Isaiah 66:3-4).

The psalmist explained God's view on this matter when he wrote: "But my people hearkened not to my voice; and Israel would not hear me. So I let them go after the stubbornness of their heart, that they might walk in their own counsels" (Psalm 81:11-12). In Romans 11:8, Paul (quoting from Isaiah 29:10) stated concerning the rebellious Israelites: "God gave them a spirit of stupor, eyes that they should not see, and ears that they should not hear."

Therefore, as Paul penned his second epistle to the young evangelist Timothy, he urged him to "give diligence to present thyself approved unto God, a workman that needeth not to be ashamed, handling aright the word of truth" (2 Timothy 2:15). Surely it behooves us today as well to "handle aright" so precious a commodity as the "word of truth." The salvation of our own souls, and the souls of those with whom we come in contact and attempt to teach (by word or by deed), will depend on the accuracy of the message.

Some, however, have elected to employ their freedom of choice to ignore and/or disobey the truth. Concerning such people, Paul repeatedly stated that "God gave them up" (Romans 1:24,26,28). They **could** have come to a knowledge of the truth, but they **would not**.

Fourth, it cannot be denied that many have abandoned their faith because of suffering in their lives or in the lives of those they know and love. Even though man cannot explain in specific detail every instance of human suffering, contrary to what many believe there are several logical reasons why people experience mental and physical pain. One of the foremost reasons is rooted in the fact that God is love (1 John 4:8), and His love allows freedom of choice. God did not create men and women as robots to serve Him slavishly without any kind of free moral agency on their part (cf. Genesis 2:16-17; Joshua 24:15; John 5:39-40). God does not control His creation as a puppeteer controls a doll. Rather, as an expression of His love, He has granted mankind free will, and that free will enables human beings to make their own choices.

Man frequently brings suffering upon himself because of the wrong decisions he makes. The apostle Peter wrote: "But let none of you suffer as a murderer, a thief, an evildoer, or as a busybody in other people's matters" (1 Peter 4:15). When people suffer the consequences of their own wrong choices, they have no one to blame but themselves. If a person decides to kill someone, he very likely will suffer the unpleasant consequences of having made a terribly wrong choice. He may spend the rest of his life in prison, or perhaps be put to death himself. If a fornicator is found to have a sexually transmitted disease, it may be because he or she made the wrong decision to engage in illicit sex with someone who was infected. Thus, frequently mankind's suffering results from a misuse or abuse of personal freedom.

On occasion, man also suffers because of the personal wrong choices of others. If God allows one person freedom of choice, then to be consistent in His love for the world (John 3:16; 1 John 4:8), He must allow everyone that same freedom. God is no respecter of persons (cf. Acts 10:34; Romans 2:11). In 2 Samuel 11, we read where Uriah the Hittite suffered because of King David's sins. Ultimately, Uriah lost his life because of David's attempt to hide the sinful decisions he had made. Today, families may be affected adversely because a father is sent to prison on a drunk driving charge, or because a mother uses drugs. In each case, a single individual is the cause of an entire family's suffering. If a man chooses to smoke cigarettes and then eventually dies of lung cancer, his family suffers because of his bad decision. But God hardly is to blame.

Another reason for the suffering that humans endure (and one that is closely related to the first two) has to do with the personal wrong choices of former generations. For example, why are hordes of people starving to death in various Third World countries today? While that admittedly is a difficult question with several possible answers, one partial answer has to do with the fact that, millennia ago, these people's ancestors taught that it was wrong to eat certain animals because they might be eating one of their ancestors. The false doctrine of reincarnation, as this idea has come to be known, thus has deprived millions throughout the world of their health. Is God to blame when people will not eat the food He has provided—food that could provide them with proper nourishment? Again, the answer is "No." There can be no doubt that many of the decisions of former generations have caused much pain and suffering for those living in the world today.

Consider this, too. We frequently hear complaints about reaping evil from the wrong choices of generations long since gone, but we rarely hear expressions of gratitude for the many blessings that have been passed down to us as a result of the hard work and sacrifices of those same people. We live longer and healthier lives because of numerous medical discoveries, and we have technological conveniences that make our daily lives all the more pleasant. Truth be told, we eat of vineyards we did not plant, and we drink of cisterns we did not dig. We owe much to many of the distant past. The fact is, while man often suffers because of the sins of former generations, he also benefits from their labors. If man truly is free, it must be possible for him to reap the benefits, as well as suffer the consequences, of his own decisions and the decisions of others.

People also suffer because of violations of natural law. Fortunately, God created a world ruled by specific laws that He established at the Creation. Those laws were implemented for man's own good, but if the laws are violated, then man will suffer the consequences. If a man steps off the roof of a five-story building, gravity will pull him to the pavement beneath. If a boy steps in front of a moving freight train, since two objects cannot occupy the same space at the same time, the train will strike the child and likely kill him. Why? Because he has (knowingly or unknowingly) violated the natural order of this world. The natural laws that God created allow man to produce fire. But the same laws that enable him to cook his food also allow him to destroy entire forests. Laws that make it possible to have things **constructive** to human life also introduce the possibility that things **destructive** to human life may occur. How can it be otherwise? A moving car is matter in motion, and takes us where we wish to go. But if someone steps in front of that car, the same natural laws that operated to our benefit will similarly operate to our detriment. The same laws that govern gravity, matter in motion, or similar phenomena also govern weather patterns, water movement, and other geological/meteorological conditions. **All** of nature is regulated by these laws—not just the parts that we find convenient. If God suspended natural laws *every* time one of His creatures was in a dangerous or life-threatening situation, chaos would corrupt the Cosmos and would argue more for a world of **atheism** than a world of **theism**! Furthermore, as Geisler noted:

> First, evil men do not really want God to intercept **every** evil act or thought. No one wants to get a headache *every* time he thinks against God. One does not want God to fill his mouth with cotton when he speaks evil of God, nor does he really desire God to explode his pen as he writes against God or destroy his books before they come off the press. At best, people really want God to intercept **some** evil actions.... Second, continual interference would disrupt the regularity of natural law and make life impossible. Everyday living depends on physical laws such as inertia or gravity. Regular interruption of these would make everyday life impossible and a human being extremely edgy! Third, it is probable that chaos would result from continued miraculous intervention. Imagine children throwing knives at parents because they know they will be turned to rubber, and parents driving through stop signs, knowing God will create crash-protection air shields to avert any ensuing collisions. The necessary intervention would finally grow in proportions that would effectively remove human freedom and responsibility (1978, p. 75, emp. in orig.).

Everyone (believer and unbeliever alike) must obey the natural laws that God established, or else suffer the consequences. In Luke 13:2-5, Jesus told the story of eighteen men who died when the tower of Siloam collapsed on them. Had these men perished because of their sins? No, they were no worse sinners than their peers. They died because a natural law was in force. Fortunately, natural laws work continually so that we can understand and benefit from them. We are not left to sort out some kind of haphazard system that works one day but not the next.

Sadly, however, we today do not inhabit a world reminiscent of the Garden of Eden; rather, we live in a world devastated by the effects of man's sin (Genesis 3:16ff.; Romans 5:12; 8:20ff.). Planet Earth is ravaged by natural disasters such as earthquakes, hurricanes, and tornadoes that often take an awful toll on both property and human life. Our bodies and minds are ravaged by an increasingly long list of maladies such as cancer, heart attacks, and Alzheimer's disease. Many through the ages have abandoned their belief in God because of the presence of evil, pain, and suffering in their lives or in the lives of those close to them.

Throughout history, for example, man has experienced great tragedies. In 526, an earthquake hit the country now known as Turkey, and left 250,000 dead. A similar earthquake in China in 1556 killed over 830,000 people. Another quake in India in 1737 annihilated 300,000, and quakes in Central China in 1920, 1927, and 1932 killed 200,000, 200,000, and 70,000 people respectively. In 1889, the famous "Johnstown Flood" occurred in Pennsylvania. The dam of the South Fork Reservoir, twelve miles east of the city, burst during heavy rains. Over 2,000 people were killed, and property damage was estimated to be over $10 million. In 1969, Hurricane Camille killed more than 250 people in seven states from Louisiana to Virginia, leaving behind over $1.5 billion in damage. In 1983, Hurricane Alicia struck near Galveston, killing 21 and causing over $2 billion in damage.

On September 21, 1989, Hurricane Hugo struck the southeastern coast of the United States. Over 25 people were killed, and over $10 billion worth of damage resulted. One month later, on October 17, an earthquake registering 7.1 on the Richter scale hit the San Francisco Bay area in California. At least 62 people were died, and damage estimates were placed at well over $1 billion. On August 24, 1992, Hurricane Andrew struck three counties in southern Florida. More than a dozen people lost their lives, and damage estimates were set at over $20 billion. A year later, on September 11, 1992, Hurricane Iniki devastated the Hawaiian islands. At least four people died, and damages reached over $1 billion. In June 1993, huge portions of numerous states along the Mississippi River and its tributaries experienced the worst flooding in their history. Entire cities stood covered with water measured not in inches, but in feet. At least 47 people died, and more than 25,000 were evacuated from their homes. The United States Congress appropriated approximately $3 billion in an attempt to cope with the tragedy. In March 1997, the Ohio River overran its banks and did a similar amount of damage.

It is rare, it seems, for a single generation in a given locale to be spared at least some kind of natural disaster. Without warning, tornadoes sweep down from the afternoon sky and destroy in a moment's fury what took decades or centuries to build. Floods cover "old home places" and remove forever any vestige of what were once storehouses of hallowed memories. In a matter of seconds, earthquakes irreparably alter once-familiar landscapes. Hurricanes come from the sea, demolish practically everything in their paths, and then dissipate as if they never had existed. Each time, humanity suffers. And each time there are those who ask **"Why?"** Why does the Earth experience natural disasters in the first place, and why are such disasters not incompatible with a benevolent God?

In the face of disasters such as those described above, there is hardly any question likely to be asked more routinely than "why?" But the question is not always asked in the same way, or with the same intent. Some stand on the charred remains of what was once their home and ask, "why me?"—and mean exactly that. Why **them** and why **now**? All they want is to **understand** the physical events that have changed their lives, and to learn what they can do to correct the situation and avoid a repeat of it. They are not looking to assign blame; they merely want an explanation of the prevailing circumstances.

Others view the destruction around them and ask "why?," but their inquiry is brief and their response immediate. They correctly view the Earth as a once-perfect-but-now-flawed home for mankind. Rather than their faith in God being diminished by the ravages of ongoing natural phenomena, it is strengthened because they: (a) know that there are rational biblical and scientific explanations for such events; (b) understand that after all is said and done, "the Judge of all the Earth will do that which is right" (Genesis 18:25); and (c) put their faith into action as they work to help themselves, or those around them whose lives have been affected by a disaster.

Still others view natural disasters and ask "why?," when what they really mean is: "If a benevolent God exists, why did He allow these things to happen?" The implication of their statement is clear. Since these things **did** happen, God must not exist.

It is not my purpose here to address the "why me, why now?" question that seeks a **physical** explanation as to what kind of swirling wind current spawns a tornado, or what kind of geological phenomena may be responsible for an earthquake. Much has been written on these and similar topics, and can provide adequate answers for those willing to research the problem. Instead, I would like to answer the more pressing **philosophical** questions of why the Earth experiences natural disasters in the first place, and why such disasters are not incompatible with a benevolent God.

At the end of His six days of creation (Genesis 1:31), God surveyed all that He had made and proclaimed it "very good"—Hebrew terminology representing that which was both complete and perfect. Rivers were running, fish were swimming, and birds were flying. Pestilence, disease, and human death were unknown. Man existed in an incomparable paradise of happiness and beauty where he shared such an intimate and blissful covenant relationship with his Maker that God came to the Garden of Eden "in the cool of the day" to commune with its human inhabitants (Genesis 3:8). Additionally, Genesis 3:22 records that man had continual access to the tree of life that stood in the garden, the fruit of which would allow him to live forever.

The peacefulness and tranquility of the first days of humanity were not to prevail, however. In Genesis 3—in fewer words than an average sportswriter would use to discuss a Friday night high school football game—Moses, through inspiration, discussed the breaking of the covenant relationship between man and God, the entrance of sin into the world, and the curse(s) that resulted therefrom. When our original parents revolted against their Creator, evil entered the world. Moses informs us that as a direct consequence of human sin, the Earth was "cursed" (Genesis 3:17). Paul, in Romans 8:20-21, declared that the entire creation was subjected to "futility" and the "bondage of corruption" as a result of the sinful events that took place in Eden on that occasion. Things apparently deteriorated rapidly. Just three chapters later, Moses wrote of the saturated wickedness of man (Genesis 6:5-7).

Genesis 6-8 records the global destruction resulting from the Great Flood sent by God as His instrument of judgment. The text indicates that the waters that caused the Flood originated from two distinct sources: (a) "the fountains of the great deep"; and (b) "the windows of heaven" (Genesis 7:11). Water fell for forty days and nights (Genesis 7:12,17), and eventually covered "all the high hills under the whole heaven" (Genesis 7:19). We may only surmise the changes that the Flood wrought upon the Earth. Local floods can cause tremendous damage in very brief periods. Imagine, then, the damage that the waters of the Flood must have caused as they covered every mountain to a height of fifteen cubits (Genesis 7:20; approximately 22½ feet). As one writer has suggested:

> The destructive power of flood-waters is evident from what flood waters in recent years have done. They moved blocks of granite weighing 350 tons more than a hundred yards. Boulders weighing 75 to 210 tons have been moved by flood waters only 15 to 20 feet deep.... What vast devastation must have been created when all those forces of the earth worked together; rain gushing down from the canopy above the firmament, earthquakes shaking the earth, many volcanoes erupting and exploding at one time, continents shifting,

> mountains lifting up, tornados, hurricanes and wild wind-
> storms raging, gigantic tidal waves with crosscurrents and
> whirlpools raising havoc.... Truly, the Flood was the greatest
> and most violent catastrophe in the history of the world, with
> total destruction of all forms of life and of the entire surface
> of the earth (Sippert, 1989, pp. 78-79).

What were conditions like on Earth prior to the Great Flood?
Numerous scientific and biblical scholars have suggested that conditions were radically different than those we see today, and that the
Earth was devoid of the many natural disasters that it presently experiences (see Rehwinkel, 1951; Whitcomb and Morris, 1961; Dillow, 1981). In their classic text, *The Genesis Flood*, John C. Whitcomb and Henry M. Morris stated:

> This is inferred from the fact that the "breaking-up of the
> fountains of the great deep" (Genesis 7:11), which implies
> this sort of activity, was one of the immediate causes of the
> Deluge; therefore it must have been restrained previously....
> Thus the Biblical record implies that the age between the fall
> of man and the resultant Deluge was one of comparative qui-
> escence geologically. The waters both above and below the
> firmament were in large measure restrained, temperatures
> were equably warm, there were no heavy rains nor winds and
> probably no earthquakes nor volcanic emissions (1961, pp.
> 242,243).

It is not unreasonable to suggest, knowing the changes caused by
local floods, that the global Flood of Genesis 6-8 not only radically
altered the face of the Earth, but simultaneously produced circumstances that are responsible for the many natural disasters experienced since that time. New, higher mountains and lower valleys were
produced by God after the Flood (Psalm 104:6-10). Approximately
71.9% of the Earth's surface remained covered with water. Tem-
perature changes occurred, producing seasonal variations unlike
any before. No doubt other factors were involved as well.

What causes natural disasters on the Earth today? One cause,
of course, is the vastly different geological and meteorological phenomena now present on our planet. Tall mountains and deep val-

leys can be conducive to localized extremes in weather. The drastically changed components of the Earth's crust (e.g., fault lines, etc.) give rise to earthquakes. Vast bodies of water, and large global climatic variations, spawn hurricanes and tropical storms. In his second epistle, the apostle Peter referred to "the world that then was" and its destruction by the Flood (3:6). Unfortunately, that world no longer exists. Today we inhabit a once-perfect-but-now-flawed Earth.

But, some will ask, why can't God "selectively intervene" to prevent disasters? Bruce Reichenbach has addressed this question:

> ...[I]n a world which operates according to divine miraculous intervention, there would be no necessary relation between phenomena, and in particular between cause and effect. In some instances one event would follow from a certain set of conditions, another time a different event, and so on, such that ultimately an uncountable variety of events would follow a given set of conditions. There would be no regularity of consequence, no natural production of effects.... Hence, we could not know or even suppose what course of action to take to accomplish a certain rationally conceived goal. Thus, we could neither propose action nor act ourselves (1976, p. 187).

How, exactly, could a livable, dependable world—governed by appropriate and understandable laws—be created and operated, other than the way ours presently is? And how, in such a world, could disasters be prevented, while maintaining both natural law and human freedom?

Upon whom should we heap blame for the suffering that results from natural catastrophes? Is it fair to accuse God, when He initially created man's home free from such things (Genesis 1:31)? In all honesty, the answer has to be no. Sin robbed us of our original garden paradise, and sin was responsible for the global deluge (Genesis 3:24; 6:7). One writer concluded: "[T]he cause of all that is wrong with the earth is **not** godliness but rather **un**godliness" (Porter, 1974, p. 467, emp. in orig.). God is not to blame.

Furthermore, one of the messages of the beautiful book of Job is that Jehovah does not necessarily shield His people from tragedy. It is a scriptural teaching that while we are the recipients of many blessings, we also are affected by calamities from time to time. But just as surely, one of the lessons to be learned here is that it does not pay to disobey our Creator.

Instead of blaming God when tragedies such as natural disasters strike, we need to turn to Him for strength and let tragedies, of whatever nature, remind us that this world never was intended to be our final home (Hebrews 11:13-16). Our time here is temporary (James 4:14), and with God's help, we can triumph over whatever comes our way (Romans 8:35-39; Psalm 46:1-3). In the end, the most important question is not "Why did this happen to me?," but rather "How can I understand what has happened, and how am I going to react to it?" With Peter, the faithful Christian can echo the sentiment that God, "who called us to His eternal glory by Christ Jesus, after you have suffered a while, perfect, establish, strengthen, and settle you. To Him be the glory and the dominion forever and ever" (1 Peter 5:10-11).

As He ended His Sermon on the Mount, Christ told a parable about two men, one of whom He labeled as wise for building his house upon a foundation of rock, and one of whom He labeled as foolish for building his house upon a foundation of sand (Matthew 7:24-27). The Lord's point was two-fold: (1) trials and tribulations will come; and (2) in order for faith to stand firm, it must be rooted in God's Word. Sometimes the trials and tribulations are literal disasters such as those Christ discussed in His parable—like floods, winds, and rains. Sometimes, however, the trials and tribulations are mental or spiritual assaults upon a person's faith that arrive in the form of persecution, the effects of disease upon a loved one, or the death of a family member. Unfortunately, on occasion such assaults raise questions in the mind of a Christian concerning the benevolence and omnipotence of God. Deep-seated emotions are stirred and the seeds of doubt begin to sprout, eventually coming into full bloom to replace what was once a vibrant, living faith. Faithfulness turns into faithlessness, and a soul is lost.

Remember, too, that there **are** times when suffering is **beneficial**. Think of the man whose chest begins to throb as he enters the throes of a heart attack. Think of the woman whose side begins to ache at the onset of acute appendicitis. Is it not true that pain often sends us to the doctor for prevention or cure? Is it not true also that at times suffering helps humankind develop the traits that people treasure the most? Bravery, heroism, altruistic love, self-sacrifice—all flourish in less-than-perfect environments, do they not?

Finally, no one can suggest—justifiably—that suffering per se is contrary to the existence or goodness of God, in light of the series of events that transpired at Calvary almost two thousand years ago. The fact that **even Jesus as the Son of God** was subjected to evil, pain, and suffering (Hebrews 5:8; 1 Peter 2:21ff.) proves that God loves and cares for His creation. He is not the unloving, angry, vengeful God depicted by atheism and infidelity. Rather, "when we were enemies we were reconciled to God through the death of His Son, much more, having been reconciled, we shall be saved by His life" (Romans 5:10). God could have abandoned us to our own sinful devices but instead, "God demonstrates His own love toward us, in that while we were still sinners, Christ died for us" (Romans 5:8; 1 John 4:9-10).

There are, to be sure, numerous other reasons why Christians leave the faith. Some place their confidence in men, only to see that those they trust also have feet of clay. As the writer of Proverbs observed: "Confidence in an unfaithful man in time of trouble is like a broken tooth and a foot out of joint" (25:19). Some abandon their faith as a result of fellow Christians whose actions may be well intentioned, but nevertheless harsh and inappropriate. For example, new Christians, through ignorance and/or weakness, may commit a sin, and yet before they can be restored lovingly and patiently (Galatians 6:1), they are (spiritually) billy-clubbed to death by some insensitive zealot. More than one sincere soul has had his or her fledgling faith bludgeoned and destroyed by a tactless saint who feels "deputized" by the Lord to right every wrong under the banner of defending the faith.

Some fall away because they do not maintain a steady diet of association with other Christians, and exposure to the world on a daily basis causes their commitment to God to wane. Regardless of the reason(s), the fact remains that as they are on their way to heaven, some Christians lose sight of the goal, become distracted or disinterested, take a detour, and end up leaving the faith altogether. But at what cost?

The High Cost of Leaving the Faith

In Romans 12:2, Paul warned: "And be not fashioned according to this world; but be ye transformed by the renewing of your mind, that ye may prove what is the good and acceptable and perfect will of God." Sad though it may be, the truth is that some Christians ultimately leave the faith, and again are "fashioned according to this world." They once were lost, but were offered salvation as the gift of God (Ephesians 2:8-9). Yet they spurned the Lord's gift, choosing instead to relinquish the treasures of a home in heaven for a meager measure of earthly pottage. What an unseemly trade—and at what a terrible price! Surely those who do such have failed to count the high cost of leaving the faith.

The Cost to the Individual Himself

In addressing the apostasy of certain Christians, the apostle Peter lamented:

> For if, after they have escaped the defilements of the world through the knowledge of the Lord and Savior Jesus Christ, they are again entangled therein and overcome, the last state is become worse than the first. For it were better for them not to have known the way of righteousness, than, after knowing it, to turn back from the holy commandment delivered unto them. It has happened unto them according to the true proverb, The dog turning to his own vomit again, and the sow that had washed to wallowing in the mire (2 Peter 2:21-22).

The apostle paints an ugly picture with his vivid description of the end state of those who leave the faith. Peter's observation that in the case of these apostates, their "last state is become worse than the first," is fitting indeed. Think of the burden of guilt that will follow them all the days of their lives. These are people who once knew the serenity of salvation. These are people who once understood the promise of an eternal life in heaven. These are people who once enjoyed the friendship and fellowship of other saints. But now, all of that is gone, having been freely relinquished and subsequently replaced with the knowledge of eventually spending an eternity in the absence of God in an eternal hell (2 Peter 2: 4; Revelation 21:8).

As the days pass by in their own fleeting fashion, what will run through the mind of the apostate? In more private moments, as he sits quietly on the park bench on a beautiful spring day, or looks pensively out the bay window of his house at the gentle rain as it falls from heaven, will his knowledge of what he knows he should do, but refuses to do, not eat away at his inner peace? Will he not remember passages such as James 4:17: "To him that knoweth to do right, and doeth it not, to him it is sin"? Will he not remember Paul's statement from Philippians 2:10-11 that "in the name of Jesus every knee should bow, or things in heaven and things on the earth and things under the earth, and that every tongue should confess that Jesus Christ is Lord, to the glory of God the father"? While his outward appearance may exhibit a confident attitude of indifference toward his present spiritual state, his true inner self may languish in the knowledge that he once was saved, but now is lost.

The Cost to Families

In Romans 14:7, Paul commented on the human condition when he noted that "none of us liveth to himself, and none dieth to himself." How true an observation that is. Hermits are few and far between. Man rarely does well when isolated from others of his kind. When God looked down from His heavenly estate on the first man,

Adam, whom He had created, He remarked, "It is not good that man should be alone" (Genesis 2:18). Nothing has changed since that initial divine diagnosis.

From the beginning to the end of our pilgrimage of life, we interact socially with those around us. We move beyond childhood and adolescence to adulthood. And as is often the case, we fall in love, marry, form a home, bear and rear children, and possibly even become grandparents or great-grandparents. Although at times we wish they did not, the truth of the matter is that more often than not the decisions we make, and the actions that stem from those decisions, inevitably affect those we love the most. Certainly this is true in a spiritual context.

For example, Peter noted that the effects of a godly wife upon her husband might be responsible for bringing his soul to the Lord. "In like manner, ye wives be in subjection to your own husbands; that, even if any obey not the word, they may without a word be gained by the behavior of their wives, beholding your chaste behavior coupled with fear" (1 Peter 3:1-2). What a sobering thought—that one person, through behavior tempered by a reverent fear of God, ultimately might influence a sinner to come to salvation.

But what is the corollary to this concept? If **faithfulness** produces such wonderful results, what results might **unfaithfulness** produce? Does not practical experience answer that question in a thousand different ways? Consider, for example, the following scenario. A young man grows up, becomes a Christian, falls in love, and marries a lovely Christian woman with whom he has two children. But during the children's impressionable years of youth, the man and his wife grow indifferent about their own spiritual conduct and welfare, and eventually leave the faith. Church attendance stops. Fellowship with Christians is severed. Years pass. Then, at the persistent urging of a friend, this couple attends a lecture on the Bible and man's responsibility according to it. The message moves both the husband and wife to repent of their years of spiritual apathy. They ask for, and are granted by God and their fellow Christians, forgiveness. They then begin their Christian life anew.

But what of their two children? These are the children who for years witnessed the callous indifference of their parents toward spiritual matters. These are the children who rarely, if ever, were taken to worship God or to attend Bible class. These are the children whose Bible knowledge would fit into a sewing thimble, because during the years when they should have been receiving spiritual instruction at home, their parents were not even capable of sustaining their own faith, much less imparting that faith to their offspring.

Their parents have returned to God. But experience tells us it is highly unlikely that these children ever will. Because of the parents' unfaithfulness at a critical time in their children's lives, the opportunity to impart a living, active faith to those children during their most impressionable years has been lost forever. And what, then, will become of this couple's grandchildren and great grandchildren? Is it not true to say that likely they, too, will be reared in an atmosphere of indifference, apathy, or outright unbelief? Thus, the spiritual condition of not one, but several generations, has been affected adversely as a result of unfaithfulness on the part of parents who failed to count the high cost of leaving the faith.

The Cost to the Church

On occasion, however, it is not just physical families that suffer due to a member's unfaithfulness. Sometimes the spiritual family of the church suffers just as well. The sin of a single individual can have severe repercussions for those around him. Paul applied this principle when he urged the Christians at Corinth to discipline one of their own members who was living in adultery. He warned them: "Know ye not that a little leaven leaveneth the whole lump?" (1 Corinthians 5:6).

Suppose, just to choose one example, that the local evangelist commits adultery and leaves his wife and family. First, there is little doubt that the church's reputation will be damaged. As he works in a local community, a preacher's influence is exhibited in a variety of ways, and his actions, rightly or wrongly, often are interpreted by non-Christians as representative of what Christians in general should be like. The fact that he has been unfaithful not only to his wife, but to his Lord, may well have a negative impact on how the church is viewed by those who are not members of it, and yet who under different circumstances would have been kindly disposed to it. This is true of any Christian, not just one who is continually in the public eye.

Second, such circumstances will provide "grist for the mill" of those who always are searching for reasons to revile the church collectively and its members individually. When he wrote his first epistle to the young evangelist Timothy, Paul urged that his instructions be carried out so that there would be "no occasion to the adversary for reviling" (1 Timothy 5:14). When Christians leave the faith, it supplies ammunition for those who have set themselves against God's work through His church.

Third, there are weak and new Christians to consider. As they see a man who was once a faithful Christian fall into sin and abandon his faith, it can have a devastating effect upon theirs. The new Christian, or the one who already is struggling, may reason as follows: If a man who is a seasoned child of God has lost his way and left the faith, then what hope is there for me? The initial unfaithfulness of a single individual may, on occasion, set off a chain reaction that decimates the body of Christ in a manner no one could have imagined.

Conclusion

Christians may freely choose to walk away from their faith in God, but no power in existence can take that faith from them without their consent. Paul assured the Christians of his day, and for all ages, that this was true when he wrote:

> Who shall separate us from the love of Christ? Shall tribulation, or anguish, or persecution, or famine, or nakedness, or peril, or sword?... Nay, in all these things we are more than

conquerors through him that loved us. For I am persuaded that neither death, nor life, nor angels, nor principalities, nor things present, nor things to come, nor powers, nor height, nor depth, nor any other creature, shall be able to separate us from the love of God, which is in Christ Jesus our Lord (Romans 8:35-37).

While it is true that some Christians fall away, it does not have to be so. Peter provided instructions from the Lord for the Christians of his day, and then reminded them: "Wherefore, brethren, give the more diligence to make your calling and election sure: for if ye do these things, ye shall never stumble" (2 Peter 1:10).

CHAPTER 13

FAITHFULLY TEACHING THE FAITH

On certain occasions, when matters of a spiritual nature are under discussion, it is not uncommon to hear someone suggest that they adhere to, or someone they know adheres to, a religion that is "better felt than told." The thrust of such a statement, of course, is that it is not the **teaching** within the person's religion that is of ultimate importance, but rather the individual's personal feelings and emotional commitment.

While this sentiment may represent a correct assessment of the religion of some, it never has been true in regard to the biblical view of faith. This is not to imply, of course, that those who trust and obey God exhibit a faith that is void of emotion, or that somehow they are less committed to their belief system than adherents of other religions. Certainly, faith in the God of the Bible always has involved both personal feelings and emotional commitment (Matthew 22:37). To suggest otherwise would be to rob man of his free moral agency, his innate right to accept or reject heaven's gracious offer of salvation, and his ability to delight in having made the correct choice.

What sets biblical faith apart from the beliefs of some other religions, however, is that instead of being rooted solely in an appeal to the emotions, it is rooted in an appeal to both the emotions and the intellect. In other words, biblical faith addresses both the heart and the mind; it is not just **felt,** but **learned** as well. This always has been the case. From the moment of man's creation, God sought to teach him how to make correct choices that would keep him in, or return him to, a covenant relationship with his Creator. Thus, as soon as man was placed in the lovely Garden of Eden, God gave the instructions necessary for man's temporal and spiritual well being (Genesis 1:28; 2:16-17). From that moment forward, God actively taught man how to build, and maintain, a proper relationship with his heavenly Father. This is evident within the pages of both the Old and New Testaments.

The Old Testament, for example, is filled with numerous instances of God's providing people with the instructions that would prompt them to serve Him with their hearts as well as with their intellects. During the Patriarchal Age, God spoke directly to the renowned men of old, and conveyed to them the commandments intended to regulate their daily lives, as well as their worship of Him. The apostle Paul, alluding to the Gentiles, spoke of those who had the law "written in their hearts, their conscience bearing witness therewith, and their thoughts accusing or else excusing them" (Romans 2: 15).

Later, during the Mosaical Age, God's instructions were given to the Hebrews in written form so that as they grew numerically, they also would possess the ability to grow spiritually. Jewish parents were instructed to teach God's Word to their children on a continuing basis (see Deuteronomy 4:10; 6:7-9; 11:18-25). Eventually, when national and spiritual reform was needed, God provided numerous kings and prophets to perform this important task (see 2 Kings 23:1-3; 2 Chronicles 7:7-9). It is said of the Old Testament prophet Ezra that he "had set his heart to seek the law of Jehovah, and to do it, and to **teach** in Israel statutes and ordinances" (Ezra

7:10, emp. added). Nehemiah 8:7-8 records that Ezra "caused the people to understand the law: and the people stood in their place, and they **read** in the book, in the law of God, distinctly; and they **gave the sense**, so that they **understood** the reading" (emp. added).

It is clear from such passages that during Old Testament times God placed a premium on knowing, understanding, obeying, and teaching His commandments. The golden thread that runs from Genesis through Malachi—the urgent message that the Savior was coming—could not be expressed through emotion alone; the intellect had to be involved as well. It was not enough for God's people merely to "feel" the message; it had to be **taught** so they could understand it, realize its importance to their ultimate salvation, and preserve it for generations yet unborn, to whom it also would be taught.

Similarly, the New Testament stresses the critical nature of teaching. In the first century A.D., the message no longer was "the Savior **is coming**"; rather, the message was "the Savior **has come**." Once Jesus began His public ministry, teaching His disciples (and others whom He encountered on almost a daily basis) became His primary task. While it is true that today we look upon Him as a miracle-worker, prophet, and preacher, He was foremost a teacher. Throughout the highways and byways of Galilee, Samaria and Judea, Jesus taught in synagogues, boats, temples, streets, marketplaces, and gardens. He taught on plains, trails, and mountainsides —wherever people were and would listen. And He taught as One possessing authority. After hearing His discourses, the only thing the people who heard Him could say was, "Never man so spake" (John 7:46).

The teaching did not stop when Christ returned to heaven. He had trained others—apostles and disciples—to continue the task He had begun. They were sent to the uttermost parts of the Earth with the mandate to proclaim the "good news" through preaching and teaching (Matthew 28:18-20). This they did daily (Acts 5:42).

The eventual result was additional disciples, who then were rooted and grounded in the fundamentals of God's Word (Acts 2:42) so they could teach others. In a single day, in a single city, over 3,000 people became Christians as a result of such teaching (Acts 2:41).

In fact, so effective was this kind of instruction that Christianity's bitterest enemies desperately tried to prohibit any further public teaching (Acts 4:18; 5:28), yet to no avail. Christianity's message, and the unwavering dedication of those into whose hands it had been placed, were too powerful for even its most formidable foes to abate or defeat. Twenty centuries later, the central theme of the Cross still is vibrant and forceful. But will that continue to be the case if those given the sobering task of teaching the Gospel act irresponsibly and alter its content, or use fraudulent means to present it? The simple fact is—Christianity's success today, just as in the first century, is dependent on the dedication, and honesty, of those to whom the Truth has been entrusted. God has placed the Gospel plan of salvation into the hands of men and women who have been instructed to teach it so that all who hear it might have the opportunity to obey it, and be saved. The apostle Paul commented on this when he wrote: "But we have this treasure in earthen vessels, that the exceeding greatness of the power may be of God, and not from ourselves" (2 Corinthians 4:7). The thrust of the apostle's statement in this particular passage was that the responsibility of taking the Gospel to a lost and dying world ultimately has been given to mortal men.

"Handling Aright the Word of Truth"

But the power is not in the men; rather, it is in the message! This, no doubt, accounts for the instructions Paul sent to Timothy in his second epistle when he urged the young evangelist to "give diligence to present thyself approved unto God, a workman that needeth not to be ashamed, **handling aright the word of truth**" (2 Timothy 2:15, emp. added). In addressing this point, Wayne Jackson wrote:

The New Testament makes it abundantly clear that Christians are to proclaim the gospel of God in a loving and positive way. We are to expose every rational creature to the good news regarding the death, burial and resurrection of Jesus of Nazareth. We should assume that each person we encounter is an honest soul until he or she demonstrates that such is not the case. Like the Lord, our mission is to seek those who are lost.... In our defense of the faith, however, we must maintain the highest level of integrity. Our argumentation must be honest and it must be sound. Any person who knowingly employs a fallacious argument in defense of some biblical truth is unworthy of the name of Christ. Truth does not need the support of misapplied scripture and invalid reasoning. It can stand on its own. There are occasions, though, when sincere people, who are honestly attempting to defend a biblical truth, unknowingly employ unsound argumentation in the process. Perhaps many of us have discovered, in retrospect, that we have made these sorts of mistakes. When such is the case, we will resolve to never repeat them—no matter how flashy or impressive the argument appears to be. Virtue demands that we attempt to prove our position correctly (1990a, 26:1).

Considering the fact that we, as God's "earthen vessels," have been made the instruments through which God offers to a lost and dying world reconciliation through His Son (John 3:16), the apostle's admonition is well taken. Surely it behooves us to "handle aright" so precious a commodity as the Word of God. The salvation of our own souls, and the souls of those we instruct, depends on the accuracy of the message.

The Unintentional Teaching of Error

Two kinds of erroneous teaching are under discussion in the above assessment. Error can result when a person inadvertently teaches something that is incorrect. The mistake is accidental and unintentional; the teacher means well, and is sincere, but is wrong. The New Testament itself records just such an incident.

In Acts 18, the story is related about Apollos, a Jew who was "fervent in spirit" and who "spake and taught accurately the things concerning Jesus" (Acts 18:25). However, when Apollos traveled to Ephesus, and began to speak "boldly in the synagogue," Aquila and Priscilla heard him and realized that he still was advocating the baptism of John the Baptizer as it looked forward to the coming of Christ (see Acts 18:25-26). That baptism, of course, no longer was valid, having been supplanted by the baptism commemorating the death and burial of Christ. Certainly, Apollos was **sincere**, but he was **sincerely wrong**. Aquila and Priscilla "took him unto them, and expounded unto him the way of God more accurately" (Acts 18:26).

When his error was pointed out to him, he corrected it and subsequently continued with his preaching and teaching about Christ —apparently with much success, since, upon his arrival in Achaia, "the brethren encouraged him; and wrote to the disciples to receive him, and when he was come, he helped them much..., for he powerfully confuted the Jews, and that publicly, showing by the scriptures that Jesus was the Christ" (Acts 18:27-28). Apollos was a good teacher. Nevertheless, he taught error. When he was shown his mistake, however, he possessed an attitude of humility, and a love for the Truth, that caused him to make the necessary correction. In so doing, he set a wonderful example for all who would be teachers of God's Word.

Many of us who teach have found ourselves in a situation akin to that of Apollos. In our earnest attempts to spread the Gospel, enlarge the borders of the kingdom, or defend the faith, we inadvertently made a mistake and taught error. When our mistake was made known to us, we corrected it, learned from it, and set about not to repeat it—consistent with the Apollos' example. Does the fact that we erred, then, necessarily make us a false teacher? In addressing the question, "Is everyone who makes mistakes a false teacher?," Steve Gibson suggested:

> No, a person receives a label when a certain behavior becomes characteristic of him. A preacher, for example, is one who preaches; a teacher is one who teaches; a criminal is one who commits crime. But not everyone who has ever

delivered a sermon deserves to be called a preacher; not everyone who has ever violated a traffic law deserves to be called a criminal. Regardless of its content, a label should be reserved for those distinguished by the corresponding behavior (1990, 10[11/12]:18).

My discussion here is not intended to center on dedicated Christian teachers who, on occasion, make (and correct) an inadvertent error as they attempt to instruct someone regarding the Gospel. Rather, it has to do with those who teach error purposely.

The Intentional Teaching of Error

Error also can result when a person intentionally teaches something he knows to be wrong. The Old Testament provides an intriguing example of this very thing. In 1 Kings 13, the story is told of an unnamed young prophet whom God sent to deliver a message to King Jeroboam. God commanded the prophet: "Thou shalt eat no bread, nor drink water, neither return by the same way that thou camest" (1 Kings 13:9). Yet an older, lying prophet met the younger prophet and said: "I also am a prophet as thou art; and an angel spake unto me by the word of Jehovah, saying, 'Bring him back with thee into thy house that he may eat bread and drink water'" (1 Kings 13:18). The young prophet accepted at face value the older prophet's instruction—false though it was—and on his return trip home was slain by a lion in punishment for his disobedience (1 Kings 13:24). The young prophet fell victim to teaching that had been presented to him intentionally by one who knew it was false. The result was the wrath of God and the loss of the young prophet's life.

Wayne Jackson, in the quotation above, suggested that "we should assume that each person we encounter is an honest soul until he or she demonstrates that such is not the case." That is good advice, and is in keeping with the apostle Paul's discussion of the concept of Christian charity that "beareth all things, believeth all things, endureth all things" (1 Corinthians 13:7). As difficult as it is for most of us to believe, however, the sad truth of the matter is that some people simply are not completely honest in their dealings. On occasion, this manifests itself even among those who profess to be Christians, and who claim that their intention is to convert the lost. The justification (even if it is not actually verbalized) usually offered for the deliberate misrepresentation of the Truth is the idea that the end justifies the means. Some apparently feel that employing **just** the truth of the matter will not impress people sufficiently to make them want to obey God's Word. Thus, the teaching is altered, and falsehood results.

While it may make the task of reaching the lost easier, and may temporarily swell the church roll, what good ultimately results from the teaching of such falsehood? Can we legitimately convert the lost through the intentional teaching of error? Can one be taught wrongly and obey correctly? The intentional teaching of error may comfort where truth offends. The person living in an adulterous marriage can be told that the marriage is acceptable to God. The person who believes that God created the Universe and populated the Earth via the process of organic evolution can be told that such a view is correct. And so on.

In the end, however, three things have occurred. First, as a result of having been taught error, the sinner may not be truly converted. Second, the church will have been filled with adulterers, theistic evolutionists, and others who hold to false views. Since "a little leaven leaveneth the whole lump" (Galatians 5:9), the church will be weakened, and others may be lured into the same error through association with those who believe it to be true. Third, the person who knowingly perpetrated the error has placed his soul, and the souls of those he taught, in jeopardy, because he knowingly taught error.

Error that Condemns, and Error that does Not

Someone might suggest that it is possible to be taught, and believe, error without endangering one's soul, since some error condemns while some does not. Such an observation is correct. As the late Bobby Duncan noted:

There are two kinds of error: (1) error which does not deter one from a course of action in harmony with the will of God, and (2) error which leads to a course of action out of harmony with the will of God....

Some in Paul's day obviously held erroneous views regarding the eating of certain meats (Rom. 14; I Cor. 8). But these views did not cause them to follow a course of action out of harmony with the will of God, and those who knew the truth were exhorted to receive them (Rom. 14:1).... One's belief of error will not damn his soul unless his erroneous views lead him into a course of action out of harmony with the will of God....

But there are other errors which, if believed, will directly affect one's life and religious practice so as to turn him aside from the will of God.... If one's belief of error caused him to worship according to the doctrines and commandments of men, his worship would be vain (Matt. 15:8-9).... If his belief of error led him to teach a perverted gospel, the curse of God would rest upon him (Gal. 1:6-9)... [1983, 19[20]:2].

Not all error, if believed, will condemn one's soul. Suppose, in the example of the two prophets (1 Kings 13), that the older prophet convinced the younger that God wanted him to rush home, carrying his staff in his left hand all the way. Would this have been a lie? Yes, but the consequences would not have been the same, for, believing and acting upon this lie, the younger prophet would not be following a course of action out of harmony with the instructions God had given him.

To suggest, however, that the intentional teaching of error does not always produce negative effects, and thus is acceptable, ignores three important points. First, error is error, regardless of the effects produced. Christians are not called to teach error, but truth (John 14:6). Surely, the question should be asked: What faithful Christian would **want** to teach, or believe, any error? God always has measured men by their attitude toward the truth. Jesus said: "Ye shall know the truth, and the truth shall make you free" (John 8:32). But the truth can free us only if we know it, accept it, and act upon it. Error never frees; it only enslaves.

Second, it is a simple fact that not all error is neutral in its effects upon a person's soul. As Bobby Duncan went on to state: "For one to be in error on some point that does not affect the faithful performance of his duty to God is one thing. But it is another for one to hold to error that would keep him from faithful obedience to God" (1983, 19[20]:2). It is possible to believe error, thinking all the while that it is true, only to discover all too late that it was not. The young prophet who lost his life because he believed a lie is a fine case in point.

Third, while it may be correct to assert that not all error condemns, such an assertion does not tell the whole story. What about the danger to the immortal soul of the person responsible for the intentional false teaching? It will not do simply to suggest that the truth was misrepresented purposely "so as to save a sinner from the error of his ways." **The end does not always justify the means!** Situation ethics has no place in the teaching, or life, of a faithful Christian. In both the Old Testament (e.g., Exodus 20:16) and New Testament (e.g., Revelation 21:8), God forbade the willful distortion of truth, and condemned those who engaged in such a practice. While positive benefits initially may seem to result from the intentional teaching of error, such benefits will be temporary at best. Ultimately the truth will win out, and those who have believed and taught error will suffer in one way or another. When those who have been taught error discover that they have believed a lie, they may become disillusioned and abandon their faith. When those who have taught the lie(s) appear before God in judgment, they will stand condemned.

In the end, who has benefited from the intentional teaching of error? The person who believed the error did not benefit, for his faith was not built upon truth, and thus his "conversion" may be called into question. The church did not benefit, but was weakened because although its numbers increased, its spirituality did not. Spiritual benefits cannot result from the intentional teaching of error. The person who taught the error did not benefit. He lied, and in so doing, incurred heaven's condemnation. Should he fail to repent, he will be delivered to "the lake that burneth with fire and brimstone, which is the second death" (Revelation 21:8).

Conclusion

In 2 Timothy 3:1-4, Paul presented his protégé with a litany of sins that characterized what he termed "grievous times." In addition to those who were selfish, boastful, haughty, disobedient, and without self-control, Paul wrote of men "holding a form of godliness, but having denied the power thereof" (2 Timothy 3:5). Paul's point was that Timothy would encounter some who, from all outward appearances, were moral, truthful, dedicated Christians. But the outward appearance was deceptive because they had become hypocrites whose lives and teachings did not conform to the Gospel.

In commenting on the sinful nature of the Pharisees, Christ said: "Ye also outwardly appear righteous unto men, but inwardly ye are full of hypocrisy and iniquity" (Matthew 23:28). The people described by Paul who exhibited "a form of godliness," but who had "denied the power thereof," possessed the same hypocritical, sinful nature as the Pharisees, which is why Paul commanded Timothy, "from these also turn away" (2 Timothy 3:5). Concerning the ill effects of this artificial "form of godliness," Raymond Hagood wrote:

> Is it not easy to see how destructive this "form of godliness" can be? It works evil under the guise of good. It wounds the sensitive consciences of babes in Christ. It corrupts the values, honesty, and integrity of our young people and it presents to the world a dim view of the church (1976, 12[40]: 1).

When James penned his New Testament epistle, he warned: "Be not many of you teachers, my brethren, knowing that we shall receive heavier judgment" (James 3:1). It is a sobering thought indeed to know that those of us who teach God's Word one day shall be held strictly accountable for how, and what, we have taught. Our teaching, therefore, should be designed to do at least three things.

First, it should present the sinner with the pure, unadulterated Gospel, in the hope that he will hear it, believe it, and obey it, thus being saved from his lost state (Luke 13:3; Romans 3:23; 6:23). The ultimate goal of our efforts is not merely to inform, but to motivate the hearer to proper action.

Second, the things we teach, publicly or privately, should equip Christians for greater maturity in the faith so that they, too, can become teachers (Hebrews 5:12). The success of Christianity in the world is dependent upon those who advocate it being able to teach it to others.

Third, our teaching should edify the entire church so that should the time come when certain saints "will not endure the sound doctrine" (2 Timothy 4:3-4), there will be those well grounded in the truth who can combat error and "contend earnestly for the faith" (Jude 3).

Certainly, those of us who teach bear a weighty responsibility (Ezekiel 33:7-9). But if we do our jobs properly, we will receive from the Lord a "crown of life" (Revelation 2:10). Equally important is the fact that if those whom we teach accept and obey God's Word, they, too, will enjoy a home in heaven, and we will have saved a soul from death (Ezekiel 33:14-16). The responsibility may indeed be weighty, but the reward is commensurate to the task. In the end, we, and those whom we have taught properly, will have built, and be able to sustain, a rock-solid faith.

REFERENCES

Ackerman, Paul D. (1990), *In God's Image After All* (Grand Rapids: Baker).

Anderson, Gary L. (1989), "The Lord..Formeth the Spirit of Man within Him," *In Hope of Eternal Life*, ed. Bobby Liddell (Pensacola, FL: Bellview Church of Christ), pp. 70-81.

Anderson, V. Elving and Bruce R. Reichenbach (1990), "Imaged Through the Lens Darkly: Human Personhood and the Sciences," *Journal of the Evangelical Theological Society*, 33:197-213, June.

Andrews, E.H. (1986), *Christ and the Cosmos* (Welwyn, Hertfordshire, England; Evangelical Press).

Aquinas, Thomas, *Summa Theologica II,* gen. ed. Robert Maynard Hutchins, *Great Books of the Western World*, 54 volumes (Chicago, IL: Encyclopaedia Britannica).

Arndt, William and F.W. Gingrich (1957), *A Greek-English Lexicon of the New Testament and Other Early Christian Literature* (Chicago, IL: University of Chicago Press).

Asimov, Isaac (1968), *Asimov's Guide to the Bible: The Old Testament* (New York: Avon).

Ayers, Tim (2000), "The Bible's Word 'Faith,'" *In the Beginning: Christian Evidences and Apologetics*, ed. Tommy J. Hicks (Lubbock, TX: Hicks Publications), pp. 163-174.

Bagster, Samuel (1970), *The Analytical Greek Lexicon* (Grand Rapids, MI: Zondervan).

Baker, William H. (1991), *In the Image of God* (Chicago, IL: Moody).

Barclay, William (1967), *The Plain Man Looks at the Apostles' Creed* (London: Collins).

Barnes, Albert (1949 edition), *Barnes' Notes on the Old and New Testaments—Job* (Grand Rapids, MI: Baker).

Barnes, Albert (1950 edition), *Barnes' Notes on the Old and New Testaments—Isaiah* (Grand Rapids, MI: Baker).

Batey, Richard (1969), *The Letter of Paul to the Romans* (Austin, TX: Sweet).

Bauer, W., W.F. Arndt, F.W. Gingrich, and F. Danker (1979), *A Greek Lexicon of the New Testament and Other Early Christian Literature* (Chicago, IL: University of Chicago Press).

Bavinck, Herman (1980), *The Certainty of Faith* (St. Catharines, Ontario, Canada: Paideia Press).

Baylis, Charles (1967), "Conscience," *The Encyclopedia of Philosophy*, ed. Paul Edwards (New York: Macmillan), 1/2:189-191.

Benton, John (1985), *How Can a God of Love Send People to Hell?* (Welwyn, Hertfordshire, England: Evangelical Press).

Bierle, Don (1992), *Surprised by Faith* (Lynnwood, WA: Emerald Books).

Blanchard, John (1993), *Whatever Happened to Hell?* (Durham, United Kingdom: Evangelical Press).

Boswell, David (1980), "Parents' Responsibility to Their Children," *Gospel Advocate*, 122:785, February 21.

Bower, Bruce (1993a), "Sudden Recall," *Science News*, 144:184-186.

Bower, Bruce (1993b), "The Survivor Syndrome," *Science News,* 144: 202-204.

Bromling, Brad T. (1989), "Satan's 'New Age' Approach," *Reason & Revelation*, 9:37-39, October.

Brown, David P. (1999), "Annihilation in Hell Error," *God Hath Spoken Affirming Truth and Reproving Error*, ed. Curtis Cates (Memphis, TN: Memphis School of Preaching), pp. 161-178.

Brown, Francis, S.R. Driver, and Charles Briggs (1907), *A Hebrew and English Lexicon of the Old Testament* (London: Oxford University Press).

Brown, T. Pierce (1974), "Some Questions and Answers About Satan," *Firm Foundation*, 91:245,251, April 16.

Brown, T. Pierce (1993), "In the Image of God," *Gospel Advocate*, 135: 50-51, August.

Brunner, Emil (1946), *Revelation and Reason* (Philadelphia, PA: Westminster).

Brunner, Emil (1954), *Eternal Hope* (Philadelphia, PA: Westminster).

Buffaloe, Neal D. and N. Patrick Murray (1981), *Creationism and Evolution* (Little Rock, AR: The Bookmark).

Camp, Ashby L. (1999), *Feet Firmly Planted* (Tempe, AZ: Ktisis Publishing).

Camp, Robert (1973), "Does Faith Contain an Element of Doubt?," *Spiritual Sword*, 4[2]:2-5, January.

Carnell, Edward John (1969), *The Case for Orthodox Theology* (Philadelphia, PA: Westminster).

Carson, Herbert M. (1978), *The Biblical Doctrine of Eternal Punishment*, Carey Conference Paper.

Carter, Tom (1988), *Spurgeon at His Best* (Grand Rapids, MI: Baker).

Causey, Bud (1992), "Who's Watching the Children?," *First Century Christian*, 14[2]:12-13, February.

Chafer, Lewis Sperry (1943), "Anthropology: Part 3," *Bibliotheca Sacra*, 100:479-496, October.

Chaney, Charles (1970), "Martin Luther and the Mission of the Church," *Journal of the Evangelical Theological Society*, 13:15-41, Winter.

Chomsky, Noam (1991), "Are Humans Born to Speak?," *Scientific American*, 264[4]:146-147, April.

Claiborne, Winford (1994), "What is Faith," *Spiritual Sword*, 25[2]:34-38, January.

Claiborne, Winford (1995), "Charles J. Sykes' *A Nation of Victims*: A Book Review," *Family, Church, and Society Restoration and Renewal*, ed. David L. Lipe (Henderson, TN: Freed-Hardeman University).

Clark, Gordon Haddon (1961), *Religion, Reason and Revelation* (Philadelphia, PA: Presbyterian and Reformed).

Clark, Gordon Haddon (1969), "The Image of God in Man," *Journal of the Evangelical Theological Society*, 12:215-222, Fall.

Clarke, Adam (no date), *Clarke's Commentary on the Bible* (Nashville, TN: Abingdon).

Clayton, John N. (1976), *The Source* (Mentone, IN: Superior Printing).

Clayton, John (1990a), "Book Reviews," *Does God Exist?*, 17[5]:20-21, September/October.

Clayton, John (1990b), *The Source: Eternal Design or Infinite Accident?* (South Bend, IN: Privately published by author).

Clayton, John (1991), *Does God Exist? Christian Evidences Intermediate Course Teacher's Guide* (South Bend, IN: Privately published by author).

Coffman, James Burton (1990), *The Major Prophets—Isaiah* (Abilene, TX: ACU Press).

Corduan, Winfried (1993), *Reasonable Faith* (Nashville, TN: Broadman and Holman).

Crawford, R.G. (1966), "Image of God," *Expository Times*, 77:233-236, May.

Custance, Arthur C. (1975), *Man in Adam and in Christ* (Grand Rapids, MI: Zondervan).

Darrow, Clarence and Wallace Rice (1929), *Infidels and Heretics: An Agnostic's Anthology* (Boston, MA: Stratford).

Davidson, Benjamin (1970 reprint), *The Analytical Hebrew and Chaldee Lexicon* (Grand Rapids, MI: Zondervan).

Deaver, Mac (1984a), "A General Study of Faith (Part 4)," *Firm Foundation*, 101:673, December 4.

Deaver, Mac (1984b), "A General Study of Faith (Part 5)," *Firm Foundation*, 101:690, December 11.

Deaver, Mac (1989), "The Meaning of Biblical Faith," *Studies in 2 Corinthians*, ed. Dub McClish (Denton, TX: Valid Publications), pp. 462-475.

Denham, Daniel (1998), "Will the Wicked Really be Punished with Eternal Fire?," *Studies in 1,2 Peter and Jude,* ed. Dub McClish (Denton, TX: Valid Publications), pp. 601-627.

Devoe, Alan (1964), *The Marvels and Mysteries of Our Animal World* (Pleasantville, NY: Readers Digest).

Dillow, Joseph C. (1982), *The Waters Above* (Chicago, IL: Moody).

Dummelow, J.R., ed. (1944), *The One-Volume Bible Commentary* (New York: MacMillan).

Duncan, Bobby (1983), "Error Which Does and Does Not Condemn," *Words of Truth*, 19[20]:2, May 20.

Dyrness, William A. (1972), "The *Imago Dei* and Christian Aesthetics," *Journal of the Evangelical Theological Society*, 15:161-172, Summer.

Ealey, Gary (1984), "The Biblical Doctrine of Hell," *The Biblical Doctrine of Last Things,* ed. David L. Lipe (Kosciusko, MS: Magnolia Bible College), pp. 20-28.

Earle, Ralph (1986), *Word Meanings in the New Testament* (Grand Rapids, MI: Baker).

East, John (1981), *Report of the Subcommittee on Separation of Powers to Senate Judiciary Committee [S-158]*, 97th Congress, first session.

Easton, M.G. (1996), *Easton's Bible Dictionary* (Oak Harbor, WA: Logos Research Systems).

Ecrement, Lloyd L. (1961), *Man, the Bible, and Destiny* (Grand Rapids, MI: Eerdmans).

Edersheim, Alfred (1971 reprint), *The Life and Times of Jesus the Messiah* (Grand Rapids, MI: Eerdmans).

England, Donald (1983), *A Scientist Examines Faith and Evidence* (Delight, AR: Gospel Light).

England, Richard (2000), "An Obedient Faith," *Gospel Advocate*, 142[12]: 36-37, December.

Feinberg, Charles Lee (1972), "Image of God," *Bibliotheca Sacra*, 129: 235-246, July–September.

Ferguson, Jesse B. (1852), *Christian Magazine*, July.

Ferguson, Kitty (1994), *The Fire in the Equations: Science, Religion, and the Search for God* (Grand Rapids, MI: Eerdmans).

Fields, Weston W. (1976), *Unformed and Unfilled* (Phillipsburg, NJ: Presbyterian and Reformed).

Fisher, Graham A. (1990), *Why Believe in Adam?* (Liverpool, England: Eye-Opener Publications).

Flew, Antony (1966), *God and Philosophy* (New York: Dell).

Flew, Antony G.N. and Thomas B. Warren (1977), *Warren-Flew Debate* (Jonesboro, AR: National Christian Press).

Foster, R.C. (1971 reprint), *Studies in the Life of Christ* (Grand Rapids, MI: Baker).

Fudge, Edward W. (1982), *The Fire That Consumes* (Houston, TX: Providential Press).

Fulford, Hugh (2001), "Why Are Our Young People Leaving the Church?," *Gospel Advocate*, 153[4]:24-25, April.

Geisler, Norman L. (1978), *The Roots of Evil* (Grand Rapids MI: Zondervan).

Geisler, Norman L. and P.D. Feinberg (1980), *Introduction to Philosophy—A Christian Perspective* (Grand Rapids, MI: Baker).

Geisler, Norman L. and Peter Bocchino (2001), *Unshakable Foundations* (Minneapolis, MN: Bethany House).

Gerstner, John H. (1990), *Repent or Perish* (Ligonier, PA: Solio Deo Gloria Publications).

Gesenius, William (1979 reprint), *Hebrew-Chaldee Lexicon to the Old Testament* (Grand Rapids, MI: Baker).

Gibson, Steve (1990), "Some Common Questions About False Teachers," *The Restorer*, 10[11/12]:17-20, November/December.

Gitt, Werner (1999), *The Wonder of Man* (Bielefeld, Germany: Christliche Literatur-Verbreitung E.V.).

Goad, Steven Clark (1981), "Keeping Our Children Saved," *Firm Foundation*, 98:297,299, May 5.

Guhrt, Joachim (1978), "Time," *The New International Dictionary of New Testament Theology,* ed. Colin Brown (Grand Rapids, MI: Zondervan).

Gunkel, Hermann (1964), *Genesis* (Gottingen: Vandenhoeck und Ruprecht).

Habermas, Gary R. (1990), *Dealing With Doubt* (Chicago, IL: Moody).

Hagood, Raymond A. (1976), "Perilous Times," *Words of Truth*, 12[40]: 1, September 17.

Hailey, Homer (1972), *A Commentary on the Minor Prophets* (Grand Rapids, MI: Baker).

Hamilton, Victor P. (1990), *The Book of Genesis* (Grand Rapids, MI: Eerdmans).

Hamlin, Hannibal (1964), "Life or Death by EEG?," *Journal of the American Medical Association*, 190[2]:112-114, October 12.

Harris, R.L., G.L. Archer, Jr., and B.K. Waltke (1980), *Theological Wordbook of the Old Testament* (Chicago, IL: Moody).

Hastings, James (1976), *The Great Texts of the Bible: Genesis-Numbers* (Grand Rapids, MI: Baker).

Hazelip, Harold (1980), "In the Image of God," *Upreach*, 2[2]:25-27, 30, March.

Hengstenberg, E.W. (no date), *Christology of the Old Testament* (MacDonald Dill AFB: MacDonald Publishing).

Henry, Carl F.H. (1967), *Evangelicals at the Brink of Crisis: Significance of the World Congress on Evangelism* (Waco, TX: Word).

Hescht, Blaine E. (1984), "What is Biblical Faith?," *Gospel Advocate*, 126:692, November 15.

Hiebert, D.E. (1975), "Satan," *The Zondervan Pictorial Encyclopedia of the Bible*, ed. Merrill C. Tenney (Grand Rapids, MI: Zondervan).

Hoekema, Anthony (1982), *The Bible and the Future* (Grand Rapids, MI: Eerdmans).

Hoekema, Anthony A (1986), *Created in God's Image* (Grand Rapids, MI: Eerdmans).

Hoover, Arlie J. (1976), *Dear Agnos: A Defense of Christianity* (Grand Rapids, MI: Baker).

Horgan, John (1995), "A Sign is Born," *Scientific American*, 273[6]:18-19, December.

Hoyles, Arthur J. (1957), "The Punishment of the Wicked after Death," *London Quarterly and Holborn Review*, April.

Hughes, Philip Edgecumbe (1989), *The True Image* (Grand Rapids, MI: Eerdmans).

Ingersoll, Robert G. (1990 reprint), *The Great Infidels* (Parsippany, NJ: American Atheist Press).

Jackson, Wayne (1974), *Fortify Your Faith in an Age of Doubt* (Stockton, CA: Courier Publications).

Jackson, Wayne (1980), "Satan," *Great Doctrines of the Bible*, ed. M.H. Tucker (Knoxville, TN: East Tennessee School of Preaching).

Jackson, Wayne (1984), "Questions and Answers," *Essays in Apologetics*, ed. Bert Thompson and Wayne Jackson (Montgomery, AL: Apologetics Press).

Jackson, Wayne (1985), "Is Man a Naked Ape?," *Reason and Revelation*, 5:5-8, February.

Jackson, Wayne (1987a), "Debate Challenge Withdrawn," *Christian Courier*, 23:31, December.

Jackson, Wayne (1987b), "Your Question & My Answer," *Christian Courier*, 23:15, August.

Jackson, Wayne (1990a), "Defending the Faith with a Broken Sword," *Christian Courier*, 26:1-2, May.

Jackson, Wayne (1990b), "Miracles," *Giving a Reason for Our Hope*, ed. Winford Claiborne (Henderson, TN: Freed-Hardeman College).

Jackson, Wayne (1991), "The Origin and Nature of the Soul," *Christian Courier*, 27:19, September.

Jackson, Wayne (1993), "Changing Attitudes Toward Hell," *Whatever Happened to Heaven and Hell?*, ed. Terry E. Hightower (San Antonio, TX: Shenandoah Church of Christ), pp. 63-67.

Jackson, Wayne (1997), "The Role of 'Works' in the Plan of Salvation," *Christian Courier*, 32:47, April.

Jackson, Wayne (1998a), "Demons: Ancient Superstition or Historical Reality?," *Reason & Revelation*, 18:25-31, April.

Jackson, Wayne (1998b), "The Use of 'Hell' in the New Testament," *Christian Courier*, 33:34-35, January.

Jacobus, Melancthon W. (1864), *Critical and Explanatory Notes on Genesis* (Philadelphia, PA: Presbyterian Board of Publication).

Jastrow, Robert (1982), "A Scientist Caught Between Two Faiths," Interview with Bill Durbin, *Christianity Today,* August 6.

Johnson, B.C. (1981), *The Atheist Debater's Handbook* (Buffalo, NY: Prometheus).

Kaufmann, Walter (1958), *Critique of Religion and Philosophy* (Garden City, NY: Doubleday).

Kearley, F. Furman (1992), "Save the Children," *Gospel Advocate*, 134 [5]:5, May.

Keil, C.F. (1996 reprint), *Commentary on the Old Testament—The Pentateuch* (Peabody, MA: Hendrickson).

Keil, C.F. and Franz Delitzsch (1968 edition), *Commentary on the Old Testament—The Pentateuch* (Grand Rapids, MI: Eerdmans).

Keil, C.F. and Franz Delitzsch (1982 edition), *Commentary on the Old Testament—Isaiah* (Grand Rapids, MI: Eerdmans).

Kelly, Douglas F. (1997), *Creation and Change* (Geanies House, Fearn, United Kingdom: Christian Focus Publications).

Key, Dalton (1992a), "Our Children," *Old Paths*, 16[4]:2, February.

Key, Dalton (1992b), "Confessions of a World-Filled Church," *Old Paths*, 16[8]:1, June.

Kierkegaard, Søren (1936), *Philosophical Fragments or a Fragment of Philosophy* (Princeton, NJ: Princeton University Press).

Knowles, Victor (1994), *Angels and Demons* (Joplin, MO: College Press).

Kreeft, Peter and Ronald K. Tacelli (1994), *Handbook of Christian Apologetics* (Downers Grove, IL: InterVarsity Press).

Kumar, Steve (1990), *Christian Apologetics: Think Why You Believe* (Auckland, New Zealand: Foundation for Life).

Kung, Hans (1980), *Does God Exist?* (New York: Doubleday).

Ladd, George Eldon (1974), *A Theology of the New Testament* (Grand Rapids, MI: Eerdmans).

Laetsch, Theo (1956), *The Minor Prophets* (St. Louis, MO: Concordia).

Lake, D.M. (1976), *Zondervan Pictorial Encyclopedia of the Bible*, ed. Merrill C. Tenney (Grand Rapids, MI: Zondervan).

Lanier, Roy H. Jr. (1981), "What is Happening to the Children?," *Rocky Mountain Christian*, 9[8]:2, July.

Lawlor, George Lawrence (1972), *The Epistle of Jude* (Nutley, NJ: Presbyterian and Reformed).

Lawrence, Robert W. (1976), "Teach the Children!," *Gospel Advocate*, 118:22-23, January 8.

Leach, Virgil (1977), *Get Thee Behind Me Satan* (Abilene, TX: Quality).

Leatherwood, Mike (1977), "A Proper View of Faith and Knowledge Points to the Crucial Need to Defend the Faith," *Spiritual Sword*, 8[3]:42-44, April.

Lemmons, Reuel (1980), "In His Image," *Firm Foundation*, 97:546, August 26.

Lenski, R.C.H. (1966), *The Interpretation of I and II Epistles of Peter, the Three Epistles of John, and the Epistle of Jude* (Minneapolis, MN: Augsburg).

Leupold, Herbert C. (1942), *Exposition of Genesis* (Grand Rapids, MI: Baker).

Lewis, C.S. (1952), *Mere Christianity* (New York: Macmillan).

Lewis, C.S. (1966), *Letters to Malcolm, Chiefly on Prayer* (London: Fontana Books).

Lewis, Jack P. (1988), "Living Soul," *Exegesis of Difficult Passages* (Searcy, AR: Resource Publications).

Lewis, Joseph (1983), *Ingersoll the Magnificent* (Austin, TX: American Atheist Press).

Lewis, Mark (1987), "Hereby Ye Shall Know...," *Joshua: A Commentary —Exegetical, Homiletical*, ed. W.S. Cline (Austin, TX: Firm Foundation), pp. 46-55.

Lindsell, Harold (1976), *The Battle for the Bible* (Grand Rapids, MI: Zondervan).

Lipe, David L. (no date), *Faith and Knowledge* (Montgomery, AL: Apologetics Press).

Lockyer, Herbert W. (1995), *All the Angels in the Bible* (Peabody, MA: Hendrickson).

Loftus, Elizabeth (1995), "Remembering Dangerously," *Skeptical Inquirer*, 19[2]:20-29, March/April.

Machen, J. Gresham (1946), *What is Faith?* (Grand Rapids, MI: Eerdmans).

MacLaine, Shirley (1983), *Out on a Limb* (New York: Bantam).

MacLaine, Shirley (1989), *Going Within* (New York: Bantam).

MacLaine, Shirley (1991), *Dancing in the Light* (New York: Bantam).

Major, Trevor J. (1994), "Chimp Speak," *Resources* (in *Reason & Revelation*), 14[3]:1, March.

Major, Trevor J. (1995a), "Do Animals Possess the Same Kind of Intelligence as Human Beings?," *Reason & Revelation*, 15:87-88, November.

Major, Trevor J. (1995b), "What Happens to Faith When We Doubt?," *Reason & Revelation*, 15:94, December.

Marais, J.L. (1939), "Anthropology," *The International Standard Bible Encyclopedia*, ed. James Orr (Grand Rapids, MI: Eerdmans).

Marais, J.L. (1956), "Spirit," *International Standard Bible Encyclopedia*, ed. James Orr (Grand Rapids, MI: Eerdmans), 5:2837-2838.

Matrisciana, Caryl and Roger Oakland (1991), *The Evolution Conspiracy* (Eugene, OR: Harvest House).

Mayberry, Thomas C. (1970), "God and Moral Authority," *The Monist*, January.

Mayhue, Linda (1992), "Day Care vs. Mother Care," *Gospel Advocate*, 134[4]:49-51, April.

McCord, Hugo (1979), "The State of the Dead," *Firm Foundation*, 96[4]:6,12, January 23.

McCord, Hugo (1983), "The Heroes of Faith," *Studies in Hebrews*, ed. Dub McClish (Denton, TX: Valid Publications), pp. 211-219.

McCord, Hugo (1995), "What is the Soul?," *Vigil*, 23:87-88, November.

McGarvey, J.W. (1875), *Commentary on Matthew-Mark* (Delight, AR: Gospel Light), reprint.

McGarvey, J.W. (1958 reprint), *Sermons* (Nashville, TN: Gospel Advocate).

Menninger, Karl (1973), *Whatever Became of Sin?* (New York: Hawthorn Books).

Miller, Dave (1988), "Blind Faith," *The Restorer*, 8[9]:10-11, September.

Miller, Dave (1987), "Anatomy of a False Teacher," *The Restorer*, 7[2]:2-3, February.

Miller, J. Maxwell (1972), "In the 'Image' and 'Likeness' of God," *Journal of Biblical Literature*, 91:289-304, September.

Moore, John N. (1983), *How to Teach Origins Without ACLU Interference* (Milford, MI: Mott Media).

Moore, Keith A. and T.V.N. Persaud (1993), *The Developing Human* (Philadelphia, PA: W.B. Saunders).

Morey, Robert A. (1984), *Death and the Afterlife* (Minneapolis, MN: Bethany House).

Morgan, G. Campbell (1903), *The Crises of the Christ* (New York: Revell).

Morris, Henry M. (1965), "The Bible is a Textbook of Science: Part 2," *Bibliotheca Sacra*, 122:63-70, January.

Morris, Henry M. (1971), *The Bible Has the Answer* (Nutley, NJ: Craig Press).

Morris, Henry M. (1976), *The Genesis Record* (Grand Rapids, MI: Baker).

Motyer, Alec (2001), *The Story of the Old Testament* (Grand Rapids, MI: Baker).

Moulton and Milligan (1976 reprint), *Vocabulary of the Greek New Testament Illustrated from the Papyri and Other Non-literary Sources* (Grand Rapids, MI: Eerdmans).

Mounce, William D. (1993), *Basics of Biblical Greek* (Grand Rapids, MI: Zondervan).

Newell, Clifford Jr. (2001), "Made in God's Image," *Encouraging Statements of the Bible*, ed. Michael Hatcher (Pensacola, FL: Bellview Church of Christ), pp. 12-20.

Newman, John Henry (1887), *An Essay in Aid of a Grammar of Assent* (London: Longmans, Green and Co.).

Nichols, Hardeman (1978), "The Binding of Satan," *Premillennialism: True or False*, ed. Wendell Winkler (Fort Worth, TX: Winkler Publications).

Nielsen, Kai (1973), *Ethics Without God* (London: Pemberton).

O'Connor, Flannery (1979), *The Habit of Being* (New York: Farrar, Stauss, and Giroux).

Orr, James (1906), *God's Image in Man* (London: Hodder and Stoughton).

Orr, James (1956), "Punishment," *International Standard Bible Encyclopedia*, ed. James Orr (Grand Rapids, MI: Eerdmans), 4:2501-2504.

Osborne, Roy F. (1964), *Great Preachers of Today—Sermons of Roy F. Osborne* (Abilene, TX: Biblical Research Press).

Otten, Herman J. (1988), *Baal or God?* (New Haven, MO: Christian News Publications), revised edition.

Overton, Basil (1976), "Satan," *The World Evangelist*, 5[4]:3, November.

Paine, Thomas (1794), *The Age of Reason* (New York: Willey Book Co.).

Parker, Gary E. (1990), *The Gift of Doubt* (San Francisco, CA: Harper & Row).

Parks, David (2000), "Building Blocks of Christian Character," *Gospel Advocate*, 142[11]:19, November.

Peele, Stanton (1989), *The Diseasing of America* (Lexington, MA: Lexington Books).

Peterson, Robert A. (1995), *Hell on Trial—The Case for Eternal Punishment* (Phillipsburg, NJ: P&R).

Pierce, Chester (1973), lecture presented at Denver, Colorado seminar on childhood education. As quoted in: Michaelsen, Johanna (1989), *Like Lambs to the Slaughter* (Eugene, OR: Harvest House).

Pink, Arthur (1976 reprint), *The Divine Inspiration of the Bible* (Grand Rapids, MI: Baker).

Pinnock, Clark (1987), "Fire, Then Nothing," *Christianity Today*, March 20.

Poe, Harry Lee and Jimmy H. Davis (2000), *Science and Faith* (Nashville, TN: Broadman and Holman).

Porter, Walter L. (1974), "Why Do the Innocent Suffer?," *Firm Foundation*, 91:467,475, July 23.

Potter, Charles Francis (1930), *Humanism: A New Religion* (New York: Simon & Schuster).

Pryor, Neale (1974), "Abortion: Soul and Spirit in the Hebrew Language," *Spiritual Sword*, 5[3]:33-35, April.

Ramtha (1985), *Voyage to the New World: An Adventure into Unlimitedness* (New York: Ballantine).

Rand, Ayn (1964), *The Virtue of Selfishness; A New Concept of Egoism* (New York: New American Library).

Rehwinkel, A.M. (1951), *The Flood* (St. Louis, MO: Concordia).

Reichenbach, Bruce (1976), "Natural Evils and Natural Laws," *International Philosophical Quarterly*, Vol. 16.

Rice, Tim (1987), "Is Hell Eternal in Nature?," *Vigil*, 15[1]:5-6, January.

Robertson, A.T. (1930), *Word Pictures in the New Testament* (Grand Rapids, MI: Baker).

Robinson, John A.T. (1949), "Universalism—Is It Heretical?," *Scottish Journal of Theology*, June.

Robinson, Richard (1964), *An Atheist's Values* (Oxford, England: Clarendon Press).

Robinson, Richard (1976), "Religion and Reason," *Critiques of God*, ed. Peter Angeles (Buffalo, NY: Prometheus).

Ross, James F. (1969), *Introduction to the Philosophy of Religion* (New York: Macmillan).

Ruby, Lionel (1960), *Logic: An Introduction* (Chicago, IL: J.B. Lippincott).

Rudin, Norah (1997), *Dictionary of Modern Biology* (Hauppauge, NY: Barrons).

Russell, Bertrand (1945), *A History of Western Philosophy* (New York: Simon & Schuster).

Russell, Bertrand (1967), *Why I am Not a Christian* (New York: Simon & Schuster).

Russell, Bertrand (1969), *Autobiography* (New York: Simon & Schuster).

Samuel, (1950), *The Impossibility of Agnosticism* [a tract] (Downers Grove, IL: InterVarsity Press).

Sanderson, L.O. (1978), "The Devil and His Wiles," *Gospel Advocate*, 120:678, October 26.

Sartre, Jean Paul, (1961), "Existentialism and Humanism," *French Philosophers from Descartes to Sartre*, ed. Leonard M. Marsak (New York: Meridian).

Sartre, Jean Paul (1966), "Existentialism," Reprinted in *A Casebook on Existentialism*, ed. William V. Spanos (New York: Thomas Y. Crowell).

Sasse, Herman (1964), "*Aion, Aionios,*" *Theological Dictionary of the New Testament,* ed. Gerhard Kittel (Grand Rapids, MI: Eerdmans), 1:208-209.

Sauer, Erich (1962), *The King of the Earth* (Grand Rapids, MI: Eerdmans).

Schaeffer, Francis A. (1968), *The God Who Is There* (Downers Grove, IL: Inter-Varsity Press).

Schaff, Phillip (1970 reprint), *History of the Christian Church* (Grand Rapids, MI: Eerdmans).

Schuller, Robert (1984), "The Hour of Prayer," February 5.

Simpson, George Gaylord (1951), *The Meaning of Evolution* (New York: Mentor).

Sippert, Albert (1989), *From Eternity to Eternity,* (North Mankato, MN: Sippert Publishing).

Smith, F. LaGard (1986), *Out on a Broken Limb* (Eugene, OR: Harvest House).

Smith, F. LaGard (1988), *A Christian Response to the New Age Movement,* Audio taped lecture presented at Pepperdine University, Malibu, California.

Smith, George H. (1979), *Atheism: The Case Against God* (Buffalo, NY: Prometheus).

Snaith, Norman Henry (1974), "Image of God," *Expository Times,* 86: 24, October.

Stacey, John (1977), *Sermons on Heaven and Hell* (Rutherford, TN: Stacey Publications).

Stevens, David (1991), "The Place of Eternal Punishment," *Therefore Stand,* 7[3]:21-22, March.

Strobel, Lee (2000), *The Case for Faith* (Grand Rapids, MI: Zondervan).

Sweet, L.M. (1939), "Satan," *International Standard Bible Encyclopedia* (Grand Rapids, MI: Eerdmans).

Sykes, Charles J. (1992), *A Nation of Victims: The Decay of the American Character* (New York: St. Martin's Press).

Sztanyo, Dick (1986), "Faith is the Substance," *Exegetical Studies of Great Bible Themes,* ed. Eddie Whitten (Bedford, TX: Christian Supply Center).

Sztanyo, Dick (1989), *The Concept of Rational Belief* (Montgomery, AL: Apologetics Press).

Sztanyo, Dick (1996), *Faith and Reason* (Montgomery, AL: Apologetics Press), revised edition.

Taylor, A.E. (1945), *Does God Exist?* (London: Macmillan).

Taylor, Robert R. Jr. (1985), *Challenging Dangers of Modern Versions* (Ripley, TN: Taylor Publications).

Thayer, J.H. (1958 reprint), *A Greek-English Lexicon of the New Testament* (Edinburgh, Scotland: T. & T. Clark).

Thiele, Gilbert (1958), "Easter Hope," *The Seminarian*, March.

Thomas, J.D. (1965), *Facts and Faith* (Abilene, TX: Biblical Research Press).

Thomas, J.D. (1974), *Heaven's Window* (Abilene, TX: Biblical Research Press).

Thompson, Bert (1995a), "The Case for the Existence of God—[Part I]," *Reason and Revelation*, 15:33-38, May.

Thompson, Bert (1995b), "The Case for the Existence of God—[Part II]," *Reason and Revelation*, 15:41-47, June.

Thompson, Bert (1997), "In Defense of...Christ's Deity," *Reason & Revelation*, 17:89-94, December.

Thompson, Bert (1998a), "In Defense of...Christ's Church," *Reason & Revelation*, 18:1-5, January.

Thompson, Bert (1998b), "In Defense of...God's Plan of Salvation," *Reason & Revelation*, 18:17-22, March.

Thompson, Bert (1999a), *In Defense of the Bible's Inspiration* (Montgomery, AL: Apologetics Press).

Thompson, Bert (1999b), *My Sovereign, My Sin, My Salvation* (Montgomery, AL: Apologetics Press).

Thompson, Bert (2000), *Rock-Solid Faith: How to Build It* (Montgomery, AL: Apologetics Press).

Thompson, Bert and Sam Estabrook (1999), "Do Animals Have Souls?," *Reason & Revelation*, 19:89-92, December.

Thompson, Bert and Wayne Jackson (1982), "The Revelation of God in Nature," *Reason & Revelation*, 2:17-24, May.

Thompson, Bert and Wayne Jackson (1992), *A Study Course in Christian Evidences* (Montgomery, AL: Apologetics Press).

Tillich, Paul (1957), *Dynamics of Faith* (New York: Harper and Brothers).

Toynbee, Arnold (1956), "Man Owes His Freedom to God," *Collier's Magazine*, March 30.

Trueblood, David Elton (1957), *Philosophy of Religion* (Grand Rapids, MI: Baker).

Turner, Rex A. Sr. (1989), *Systematic Theology* (Montgomery, AL: Alabama Christian School of Religion).

Vincent, M.R. (1946), *Word Studies in the New Testament* (Grand Rapids, MI: Eerdmans).

Vine, W.E. (1940), *An Expository Dictionary of New Testament Words* (Old Tappan, NJ: Revell).

Vine, W.E. (1966 reprint), *An Expository Dictionary of New Testament Words* (Old Tappan, NJ: Revell).

Vine, W.E. (1991), *Amplified Expository Dictionary of New Testament Words* (Iowa Falls, IA: World).

Vine, W.E., Merrill F. Unger, and William White (1985), *Vine's Complete Expository Dictionary of Old and New Testament Words* (Nashville, TN: Nelson).

Vos, Geerhardus (1956), "Gehenna," *International Standard Bible Encyclopedia*, ed. James Orr (Grand Rapids, MI: Eerdmans), 2:1183.

Wacaster, Tom (1987), "How is Man the Image of God?" *Questions Men Ask About God*, ed. Eddie Whitten (Bedford, TX: Christian Supply Center).

Walker, T. Stuart (1991), "Animal Rights and the Image of God—Part II," *Journal of Biblical Ethics in Medicine*, 5[2]:21-27, Spring.

Wallace, Robert A. (1975), *Biology: The World of Life* (Pacific Palisades, CA: Goodyear).

Ward, Rita Rhodes (1986), "Educating Children in an Anti-Christian Environment," *Gospel Advocate*, 128:520, September 4.

Warren, Thomas B. (1992), *Immortality—All of Us Will be Somewhere Forever* (Moore, OK: National Christian Press).

Whately, Richard (1856), *Introductory Lessons on Morals and Christian Evidences* (Cambridge, England: Cambridge University Press).

Whitcomb, John C. (1972), *The Early Earth* (Grand Rapids, MI: Baker).

Whitcomb, John C. and Henry M. Morris (1961), *The Genesis Flood* (Grand Rapids, MI: Baker).

Whitelaw, Robert L. (1991), *Can There be Eternal Life Apart from Christ?* (Sterling, VA: GAM Publications).

Willis, John T. (1979), "Introduction," *The World and Literature of the Old Testament* (Austin, TX: Sweet).

Wilson, Edward O. (1978), *On Human Nature* (Cambridge, MA: Harvard University Press).

Wilson, S.G. (1974), "New Wine in Old Wineskins," *Expository Times*, 85:356-361, September.

Woods, Guy N. (1976), *Questions and Answers* (Henderson, TN: Freed-Hardeman College).

Woods, Guy N. (1980), "What is the Difference Between the Soul and the Spirit of Man?," *Gospel Advocate*, 122:163, March 20.

Woods, Guy N. (1985a), "Do the Scriptures Teach that the Wicked are to Experience Endless Suffering in Hell?," *Gospel Advocate*, 127:278, May 2.

Woods, Guy N. (1985b), "What is the Soul of Man?," *Gospel Advocate*, 127:691-692, November 21.

Woods, Guy N. (1994), "Faith vs. Knowledge?," *Gospel Advocate*, 136:31, February.

Woodson, Leslie (1973), *Hell and Salvation* (Old Tappan, NJ: Revell).

Workman, Gary (1981a), "Is the Devil a Fallen Angel?," *The Restorer*, 1[5]:4, April.

Workman, Gary (1981b), "Twenty Suggestions on Raising Your Kids for Christ," *The Restorer*, 1[7]:2, June.

Workman, Gary (1992), "Is There An Eternal Hell?," *Spiritual Sword*, 23[3]:30-34, April.

Workman, Gary (1993), "Will the Wicked Be Eternally Punished or Annihilated?," *Whatever Happened to Heaven and Hell?*, ed. Terry E. Hightower (San Antonio, TX: Shenandoah Church of Christ), pp. 495-503.

Young, Edward J. (1965), *Psalm 139* (London: The Banner of Truth Trust).

Young, Warren C. (1954), *A Christian Approach to Philosophy* (Grand Rapids, MI: Baker).

Zacharias, Ravi (1994), *Can Man Live Without God?* (Dallas, TX: Word).

Zenos, Andrew C. (1936), "Satan," *A New Standard Bible Dictionary*, ed. Melancthon W. Jacobus (New York: Funk and Wagnalls).

Zerr, E.M. (1952), *Bible Commentary—New Testament* (Bowling Green, KY: Guardian of Truth Publications).

Zerr, E.M. (1954), *Bible Commentary—Psalms, Proverbs, Ecclesiastes, Song of Solomon, and Proverbs* (Bowling Green, KY: Guardian of Truth Publications).

SUBJECT INDEX

G

Holy nature of—226
Image and likeness of, man
created in—85-132
Justice of—226,228
Knowing He exists—14-16
Mercy of—226,228
Omnipotence of—142-143
Omnipresence of—143
Omniscience of—143
Greek, universal language—1

H

Hades, definition of in
Scripture—186-
187,241-242,244
"Hall of Fame" of faith—42
Heaven
Eternal nature of—
212-220,260-262
Hell and, equal duration of—
256-260
Hēlēl (Hebrew word for
Lucifer)—148
Hell
Consciousness and—
246-248
Definition of—241
Eternal nature of—252-256
Fire, unquenchable and—
249-251
Modern views of—239-240
Opposition to—208-209

Punishment, place of—
245-246
Sorrow and torment,
place of—246-248
Universalism and—204-205
Worms, undying and—
249-250
Hinnom, Valley of—242
Humanism
Children and—271
Public schools and—
270-271
Hupostasis (Greek word
for substance)—63
Hurricanes, suffering and—
293

I

Image and likeness of God
Domination of lower crea-
tion, man's and—94-95
Man created in—85-132
Murder and—100-101
Physical image of man
and—90-92
Posture, man's and—91-92
Sexual distinction and—94
Sin destroyed the?—95-107
Imago Dei—109,129,134
Instinct, animals and—
118,122-123
Intuition, knowledge and—44

M

Man
  Animals, kinship with?—
    130-131
  Conscience and—125-127
  Creation of by God—
    109-113
  Creative nature of—
    117-119
  Emotions and—127-128
  Free will and—121-123
  Morality and—123-127
  Religious inclination of—
    128-130
  Right and wrong, ability to
    distinguish between—
    123-125
  Soul of—112-113,129-
    130,171-262
  Speech and—114-116
  Writing ability of—116
Means, end, not always
    justified by the—316
Metaphysical deduction,
    knowledge and—45
Miracles—67
Miscarriage, Old Testa-
    ment laws and—198
Moral oughtness
  Animals and—123-124
  Man and—123-125,229
Morality
  Definition of—229

  Differences in—231-232
  God as basis of—124-125
  Man's concept of—126
Moses, Law of—226
Murder, image of God and—
    100-101,131-132
Mustard seed, faith like a—24

N

Nephesh (Hebrew word
    for soul)—131,176-178,
    180-181,183,186-187,
    189-191,213
New Age Movement—87

O

Obedience, faith and—
    28,42-45,72
Oida (Greek word
    for know)—40

P

Paradeisos (Greek word
    for paradise)—187
Parents
  God's word, incorrect
    view of—273-275
  Priorities, improper—
    277-278

R

S

Y

NAME INDEX

A

Ackerman, Paul—118
Anderson, Gary—132
Anderson, V. Elving—110,129
Andrews, E.H.—32
Angeles, Peter—9
Aquinas, Thomas—122
Arndt, William—23,63,
    176, 183,250
Asimov, Isaac—137
Ayers, Tim—22

B

Bagster, Samuel—249
Baker, William—95
Barclay, William—203
Barnes, Albert—146,149
Barth, Karl—94
Bavinck, Herman—37
Baylis, Charles—231
Benton, John—203,206
    239,247,250-251
    258-259
Bierle, Don—26,53,79-80
Blanchard, John—251
Bocchino, Peter—13,46
Bonaparte, Napoleon—59

Boswell, David—269
Briggs, Charles—177,182
Bromling, Brad—87
Brown, David—207-208,
    218,241,245,255
Brown, Francis—177,182
Brown, T. Pierce—91,107
Browning, Elizabeth—236
Brunner, Emil—31,205
Buffaloe, Neal—137

C

Calvin, John—95
Camp, Ashby—92,99,105-
    106,110,127
Camp, Robert—77
Carnell, Edward—51
Carson, Herbert—241
Causey, Bud—268
Chafer, Lewis—91,94,97,
    100,113
Chaney, Charles—109
Chomsky, Noam—115
Claiborne, Winford—41,63
Clark, Gordon—51,91,
    93,96,121
Clarke, Adam—253

H

I

J

K

L

SCRIPTURE INDEX

Nehemiah
11:30—242
8:7-8—309
9:6—152

Job
1-2—155
1:6-11—162
1:12—162
2:1-2—139
2:3-6—162
2:6—162
2:7—162
2:10—145
3:11—197
3:13-16—197
4:15—183
4:18—146
6:7-11—180
9:32—124
10:8-12—99
12:10—124
14:11—135
14:13-15—186
19:25—39
19:25-27—213
21:1-5—162
26:5—183
26:13-14—142
30:16—180
38:1—67
38:1-7—151
38:4-7—153
38:6,7—152

40:6—67
40:15—242
41:23—242
42:2—142,154

Psalms
1:2—284
4:5—22
8:4—225
9:17—186,245
16:10—186-188
18:10-16—67
19:1—67,121
19:1-6—45
31:5—183
33:6-9—114
41:4—181
46:1-3—299
46:10—16,279
49:15—181
73:2-5,12-14—240
75:7-9—235
77:6—183
78:14—67
78:50—179
80:1—67
81:11-12—289
89:14—124,226
90:2—124
99:1—67
99:7—67
100:3—124
102:27—142
104:2-5—153